LAWS OF

VERMONT

1777-1780

State Papers of Vermont

I. INDEX TO THE PAPERS OF THE SURVEYORS-GENERAL. Prepared by Franklin H. Dewart. 170 pp. 1918.

II. CHARTERS GRANTED BY THE STATE OF VERMONT: being Transcripts of Early Charters of Townships and Smaller Tracts of Land Granted by the State of Vermont; with an appendix containing . . . Historical and Bibliographical Notes Relative to Vermont Towns, Continued and Brought up to Date. [In front: Map of Vermont by James Whitelaw, 1796.] Edited by Franklin H. Dewart. 424 pp. Indexed. 1922.

III. JOURNALS AND PROCEEDINGS OF THE GENERAL ASSEMBLY OF THE STATE OF VERMONT . . . with explanatory notes. Edited by Walter H. Crockett. In four separate parts or volumes, all indexed:

> PART I: March, 1778 through June, 1781. With an Introduction by James B. Wilbur. 288 pp. 1924.
> PART II: October, 1781 through October, 1783. 232 pp. 1925.
> PART III: February, 1784 through March, 1787. 359 pp. 1928.
> PART IV: October, 1787 through January, 1791. 307 pp. 1929.

IV. REPORTS OF COMMITTEES TO THE GENERAL ASSEMBLY OF THE STATE OF VERMONT: March 9, 1778 to October 16, 1801; with Explanatory Notes. Edited by Walter H. Crockett. 257 pp. Indexed. 1932.

V. PETITIONS FOR GRANTS OF LAND 1778-1811. Edited by Mary Greene Nye. 547 pp. Indexed. 1939.

VI. SEQUESTRATION, CONFISCATION AND SALE OF ESTATES [*Loyalist material, 1777-1822*]. Edited by Mary Greene Nye. 476 pp. Indexed. 1941.

VII. NEW YORK LAND PATENTS 1688-1786. Covering Land Now Included in the State of Vermont (Not including Military Patents). Edited by Mary Greene Nye. 537 pp. Indexed. 1947.

VIII. GENERAL PETITIONS 1778-1787. Edited by Edward A. Hoyt. 458 pp. Indexed. 1952.

IX. GENERAL PETITIONS 1788-1792. Edited by Edward A. Hoyt. 506 pp. Indexed. 1955.

X. GENERAL PETITIONS 1793-1796. Edited by Allen Soule. 470 pp. Indexed. 1958.

XI. GENERAL PETITIONS 1797-1799. Edited by Allen Soule. 494 pp. Indexed. 1962.

LAWS OF VERMONT

EDITED BY ALLEN SOULE

State Papers of Vermont

VOLUME TWELVE

HOWARD E. ARMSTRONG

Secretary of State, Montpelier, Vermont

1964

PRINTED IN THE UNITED STATES OF AMERICA

BY THE VERMONT PRINTING COMPANY • BRATTLEBORO • VERMONT

FOREWORD

THIS volume, the twelfth of the *State Papers of Vermont,* is the first in a series which will include all the laws which governed Vermont in the years prior to 1800. These laws are taken from the bound manuscript volumes in the Secretary of State office, which have come to be known as the *Manuscript Laws of Vermont.* While the laws were originally published at the close of the Legislative session, few copies remain extant today. Thus these publications will make available, for study and research in Vermont and its history, a basic source of material hitherto available only in rare imprint or in the bound manuscript volumes in the Secretary's office.

Authority for publication is contained in Number 259 of the Acts of 1912 entitled "An Act to Provide for the Publication of State Papers." This act provides that the Secretary of State direct publication of certain material and "Such other of the manuscript records of his office as in his judgment are of general public interest."

The design of this volume is to fit the needs of the general reader, whether he be scholar or student, historian or reader of history. The few archaic spellings which occurred in the manuscript have been modernized, as has the punctuation. No attempt has been made to trace the origin of the laws passed, beyond a general introduction for each section. These essays give some idea of the material and its place in the history of the times. Suggestions for further readings may be found in the bibliographical notes. This method has made it possible for the editor to omit (with a great deal of pleasure) that scholar's prop, the footnote; sources are mentioned in the text in the few cases where it seems necessary.

Many individuals and institutions have given generously of advice and aid in the preparation of this volume, including Lawrence Turgeon and the Vermont State Library; T. D. S. Bassett of the Wilbur Library at U. V. M.; Virginia Knox, Connecticut State Librarian; and Richard Wood and staff of the Vermont Historical Society. The final stages of proofing were completed, and the indexing done, by Harrison J. Conant, former State Librarian who also edited the 1780 laws.

The editor would pause for a moment of silent gratitude to the many writers, researchers, students and historians from all walks of life who have preceded us in ferreting out the hidden by-ways of our early history. The story of the past is kept alive only by those who take an active interest in its preservation; our understanding of the present and our hope for the future would not be possible without their efforts and their records.

TABLE OF CONTENTS

INTRODUCTION

THE struggle for independence often amounts to little more than a struggle for self-government, usually accompanied by the stimulus for economic betterment; on these principles the American Revolution was fought. Vermont participated spiritedly in this Revolution, while involved in a similar revolution of its own—a less bloody but much longer struggle for independence, which began with the first of the New Hampshire land grants in 1749 and ended only with the achievement of statehood in 1791.

The early history of Vermont is the story of this 42 year struggle, which happens to be conveniently divided into three periods of about fourteen years each. The "New Hampshire Grants" era covers the years between 1749 and 1763, with settlement proceeding slowly on Governor Wentworth's 128 land grants, over which the Colony of New York was also claiming jurisdiction. In 1764, King George issued an Order in Council to the effect that New York did indeed have jurisdiction over the territory, and the following years saw the Yorkers try to exercise this jurisdiction. Finally, the "Vermont Republic" period lasts from 1777, when the settlers declared themselves independent, until 1791, when Vermont became the fourteenth state in the Union.

Thus 1777 was a momentous year for Vermont. In January, independence was declared; in July, a convention adopted a Constitution. The Legislature met the following year, and a code of Statute Law was soon adopted. The first of these fruits of self-government are reprinted in this volume, many of them for the first time since they were enacted nearly two hundred years ago. By way of introduction, we may briefly review the chain of events which led the settlers, in 1777, to declare for independence.

On the third day of January, 1749, Benning Wentworth, colonial governor of New Hampshire, made the first of his many land grants in the Green Mountain wilderness, modestly naming the remote township "Bennington." Governor Clinton of New York immediately protested, claiming that all the land west of the Connecticut River was under New York jurisdiction, and the struggle was on.

At first it was a battle of correspondence. Wentworth wrote ambiguous letters to the Board of Trade in London and to the New York governors. The latter were lax in protecting their interest, both on the Grants and to London. Settlement in the Grants was slow because of the French and Indian War. There was no great demand for land, for settlement or speculation, until 1761. When peace came that year, a new wave of land hunger swept the country and Wentworth, who had granted but sixteen townships in the region, chartered over a hundred in the following three years, much to the chagrin of Lieutenant-Governor Cadwallader Colden of New York.

Showing its customary lack of effective leadership in colonial matters, England delayed any decision on the land question until its 1764 Order in Council, which stated that the land west of the Connecticut River did indeed belong to the colony of New York. With this order, whatever jurisdiction New Hampshire held over the Grants ceased. Except for sporadic occasions later, when Vermont's independence was endangered, New Hampshire made no further pretense to ownership. But New York was to find it impossible to establish effective jurisdiction over the area, even after the 1764 Order in Council.

The basic authority in the early settlements had been that inherent in the town charter. Under its provisions, the proprietors and subsequent settlers were granted certain rights in establishing the pattern of local government common to the New England township system. Naturally there was little "governing" necessary under early frontier conditions, which persisted largely up until Revolutionary times. Nor was any significant governing authority exercised over the Grants by the chartering authority, New Hampshire. This was due in part to the dispute over jurisdiction, lack of need for authority, and the decline of the New England proprietorship system generally.

The great influx of settlers onto Wentworth's grants started after the peace of 1761. Primarily they came from New England states— Connecticut, Massachusetts, Rhode Island—and were partial to the "town meeting" form of government. They did not relish the thought of New York jurisdiction, nor did they like the "patroon system," whereby New York granted large areas to individuals who rented in turn to tenant farmers.

New York also made several errors in judgment. Some grants were made of land on which settlers were already established under New Hampshire grants, and against whom ejectment suits were brought; New York courts did not allow the New Hampshire titles to be given in evidence. New York required that confirmatory charters be taken out; about seventy townships started this process, as the costs were not exorbitant for small landowners. But for those who owned thousands of acres—significantly, the Onion River land company of the Allens—the cost was too great. They had no intentions of paying confirmatory fees, and sought to dissuade others from doing so.

And so resistance developed, spearheaded by the "Green Mountain Boys." The officials appointed by New York found it increasingly difficult to maintain any semblance of jurisdiction. A final blow to New York authority was the "Westminster Massacre," in which two settlers were fatally wounded in 1775 in an attempt to prevent the sitting of a court of New York officials. And with the growing resentment of the country towards British rule, it became a simple matter to lump the "Tories" and the "Yorkers" together as common enemies of freedom.

This growing resistance of the other colonies to British rule aided the cause of freedom in the Grants. Meetings of Committees of Correspondence had led to the first Continental Congress at Philadelphia in 1774, and the news spread quickly to the Grants. Town and county Committees of Safety met in 1774 and 1775, principally to discuss relations with New York but increasingly to consider relations with the mother country. Records of their early meetings are scattered, but we do have the record of the conventions of 1775-1776 which led to the Grants' declaration of independence. The clerk of these conventions, Jonas Fay, kept a journal which is now in the Secretary of State office. It was reproduced in facsimile in 1904 by Redfield Proctor and was printed in *Governor and Council* in volume I, pp. 3-48 (E. P. Walton, ed., Montpelier, 1873).

A warrant of 20 December 1775 called for a convention of representatives from the towns west of the Green Mountains to meet at Dorset on 16 January 1776; one of the articles was "to see whether the convention will consent to associate with New York, or by themselves in the cause of America." This was not the first time independence had been considered; as early as 1 March 1775 Ethan Allen had proposed the possibility in a letter to Oliver Wolcott (Matt Jones, *Vermont in the Making*, Cambridge, 1939, p. 341).

Later conventions were held at Dorset in July and September, 1776. And on January 15, 1777—six months after the American declaration of independence—a convention met at Westminster. They appointed a committee to count the number voting for a new state, and this committee reported that three fourths of those who acted were in favor of the new state—"the rest we view as neuters." The convention then voted unanimously to form a new state, and a committee was appointed to draft a declaration of independence, which was accepted. A slightly revised declaration, printed in the *Connecticut Courant* of 17 March 1777, was prepared by a committee appointed for that purpose. Still a third version was adopted by a convention on 4 June 1777, differing in the inclusion of detailed causes for separation from New York and the first adoption of the name of the new state—Vermont. This convention also adopted a resolution that, as it was necessary for the

> "safety, well-being and happiness of the inhabitants of this state to form such a government as shall, in the opinion of the representatives of the people of this state, best conduce to the happiness and safety of their constituents in particular and America in general . . ."

that the inhabitants of each town meet on June 23 to choose representatives to attend a convention in Windsor on July 2, whose business it would be to choose delegates to attend the general congress, a committee of safety,—and to form a constitution.

And while the hardy settlers had been demonstrating their talents at self-government for some time, it is with the adoption of a constitution that the story of the Laws of Vermont begins.

ALLEN SOULE
State Historian
Plainfield, Vermont
December, 1963

BIBLIOGRAPHICAL NOTE

There are numerous sources for the study of this period, perhaps the most important and certainly the most interesting of Vermont's history. Because of the many factors involved, the interweaving of cause and effect, and the need for careful interpretation of the many forces in action, it is difficult to portray these 42 years of struggle except in a "serious" work.

Vermont in the Making (Matt Jones, Cambridge, 1939) covers the period 1749-1777 most thoroughly. *Vermont in Quandary, 1763-1825* (Chilton Williamson, Montpelier, 1949) tends toward an "economic" interpretation of events. *History of Vermont* (Walter Crockett,

New York, 1921, in five volumes) is a comprehensive source, though stodgy. *Ira Allen, Founder of Vermont, 1751-1814* (James Wilbur, New York and Boston, 1928, in two volumes) stresses the contribution of the Allens; a critical view of their activities is in *The Birthplace of Vermont. A History of Windsor to 1781* (Henry S. Wardner, New York, 1927). *The Town Proprietors in Vermont: The New England Proprietorship in Decline* (Florence Woodard, New York, 1936) shows how the township system worked, as does *Vermont Lease Lands* (Walter Bogart, Montpelier, 1950), which contains an analysis of the land ownership problem and an extensive bibliography.

Well over a hundred town histories of varying quality have been written, many of which provide interesting accounts of early Vermont history. Nor should the reader neglect the *Vermont Historical Gazeteer* (Abby M. Hemenway, 1867-91, five volumes), with its many anecdotes of early town history.

The first of the official compilations, *Vermont State Papers* (William Slade, Montpelier, 1823) includes a miscellany of official documents of the early period, including many of the laws. Other official documents are found in the *Governor and Council* series (E. P. Walton, Montpelier, 1873-1880, in 8 volumes). Finally, there is the current *State Papers of Vermont* series (various editors, 1918-   ), of which this volume is the twelfth.

LAWS OF VERMONT

THE CONSTITUTION OF 1777

JULY 2-8, 1777

THE CONSTITUTION OF 1777

THE road to revolution is a fortuitous route with cause and effect often not readily discernible. Certainly the "coercive acts" of 1774 were major factors in an environment partially disenchanted with British rule. Almost spontaneously, committees of safety and committees of correspondence were formed and delegates appointed to Continental Congresses. Gradually they assumed operation of the government, as the power of royal governments waned. Increased local functions made the adoption of Constitutions necessary—Constitutions in which sanction of the people was substituted for royal sanction. Except for this basic change, the states generally adopted constitutions which mirrored their previous government, with emphasis on the democratic aspects. Vermont's first constitution reflects this trend.

In mid-summer of 1777, some forty delegates from about 30 Vermont towns journeyed to Windsor for what must have been a rather hectic convention. Their chief purpose was to adopt a constitution, but they were called to other duty as well. Unfortunately, no official account of this convention exists. Ira Allen wrote a short account many years later; it is included in a section of volume I, *Governor and Council* (pp. 62-79), which considers other aspects of the Convention as well.

On the second day of the session, July 3, they received a desperate call from Seth Warner, Commandant of the Green Mountain Boys, warning of imminent danger to Fort Ticonderoga from the forces of General Burgoyne:

> "The enemy have come up the lake, with 17 or 18 gunboats, two large ships, and other craft, and lie at Three Mile Point. The General Expects an attack every hour. He orders me to call out the militia of this state, of Massachusetts, and New Hampshire. . . . I know not to whom to apply except to your honorable body to call out the militia on the east side of the mountain. . . . I should be glad if a few hills of corn unhoed should not be a motive sufficient to detain men at home, considering the loss of such an important post might be irretrievable. . . ."

The Convention forwarded a copy of this message to the General Assembly of New Hampshire, then in session at Exeter, with a covering letter:

"We have no knowledge that any express has been sent you. Therefore as the matter nearly concerns the Liberties of the United States
in general, this house flatter themselves that their forwarding this
intelligence may not prove unacceptable. The militia from this state
are principally with the officer commanding the continental army at
Ticonderoga, the remainder on their march for the relief of that distressed post . . . every prudent step ought to be immediately taken
for their relief. . . ."

The convention then resumed its consideration of the proposed
constitution, concluding its work on July 8, when word arrived of the
evacuation of Ticonderoga. Ira Allen's account of the event follows,
taken from *Governor and Council* (p. 62):

"A draft of a constitution was laid before the Convention, and read.
The business being new, and of great consequence, required serious
deliberation. The Convention had it under consideration when the
news of the evacuation of Ticonderoga arrived, which alarmed them
very much, as thereby the frontiers of the State were exposed to the
inroads of an enemy. The family of the President of the Convention,
as well as those of many other members, were exposed to the foe. In
this awful crisis the Convention was for leaving Windsor, but a
severe thunderstorm came on, and gave them time to reflect, while
other members, less alarmed at the news, called the attention of the
whole to finish the Constitution, which was then reading paragraph
by paragraph for the last time. This was done, and the Convention
then appointed a Council of Safety to act during the recess, and the
Convention adjourned."

Thus in the short period of time between the 2nd and 8th of July,
1777, a constitution was adopted for the state of Vermont—a constitution which, in many respects, remains unchanged to this day. The fact
that it was copied almost word for word from the constitution which
Pennsylvania had adopted a year earlier should not detract from the
work of the convention, which must have realized the sound democratic principles upon which it was founded.

Just how the constitution of Pennsylvania came into the hands of
the Vermont convention is a mystery. Previous conventions had sent
emissaries to the Continental Congress in Philadelphia, who could have
become imbued with the liberal spirit in that neighborhood. The finger
of suspicion points to Thomas Young, boyhood friend of Ethan Allen
and member of the Pennsylvania constitutional convention. A friend to
Vermont and strong advocate of its independence, Young is credited

with having suggested the very name "Vermont," according to a petition written by Ethan Allen, Thomas Chittenden, and Joseph Fay for the benefit of Young's heirs ten years later (see Volume VIII, *State Papers of Vermont,* pp. 272-3).

Some changes were made from the Pennsylvania version—but these changes were in the direction of greater individual freedom, such as the universal suffrage article and the deservedly famous First Article, prohibiting slavery; the first such Article adopted in this country.

BIBLIOGRAPHICAL NOTE

The most complete source concerning the Pennsylvania Constitution known to the editor is *The Pennsylvania Constitution of 1776—A Study in Revolutionary Democracy* (J. Paul Selsam, Philadelphia, 1936). Its extensive bibliography lists sources for further study of state constitutions and their adoption. *A Memorial to Thomas Chittenden* (Daniel Chipman, Middlebury, 1849), in spite of its title, contains much material on the Vermont constitution and compares it with that of Pennsylvania. A readily available source containing the constitution and notes on its adoption is the *Vermont Legislative Directory,* published biennially by the Secretary of State, Montpelier. As already mentioned, volume 1 of *Governor and Council* contains notes on the adoption of the constitution, including probable members to the convention and the constitution itself.

PREAMBLE

Whereas, all government ought to be instituted and supported for the security and protection of the community as such and to enable the individuals who compose it, to enjoy their natural rights, and the other blessings which the Author of existence has bestowed upon man; and whenever those great ends of government are not obtained, the people have a right, by common consent, to change it, and take such measures as to them may appear necessary to promote their safety and happiness.

And whereas, the inhabitants of this State have, (in consideration of protection only) heretofore acknowledged allegiance to the King of Great Britain, and the said King has not only withdrawn that protection, but commenced, and still continues to carry on, with unabated vengeance, a most cruel and unjust war against them; employing therein, not only the troops of Great Britain, but foreign mercenaries, savages and slaves, for the avowed purpose of reducing them to a total and abject submission to the despotic dominion of the British parliament, with many other acts of tryanny (more fully set forth in the declaration of Congress), whereby all allegiance and fealty to the said King and his successors, are dissolved and at an end; and all power and authority derived from him, ceased in the American Colonies.

And whereas, the territory which now comprehends the State of Vermont, did antecedently, of right, belong to the government of New Hampshire; and the former Governor thereof, viz. his excellency Benning Wentworth, Esq., granted many charters of lands and corporations, within this State, to the present inhabitants and others. And whereas, the late Lieutenant Governor Colden, of New York, with others, did, in violation of the tenth command, covet those very lands; and by a false representation made to the court of Great Britain (in the year 1764, that for the convenience of trade and administration of justice, the inhabitants were desirous of being annexed to that government), obtained jurisdiction of those very identical lands, ex-parte; which ever was, and is disagreeable to the inhabitants. And whereas, the legislature of New York, ever have, and still continue to disown the good people of this State, in their landed property, which will appear in the complaints hereafter inserted, and in the 36th section of their present constitution, in which is established the grants of land made by that government.

They have refused to make re-grants of our lands to the original proprietors and occupants, unless at the exorbitant rate of 2300 dollars fees for each township; and did enhance the quitrent, three fold, and demanded an immediate delivery of the title derived before, from New Hampshire.

The judges of their supreme court have made a solemn declaration, that the charters, conveyances, &c., of the lands included in the before described premises, were utterly null and void, on which said title was founded; in consequence of which declaration, writs of possession have been by them issued, and the sheriff of the county of Albany sent, at the head of six or seven hundred men, to enforce the execution thereof.

They have passed an act, annexing a penalty thereto, of thirty pounds fine and six months imprisonment, on any person who should refuse assisting the sheriff, after being requested, for the purpose of executing writs of possession.

The Governors, Dunmore, Tryon and Colden, have made re-grants of several tracts of land, included in the premises, to certain favorite land jobbers in the government of New-York, in direct violation of his Britannic majesty's express prohibition, in the year 1767.

They have issued proclamations, wherein they have offered large sums of money, for the purpose of apprehending those very persons who have dared boldly, and publicly, to appear in defence of their just rights.

They did pass twelve acts of outlawry, on the 9th day of March, A. D. 1774, impowering the respective judges of their supreme court, to award execution of death against those inhabitants in said district that they should judge to be offenders, without trial.

They have, and still continue, an unjust claim to those lands, which greatly retards emigration into, and the settlement of, this State.

They have hired foreign troops, emigrants from Scotland, at two different times, and armed them, to drive us out of possession.

They have sent the savages on our frontiers, to distress us.

They have proceeded to erect the counties of Cumberland and Gloucester, and establish courts of justice there, after they were discountenanced by the authority of Great Britain.

The free Convention of the State of New-York, at Harlem, in the year 1776, unanimously voted, "That all quit-rents formerly due to the King of Great Britain, are now due and owing to this convention, or such future government as shall be hereafter established in this State."

In the several stages of the aforesaid oppressions, we have petitioned his Britannic majesty, in the most humble manner, for redress, and have, at very great expense, received several reports in our favor; and in other instances, wherein we have petitioned the late legislative authority of New-York, those petitions have been treated with neglect.

And whereas, the local situation of this State, from New-York, at the extreme part, is upwards of four hundred and fifty miles from the seat of that government, which renders it extreme difficult to continue under the jurisdiction of said State,

Therefore, it is absolutely necessary, for the welfare and safety of the inhabitants of this State, that it should be, henceforth, a free and independent State; and that a just, permanent and proper form of government, should exist in it, derived from, and founded on, the authority of the people only, agreeable to the direction of the honorable American Congress.

We the representatives of the freemen of Vermont, in General Convention met, for the express purpose of forming such a government, confessing the goodness of the Great Governor of the Universe (who alone, knows to what degree of earthly happiness, mankind may attain, by perfecting the arts of government), in permitting the people of this State, by common consent, and without violence, deliberately to form for themselves, such just rules as they shall think best for governing their future society; and being fully convinced that it is our indispensable duty, to establish such original principles of government, as will best promote the general happiness of the people of this State, and their posterity, and provide for future improvements, without partiality for, or prejudice against, any particular class, sect, or denomination of men whatever: Do, by virtue of authority vested in us, by our constituents, ordain, declare, and establish, the following declaration of rights, and frame of government, to be the Constitution of this Commonwealth, and to remain in force therein, forever, unaltered, except in such articles, as shall, hereafter, on experience, be found to require improvement, and which shall, by the same authority of the people, fairly delegated, as this frame of government directs, be amended or improved, for the more effectual obtaining and securing the great end and design of all government, herein before mentioned.

CHAPTER I

A DECLARATION OF THE RIGHTS OF THE INHABITANTS OF THE STATE OF VERMONT

I. That all men are born equally free and independent, and have certain natural, inherent and unalienable rights, amongst which are the enjoying and defending life and liberty; acquiring, possessing and protecting property, and pursuing and obtaining happiness and safety. Therefore, no male person, born in this country, or brought from over sea, ought to be holden by law, to serve any person, as a servant, slave or apprentice, after he arrives to the age of twenty-one years, nor female, in like manner, after she arrives to the age of eighteen years, unless they are bound by their own consent, after they arrive at such age, or bound by law, for the payment of debts, damages, fines, costs, or the like.

II. That private property ought to be subservient to public uses, when necessity requires it; nevertheless, whenever any particular man's property is taken for the use of the public, the owner ought to receive an equivalent in money.

III. That all men have a natural and unalienable right to worship

Almighty God, according to the dictates of their own consciences and understanding, regulated by the word of God; and that no man ought, or, of right, can be compelled to attend any religious worship, or erect, or support any place of worship, or maintain any minister, contrary to the dictates of his conscience; nor can any man who professes the protestant religion be justly deprived or abridged of any civil right as a citizen, on account of his religious sentiment, or peculiar mode of religious worship, and that no authority can, or ought to be vested in, or assumed by, any power whatsoever, that shall in any case, interfere with, or in any manner control, the rights of conscience, in the free exercise of religious worship; nevertheless, every sect or denomination of people ought to observe the Sabbath, or the Lord's day, and keep up, and support, some sort of religious worship, which to them shall seem most agreeable to the revealed will of God.

IV. That the people of this State have the sole, exclusive and inherent right of governing and regulating the internal police of the same.

V. That all power being originally inherent in, and consequently, derived from, the people; therefore, all officers of government, whether legislative or executive, are their trustees and servants, and at all times accountable to them.

VI. That government is, or ought to be, instituted for the common benefit, protection, and security of the people, nation or community; and not for the particular emolument or advantage of any single man, family or set of men, who are a part only of that community; and that the community hath an indubitable, unalienable and indefeasible right to reform, alter, or abolish government, in such manner as shall be, by that community, judged most conducive to the public weal.

VII. That those who are employed in the legislative and executive business of the State, may be restrained from oppression, the people have a right, at such periods as they may think proper, to reduce their public officers to a private station, and supply the vacancies by certain and regular elections.

VIII. That all elections ought to be free; and that all freemen, having a sufficient evident common interest with, and attachment to, the community, have a right to elect officers, or be elected into office.

IX. That every member of society hath a right to be protected in the enjoyment of life, liberty and property, and therefore, is bound to contribute his proportion towards the expense of the protection, and yield his personal service, when necessary, or an equivalent thereto; but no part of a man's property can be justly taken from him, or applied to public uses, without his own consent, or that of his legal representatives;

nor can any man who is conscientiously scrupulous of bearing arms, be justly compelled thereto, if he will pay such equivalent; nor are the people bound by any law, but such as they have in like manner, assented to, for their common good.

X. That, in all prosecutions for criminal offences, a man hath a right to be heard, by himself and his counsel—to demand the cause and nature of his accusation—to be confronted with the witnesses—to call for evidence in his favor, and a speedy public trial, by an impartial jury of the country; without the unanimous consent of which jury he cannot be found guilty; nor can he be compelled to give evidence against himself; nor can any man be justly deprived of his liberty, except by the laws of the land or the judgment of his peers.

XI. That the people have a right to hold themselves, their houses, papers and possessions free from search or seizure; and therefore warrants, without oaths or affirmations first made, affording a sufficient foundation for them, and whereby any officer or messenger may be commanded or required to search suspected places, or to seize any person or persons, his, her or their property, not particularly described, are contrary to that right, and ought not to be granted.

XII. That no warrant or writ to attach the person or estate of any freeholder within this state, shall be issued in civil action, without the person or persons, who may request such warrant or attachment, first make oath, or affirm, before the authority who may be requested to issue the same, that he, or they, are in danger of losing his, her or their debts.

XIII. That, in controversies respecting property, and in suits between man and man, the parties have a right to a trial by jury; which ought to be held sacred.

XIV. That the people have a right to freedom of speech, and of writing and publishing their sentiments; therefore, the freedom of the press ought not to be restrained.

XV. That the people have a right to bear arms for the defence of themselves and the State; and, as standing armies, in the time of peace, are dangerous to liberty, they ought not to be kept up; and that the military should be kept under strict subordination to, and governed by, the civil power.

XVI. That frequent recurrence to fundamental principles, and a firm adherence to justice, moderation, temperance, industry and frugality, are absolutely necessary to preserve the blessings of liberty, and keep government free. The people ought, therefor, to pay particular attention to these points, in the choice of officers and representatives, and have a right to exact a due and constant regard to them from their legislators and magistrates, in the making and executing such laws as are necessary for the good government of the State.

XVII. That all people have a natural and inherent right to emigrate from one State to another, that will receive them; or to form a new State in vacant countries, or in such countries as they can purchase, whenever they think that thereby they can promote their own happiness.

XVIII. That the people have a right to assemble together, to consult for their common good—to instruct their representatives; and to apply to the legislature for redress of grievances, by address, petition or remonstrance.

XIX. That no person shall be liable to be transported out of this State, for trial, for any offence committed within this State.

CHAPTER II
PLAN OR FRAME OF GOVERNMENT

SECTION I

The Commonwealth or State of Vermont, shall be governed hereafter, by a Governor, Deputy Governor, Council, and an Assembly of the Representatives of the Freemen of the same, in manner and form following.

SECTION II

The supreme legislative power shall be vested in a House of Representatives of the Freemen or Commonwealth or State of Vermont.

SECTION III

The supreme executive power shall be vested in a Governor and Council.

SECTION IV

Courts of justice shall be established in every county in this State.

SECTION V

The freemen of this Commonwealth, and their sons, shall be trained and armed for its defence, under such regulations, restrictions and exceptions, as the General Assembly shall, by law, direct; reserving always to the people, the right of choosing their colonels of militia, and all commissioned officers under that rank, in such manner, and as often, as by the said laws shall be directed.

SECTION VI

Every man of the full age of twenty-one years, having resided in this State for the space of one whole year, next before the election of representatives, and who is of a quiet and peaceable behaviour, and will take the following oath (or affirmation), shall be entitled to all the privileges of a freeman of this State.

I .... solemnly swear, by the ever living God (or affirm in the presence of Almighty God), that whenever I am called to give my vote or suffrage, touching any matter that concerns the State of Vermont, I will do it so, as in my conscience, I shall judge will most conduce to the best good of the same, as established by the constitution, without fear or favor of any man.

SECTION VII

The House of Representatives of the Freemen of this State, shall consist of persons most noted for wisdom and virtue, to be chosen by the freemen of every town in this State, respectively. And no foreigner shall be chosen, unless he has resided in the town for which he shall be elected, one year immediately before said election.

SECTION VIII

The members of the House of Representatives, shall be chosen annually, by ballot, by the freemen of this State, on the first Tuesday of September, forever (except this present year), and shall meet on the second Thursday of the succeeding October, and shall be stiled the General Assembly of the Representatives of the Freemen of Vermont; and shall have power to choose their Speaker, Secretary of the State, their Clerk, and other necessary officers of the house—sit on their own adjournments—prepare bills and enact them into laws—judge of the elections and qualifications of their own members—they may expel a member, but not a second time for the same cause—They may administer oaths (or affirmations) on examination of witnesses—redress grievances—impeach State criminals—grant charters of incorporation—constitute towns, boroughs, cities and counties, and shall have all other powers necessary for the legislature of a free State; but they shall have no power to add to, alter, abolish, or infringe, any part of this constitution. And for this present year the members of the General Assembly shall be chosen on the first Tuesday of March next, and shall meet at the meeting-house, in Windsor, on the second Thursday of March next.

SECTION IX

A quorum of the house of representatives shall consist of two thirds of the whole number of members elected; and having met and chosen their speaker, shall, each of them, before they proceed to business, take and subscribe, as well the oath of fidelity and allegiance hereinafter directed, as the following oath or affirmation, viz.

I .... do solemnly swear, by the ever living God (or I do solemnly affirm in the presence of Almighty God), that as a member of this assembly, I will not propose or assent to any bill, vote or resolution which shall appear to me injurious to the people; nor do or consent to any act or thing whatever, that shall have a tendency to lessen or abridge their rights and privileges, as declared in the Constitution of this State; but will in all things, conduct myself as a faithful, honest representative and guardian of the people, according to the best of my judgment and abilities.

And each member, before he takes his seat, shall make and subscribe the following declaration, viz.

I do believe in one God, the Creator and Governor of the universe, the rewarder of the good and punisher of the wicked. And I do acknowledge the scriptures of the old and new testament to be given by divine inspiration, and own and profess the protestant religion.

And no further or other religious test shall ever, hereafter, be required of any civil officer or magistrate in this State.

SECTION X

Delegates to represent this State in Congress shall be chosen, by ballot, by the future General Assembly, at their first meeting, and annually, forever afterward, as long as such representation shall be necessary. Any Delegate may be superceded, at any time, by the General Assembly appointing another in his stead. No man shall sit in Congress longer than two years successively, nor be capable of re-election for three years afterwards; and no person who holds any office in the gift of the Congress, shall, thereafter, be elected to represent this State in Congress.

SECTION XI

If any town or towns shall neglect or refuse to elect and send representatives to the General Assembly, two thirds of the members of the towns that do elect and send representatives (provided they be a majority of the inhabited towns of the whole State), when met, shall have all the powers of the General Assembly, as fully and amply as if the whole were present.

SECTION XII

The doors of the house in which the representatives of the freemen of this State, shall sit, in General Assembly, shall be and remain open for the admission of all persons, who behave decently, except only, when the welfare of this State may require the doors to be shut.

SECTION XIII

The votes and proceedings of the General Assembly shall be printed, weekly, during their sitting, with the yeas and nays, on any question, vote or resolution, where one third of the members require it; (except when the votes are taken by ballot) and when the yeas and nays are so taken, every member shall have a right to insert the reasons of his votes upon the minutes, if he desire it.

SECTION XIV

To the end that laws, before they are enacted, may be more maturely considered, and the inconveniency of hasty determination as much as possible prevented, all bills of public nature, shall be first laid before the Governor and Council, for their perusal and proposals of amendment, and shall be printed for the consideration of the people, before they are read in General Assembly for the last time of debate and amendment; except temporary acts, which, after being laid before the Governor and Council, may (in the case of sudden necessity) be passed into laws; and no other shall be passed into laws, until the next session of Assembly. And for the more perfect satisfaction of the public, the reasons and motives for making such laws, shall be fully and clearly expressed and set forth in their preambles.

SECTION XV

The style of the laws of this State shall be,—"Be it enacted, and it is hereby enacted, by the Representatives of the Freemen of the State of Vermont, in General Assembly met, and by the Authority of the same."

SECTION XVI

In order that the Freemen of this State might enjoy the benefit of election, as equally as may be, each town within this State, that consists, or may consist, of eighty taxable inhabitants, within one septenary or seven years, next after the establishing this constitution, may hold elections therein, and choose each, two representatives; and each other inhabited town in this State may, in like manner, choose each, one representative, to represent them in General Assembly, during the said septenary or seven years; and after that, each inhabited town may, in like manner, hold such election, and choose each, one representative, forever thereafter.

SECTION XVII

The Supreme Executive Council of this State, shall consist of a Governor, Lieutenant-Governor, and twelve persons, chosen in the following manner, viz. The Freemen of each town, shall, on the day of election for choosing representatives to attend the General Assembly, bring in their votes for Governor, with his name fairly written, to the constable, who shall seal them up, and write on them, votes for the Governor, and deliver them to the representative chosen to attend the General Assembly; and, at the opening of the General Assembly, there shall be a committee appointed out of the Council, and Assembly, who, after being duly sworn to the faithful discharge of their trust, shall proceed to receive, sort, and count, the votes for the Governor, and declare the person who has the major part of the votes, to be Governor, for the year ensuing. And if there be no choice made, then the Council and General Assembly, by their joint ballot, shall make choice of a Governor.

The Lieutenant Governor and Treasurer, shall be chosen in the manner above directed; and each freeman shall give in twelve votes for twelve councillors, in the same manner; and the twelve highest in nomination shall serve for the ensuing year as Councillors.

The council that shall act in the recess of this Convention, shall supply the place of a council for the next General Assembly, until the new Council be declared chosen. The Council shall meet annually, at the same time and place with the General Assembly; and every member of the Council shall be a Justice of the Peace for the whole State, by virtue of his office.

SECTION XVIII

The Governor, and in his absence, the Lieutenant or Deputy Governor, with the Council—seven of whom shall be a quorum—shall have power to appoint and commissionate all officers (except those who are appointed by the General Assembly), agreeable to this frame of government, and the laws that may be made hereafter; and shall supply every vacancy in any office, occasioned by death, resignation, removal or disqualification, until the office can be filled, in the time and manner directed by law or this constitution. They are to correspond with other

States, and transact business with officers of government, civil and military; and to prepare such business as may appear to them necessary to lay before the General Assembly. They shall sit as judges to hear and determine on impeachments, taking to their assistance, for advice only, the justices of the supreme court; and shall have power to grant pardons, and remit fines, in all cases whatsoever, except cases of impeachment, and in cases of treason and murder—shall have power to grant reprieves, but not to pardon, until the end of the next session of the Assembly: but there shall be no remission or mitigation of punishment, on impeachment, except by act of legislation. They are also, to take care that the laws be faithfully executed. They are to expedite the execution of such measures as may be resolved upon by General Assembly; and they may draw upon the Treasurer for such sums as may be appropriated by the House: they may also lay embargoes, or prohibit the exportation of any commodity for any time, not exceeding thirty days, in the recess of the House only: they may grant such licences as shall be directed by law, and shall have power to call together the General Assembly, when necessary, before the day to which they shall stand adjourned. The Governor shall be commander in chief of the forces of the State; but shall not command in person, except advised thereto by the Council, and then, only, as long as they shall approve thereof. The Governor and Council shall have a Secretary, and keep fair books of their proceedings, wherein any Councillor may enter his dissent, with his reasons to support it.

SECTION XIX

All commissions shall be in the name of the freemen of the State of Vermont, sealed with the State seal, signed by the Governor, and in his absence the Lieutenant Governor, and attested by the Secretary; which seal shall be kept by the Council.

SECTION XX

Every officer of State, whether judicial or executive, shall be liable to be impeached by the General Assembly, either when in office, or after his resignation, or removal for mal-administration. All impeachments shall be before the Governor or Lieutenant Governor and Council, who shall hear and determine the same.

SECTION XXI

The supreme court, and the several courts of common pleas of this State shall, besides the powers usually exercised by such courts, have the powers of a court of chancery, so far as relates to perpetuating testimony, obtaining evidence from places not within this State, and the care of persons and estates of those who are non compotes mentis, and such other powers as may be found necessary by future General Assemblies, not inconsistent with this constitution.

SECTION XXII

Trials shall be by jury; and it is recommended to the legislature of this State to provide by law, against every corruption or partiality in the choice, and return, or appointment, of juries.

SECTION XXIII

All counts shall be open, and justice shall be impartially administered, without corruption or unnecessary delay; all their officers shall be paid an adequate, but moderate, compensation for their services; and if any officer shall take greater or other fees than the laws allow him, either directly or indirectly, it shall ever after disqualify him from holding any office in this State.

SECTION XXIV

All prosecutions shall commence in the name and by the authority of the freemen of the State of Vermont, and all indictments shall conclude with these words, "against the peace and dignity of the Same." The style of all process hereafter, in this State, shall be,—The State of Vermont.

SECTION XXV

The person of a debtor, where there is not a strong presumption of fraud, shall not be continued in prison, after delivering up, bona fide, all his estate, real and personal, for the use of his creditors, in such manner as shall be hereafter regulated by law. All prisoners shall be bailable by sufficient securities, unless for capital offences, when the proof is evident or presumption great.

SECTION XXVI

Excessive bail shall not be exacted for bailable offences; and all fines shall be moderate.

SECTION XXVII

That the General Assembly, when legally formed, shall appoint times and places for county elections, and at such times and places, the freemen in each county respectively, shall have the liberty of choosing the judges of inferior court of common pleas, sheriff, justices of the peace, and judges of probate, commissioned by the Governor and council, during good behavior, removable by the General Assembly upon proof of mal-administration.

SECTION XXVIII

That no person, shall be capable of holding any civil office, in this State except he has acquired, and maintains a good moral character.

SECTION XXIX

All elections, whether by the people or in General Assembly, shall be by ballot, free and voluntary; and any elector who shall receive any gift or reward for his vote, in meat, drink, monies or otherwise, shall forfeit his right to elect at that time, and suffer such other penalty as future laws shall direct. And any person who shall, directly or indirectly, give, promise, or bestow, any such rewards to be elected, shall, thereby, be rendered incapable to serve for the ensuing year.

SECTION XXX

All fines, licence money, fees and forfeitures, shall be paid, according to the direction hereafter to be made by the General Assembly.

SECTION XXXI

All deeds and conveyances of land shall be recorded in the town clerk's office, in their respective towns.

SECTION XXXII

The printing presses shall be free to every person who undertakes to examine the proceedings of the legislature, or any part of government.

SECTION XXXIII

As every freeman, to preserve his independence (if without a sufficient estate), ought to have some profession, calling, trade or farm, whereby he may honestly subsist, there can be no necessity for, nor use in, establishing offices of profit, the usual effects of which are dependence and servility, unbecoming freemen, in the possessors or expectants; faction, contention, corruption and disorder among the people. But if any man is called into public service, to the prejudice of his private affairs, he has a right to a reasonable compensation; and whenever an office, through increase of fees, or otherwise, becomes so profitable as to occasion many to apply for it, the profits ought to be lessened by the legislature.

SECTION XXXIV

The future legislature of this State, shall regulate entails, in such manner as to prevent perpetuities.

SECTION XXXV

To deter more effectually from the commission of crimes, by continued visible punishment of long duration, and to make sanguinary punishments less necessary; houses ought to be provided for punishing, by hard labor, those who shall be convicted of crimes not capital; wherein the criminal shall be employed for the benefit of the public, or for reparation of injuries done to private persons; and all persons, at proper times, should be admitted to see the prisoners at their labor.

SECTION XXXVI

Every officer, whether judicial, executive or military, in authority under this State, shall take the following oath or affirmation of allegiance, and general oath of office, before he enter on the execution of his office.

THE OATH OR AFFIRMATION OF ALLEGIANCE

"I .... do solemnly swear by the ever living God (or affirm in presence of Almighty God), that I will be true and faithful to the State of Vermont; and that I will not, directly or indirectly, do any act or thing, prejudicial or injurious, to the constitution or government thereof, as established by Convention."

THE OATH OR AFFIRMATION OF OFFICE

"I .... do solemnly swear by the ever living God (or affirm in presence of Almighty God), that I will faithfully execute the office of .... for the .... of ....; and will do equal right and justice to all men, to the best of my judgment and abilities, according to law."

SECTION XXXVII

No public tax, custom or contribution shall be imposed upon, or paid by, the people of this State, except by a law for that purpose; and before any law be made for raising it, the purpose for which any tax is to be raised ought to appear clear to the legislature to be of more service to the community than the money would be, if not collected; which being well observed, taxes can never be burthens.

SECTION XXXVIII

Every foreigner of good character, who comes to settle in this State, having first taken an oath or affirmation of allegiance to the same, may purchase, or by other just means acquire, hold, and transfer, land or other real estate; and after one years residence, shall be deemed a free denizen of this State; except that he shall not be capable of being elected a representative, until after two years residence.

SECTION XXXIX

That the inhabitants of this State, shall have liberty to hunt and fowl, in seasonable times, on the lands they hold, and on other lands (not enclosed); and, in like manner, to fish in all boatable and other waters, not private property, under proper regulations, to be hereafter made and provided by the General Assembly.

SECTION XL

A school or schools shall be established in each town, by the legislature, for the convenient instruction of youth, with such salaries to the masters, paid by each town, making proper use of school lands in each town, thereby to enable them to instruct youth at low prices. One grammar school in each county, and one university in this State, ought to be established by direction of the General Assembly.

SECTION XLI

Laws for the encouragement of virtue and prevention of vice and immorality, shall be made and constantly kept in force; and provision shall be made for their due execution; and all religious societies and bodies of men, that have or may be hereafter united and incorporated, for the advancement of religion and learning, or for other pious and charitable purposes, shall be encouraged and protected in the enjoyment of the privileges, immunities and estates which they, in justice, ought to enjoy, under such regulations, as the General Assembly of this State shall direct.

SECTION XLII

All field and staff officers, and commissioned officers of the army, and all general officers of the militia, shall be chosen by the General Assembly.

SECTION XLIII

The declaration of rights is hereby declared to be a part of the Constitution of this State, and ought never to be violated on any pretence whatsoever.

SECTION XLIV

In order that the freedom of this Commonwealth may be preserved inviolate, forever, there shall be chosen, by ballot, by the freemen of this State, on the last Wednesday in March, in the year one thousand seven hundred and eighty-five, and on the last Wednesday in March, in every seven years thereafter, thirteen persons, who shall be chosen in the same manner the council is chosen—except they shall not be out of the Council or General Assembly—to be called the Council of Censors; who shall meet together, on the first Wednesday of June next ensuing their election; the majority of whom shall be a quorum in every case, except as to calling a Convention, in which two thirds of the whole number elected shall agree; and whose duty it shall be to enquire whether the legislative and executive branches of government have performed their duty as guardians of the people; or assumed to themselves, or exercised, other or greater powers, than they are entitled to by the constitution. They are also to enquire whether the public taxes have been justly laid and collected, in all parts of this Commonwealth—in what manner the public monies have been disposed of, and whether the laws have been duly executed. For these purposes they shall have power to public censures—to order impeachments, and to recommend to the legislature the repealing such laws as appear to them to have been enacted contrary to the principles of the constitution. These powers they shall continue to have, for and during the space of one year from the day of their election, and no longer. The said Council of Censors will also have power to call a Convention, to meet within two years after their sitting, if there appears to them an absolute necessity of amending any article of this constitution which may be defective—explaining such as may be thought not clearly expressed, and of adding such as are necessary for the preservation of the rights and happiness of the people; but the articles to be amended, and the amendments proposed, and such articles as are proposed to be added or abolished, shall be promulgated at least six months before the day appointed for the election of such convention, for the previous consideration of the people, that they may have an opportunity of instructing their delegates on the subject.

LAWS OF 1778

LAWS OF 1778

O N the third day of March, 1778, the first state elections were held, and nine days later about fifty newly elected representatives journeyed to Windsor for the first of the new state's legislative sessions. It lasted from March 12 through 26; later sessions that year were held from June 4 through 18 and from October 8 through 24.

The deliberations and activities of these 44 days were significant. Tasks were not limited to legislative acts, for the Assembly, with the Governor and Council, were in a real sense responsible for the survival of the state. Prior service on the councils and committees which preceded independence qualified many of them for the tasks at hand. In addition, many had been leaders in the other New England towns from whence they migrated to the Grants.

The Journals of these and subsequent sessions have been published as Volume III of the *State Papers* series, in four parts. In his Introduction to Part 1, James Wilbur discusses the difficulties under which the state was laboring, as well as the vicissitudes of early record-keeping; the Journals of 1778 seem never to have been published until taken from the manuscript journal in 1924 when Volume III was published.

Nor do the Laws of 1778 ever seem to have been published. The Journal notes on page 48 that a committee was appointed on October 24, 1778 "to prepare the acts passed at the former sessions and likewise the present session, for the press, and get them printed." And a committee report among the manuscript Vermont State Papers (Volume 74, page 96, in the Secretary of State office) dated 7 November 1821 states in part:

"Some of your committee recollect that the laws which were passed in 1778 were printed in a small pamphlet and as they are not found in the Secretary's office, it is probable that they were all temporary . . ."

While such a pamphlet might be even now lurking about in the dismal confines of some obscure town clerk office, none is known to exist. We are thus limited to the Assembly Journals, as published in Part 1, Volume III of the *State Papers,* in our search for the legislation of 1778.

Most of the acts which follow were preceded in the Journals by the terminology "Passed the Act . . ." In addition, the Assembly "Voted . . ." a number of actions, some of which were legislative, some judicial and some executive. Such was the nature of the times in the new state. For example, one of the major concerns of the first session was defense of the frontiers, and it was variously voted to raise militia pay, alter regiments, and leave the establishment of defense lines to the Governor and Council. And at the October session, the union with several New Hampshire towns seems to have been dissolved by the simple expedient of voting on three questions concerning county lines. Other executive actions taken by the Assembly included appointment of state printers, establishment of state loan offices, taking of Dartmouth College under the patronage of the state, and the appointment of judges, ambassadors, and a raft of other officials.

It should be noted that the Journals were probably incomplete, as Wilbur suggests. Many acts were ordered to be brought in of which there is no subsequent record during the 1778 sessions. These acts concern the following (page numbers refer to the Assembly Journals, Volume III, Part 1):

preservation of timber, 11; safeguarding troop supplies at Bennington, 24; keeping the Sabbath, 13, 22-3; raising troops, 26; supplying the towns with gunpowder, lead, and flints, 26; counterfeiting, 27; county elections, 27; pine timber, 28; bounty on wolves, 23; freedom of slaves, as established in the Bill of Rights, 48; division of the state into four counties, 40; town representation, 47. Some of these acts were undoubtedly passed at the 1778 sessions; others were passed at the February, 1779 session.

The titles of the Acts of 1778 are listed alphabetically, by session. We have included notes taken from the Journals relating to the passage of the acts. Many references in the Journals are vague as to which legislation is referred to and have been omitted. Finally, it should be kept in mind that these public acts were considered temporary, and all of them except for a few private acts seem to have been passed at the February, 1779 session.

LAWS OF VERMONT
PASSED DURING THE SESSION OF THE GENERAL ASSEMBLY
MARCH 12-MARCH 26, 1778

AN ACT REGULATING ATTORNIES AND THEIR FEES
17 MARCH 1778

A.J.1778: committee appointed to prepare a bill regulating attornies; their report providing attornies for the county courts and regulating their fees accepted, page 7.

AN ACT TO ESTABLISH THE COMMON LAW AS THE LAW OF THE STATE
21 MARCH 1778

A.J.1778: Council bill establishing the common law as the law of the state read, debated, and passed, page 13.

AN ACT AGAINST TREACHEROUS CONSPIRACIES
26 MARCH 1778

A.J.1778: an act against treacherous conspiracies passed as said act appears in the Connecticut Law Book, page 17.

ACTS CONCERNING COUNTY ELECTIONS
MARCH 1778

A.J.1778: committee appointed to select places to count county election votes, page 8; time appointed for holding county elections, pages 8, 10; committee report selecting places for holding county elections accepted, page 10; county elections postponed, page 16.

ACTS ESTABLISHING TWO COUNTIES WITHIN THE STATE
17 MARCH 1778

A.J.1778: a bill of the Governor and Council establishing a county west of the mountains accepted, page 7; a bill concerning a county east of the mountains altered, page 7; bill with alterations accepted, page 8.

ACTS NAMING THE COUNTIES WITHIN THE STATE
MARCH 1778

A.J.1778: county west of the mountains named Bennington (March 17), page 8; county east of the mountains named Unity (March 17), page 8; Unity county renamed Cumberland county (March 21), page 13.

AN ACT TO REGULATE FISHING IN THE WHITE RIVER
24 MARCH 1778

A.J.1778: committee appointed to prepare a bill concerning fishing in the White River, page 13; act passed, page 15.

AN ACT REGULATING HIGHWAYS
20 MARCH 1778

A.J.1778: an act providing, altering, regulating and mending highways voted, page 9; committee appointed to prepare a bill, page 9; highway act passed, page 12.

AN ACT RELATING TO THE COPYING OF THE JOURNALS
26 MARCH 1778

A.J.1778: committee appointed to prepare the papers passed by the House for copying, page 16-17; committees appointed to copy the proceedings of the House and distribute to the towns, page 17.

AN ACT RELATING TO THE DUTIES OF THE LISTERS
23 MARCH 1778

A.J.1778: the list act read and passed by paragraphs, pages 13-14.

AN ACT REGULATING THE MILITIA
25 MARCH 1778

A.J.1778: Governor and Council requested to prepare a militia bill, page 7; militia bill passed, page 16.

AN ACT FOR THE ESTABLISHMENT OF PROBATE DISTRICTS
24 MARCH 1778

A.J.1778: four probate districts for each county voted; committee appointed to draw lines between districts, page 8; committee report accepted, page 9; act establishing probate districts passed, page 16.

AN ACT FOR THE ESTABLISHMENT OF PROBATE FEES
24 MARCH 1778

A.J.1778: probate fees established as being three times as much as those established by Connecticut law, page 16.

AN ACT CONCERNING PROBATE JUDGES
25 MARCH 1778

A.J.1778: committee appointed to bring in a bill concerning appointment of probate judges; their report accepted, page 16.

AN ACT OF AFFIRMATION FOR QUAKERS
20 MARCH 1778

A.J.1778: act of affirmation for Quakers passed, page 10.

AN ACT ESTABLISHING THE FEES OF THE SECRETARY OF STATE
25 MARCH 1778

A.J.1778: fees of the Secretary of State to be generally three times those allowed by Connecticut law, page 16.

ACTS RELATING TO THE DESIGNATION OF SHIRE TOWNS AND THE
APPOINTMENT OF JUDGES FOR SHIRE TOWNS
24 MARCH 1778

A.J.1778: committee appointed to designate shire towns, page 7; lines between shire towns adopted; judges appointed for the different shires, page 15.

AN ACT RELATING TO TORIES
26 MARCH 1778

A.J.1778: committee appointed to prepare Tory bill, page 10; act passed allowing the Governor and Council to dispose of Tory estates, 17.

AN ACT FOR THE REGULATION OF TOWN MEETINGS
24 MARCH 1778

A.J.1778: committee appointed to establish town meeting day, page 10; act passed regulating town meetings, page 15.

AN ACT AGAINST TREASON
26 MARCH 1778

A.J.1778: act against treason passed, based on Connecticut law, page 17.

LAWS OF VERMONT
PASSED DURING THE SESSION OF THE GENERAL ASSEMBLY
JUNE 4-JUNE 18, 1778

AN ACT FOR THE ERECTION OF TOLL GATES
6 JUNE 1778

A.J.1778: committee appointed to consider a petition from Pownal, page 22; act passed allowing the erection of toll gates on the Albany Road in Pownal, page 22.

AN ACT ADOPTING A UNION WITH CERTAIN NEW HAMPSHIRE TOWNS

11 JUNE 1778

A.J.1778: referendum voted concerning union with several New Hampshire towns, page 9; committee appointed to count votes concerning union, page 23; voted that union take place, page 24; act concerning union adopted, page 24.

LAWS OF VERMONT

PASSED DURING THE SESSION OF THE GENERAL ASSEMBLY

OCTOBER 8-OCTOBER 24, 1778

AN ACT REVIVING CERTAIN ACTS PASSED AT PREVIOUS SESSIONS

23 OCT 1778

A.J.1778: acts passed at the March and June sessions, except those concerning special courts and banishment, revived until next session, page 47.

AN ACT FOR THE RELIEF OF EUNICE COOK

15 OCT 1778

A.J.1778: report of the committee appointed on the petition of Eunice Cook read and accepted, page 37; a bill accordingly brought in and passed, page 38.

AN ACT FOR AUTHENTICATING DEEDS AND CONVEYANCES

20 OCT 1778

A.J.1778: committee appointed to prepare a form for a deed, page 29; act for authenticating deeds and conveyances passed, page 40.

AN ACT FOR THE ESTABLISHMENT OF FEES AND FINES

24 OCT 1778

A.J.1778: committee appointed to draw up a bill for establishment of fees and fines, page 41; act concerning fees, fines, and penalties passed, page 41(?); committee membership changed, page 46; act concerning fees passed, page 48.

AN ACT FOR REVIVING THE MILITIA ACT

22 OCT 1778

A.J.1778: resolved that the militia act be revived, page 45.

AN ACT FOR REVIVING THE GENERAL PRIVILEGES ACT
22 OCT 1778

A.J.1778: resolved to revive the act for securing the general privileges of the freemen of the state.

AN ACT TO PROHIBIT THE EXPORT OF PROVISIONS
20 OCT 1778

A.J.1778: an act prohibiting the export of provisions passed, page 40.

AN ACT FOR THE IMPROVEMENT OF A ROAD
24 OCT 1778

A.J.1778: petition read, granted, and bill ordered brought in for repair of a road through Wilmington, page 38; resolved to make a road from Wilmington to Bennington, page 48.

AN ACT FOR THE RELIEF OF NICHOLAS TURNER
15 OCT 1778

A.J.1778: a report of the committee appointed on the petition of Nicholas Turner read and approved; bill brought in and passed, page 38.

AN ACT FOR THE RELIEF OF LEMUEL WHITE
17 OCT 1778

A.J.1778: petition of Lemuel White read; ordered that a rehearing be granted and a bill brought in, page 38.

AN ACT REVIVING THE ACT RELATING TO WRITS
22 OCT 1778

A.J.1778: resolved to revive the act relating to the abatement and amendment of writs, page 45.

LAWS OF 1779

LAWS OF 1779

IN 1779, as in 1778, the General Assembly met three times. At the first of these sessions, February 11 through 26, there was passed a body of statute law, based on English common law, similar to the legislation in force in the other New England states. The second session lasted merely from June 2 through 4; the October session lasted from the 14th through the 27th.

The body of statute law passed in February was accompanied by almost no discussion, as we can see from the Assembly Journal. This was because the same laws were passed that were in the Connecticut law book (1769 edition) with a few exceptions; these were the same laws that had been in usage for many years. Most of the settlers had come from Connecticut, and the other New England states; they figured the old laws would serve the new state as well. Significantly, the new state of Connecticut was also to copy the old laws almost verbatim in their revision of 1784.

For a study of the development of common law, see *The Common Law*, by Oliver Wendell Holmes. Originally written in 1881, a recent edition (ed. Mark de Wolfe Howe, Cambridge, 1963) contains an essay on the place of common law in our history. Other readings, suggested by Austin Noble, Esq., include *The Formative Era in American Law* (Roscoe Pound, New York, 1938); *Readings on the History and System of the Common Law* (Pound and Theodore Plucknett, Rochester, 1927, 3rd edition); *Sketches on the Principles of Government* (Nathaniel Chipman, Rutland, 1793); and *Life of Nathaniel Chipman* (Daniel Chipman, about 1845).

LAWS OF VERMONT
PASSED DURING THE SESSION OF THE GENERAL ASSEMBLY
FEBRUARY 11-FEBRUARY 26, 1779

AN ACT FOR SECURING THE GENERAL PRIVILEGES OF THE PEOPLE, AND ESTABLISHING COMMON LAW AND THE CONSTITUTION, AS PART OF THE LAWS OF THIS STATE

13 FEB 1779

Forasmuch as the free fruition of such liberties and privileges as humanity, civility and christianity call for, as due to every man, in his place and proportion, without impeachment and infringement, hath been, and ever will be, the tranquility and stability of churches and commonwealth; and the denial or deprival thereof, the disturbance, if not ruin of both:

Be it enacted, and it is hereby enacted, by the representatives of the freemen of the state of Vermont, in general assembly met, and by the authority of the same, that no man's life shall be taken away; no man's honor or good name stained; no man's person shall be arrested, restrained, banished, dismembered, nor anyway punished; no man shall be deprived of his wife or children; no man's goods or estate shall be taken away from him, nor any way indamaged, under colour of law, or countenance of authority; unless it be by virtue of some express law of this state, warranting the same, established by the general assembly; or in case of the defect of such law in any particular case, by some plain rule warranted by the word of God.

That all the people of the American states within this state, whether they be inhabitants or not, shall enjoy the same justice and law that is general for this state; in all cases proper for the cognizance of the civil authority and courts of judicature in the same, and that without partiality or delay: and that no man's person shall be restrained or imprisoned by any authority whatever, before the law hath sentenced him thereto, if he can and will put in sufficient security, bail or main-prize for his appearance, and good behaviour in the meantime; unless it be for capital crimes, contempt in open court, or in such cases wherein some express law doth allow of or order the same.

Be it further enacted by the authority aforesaid, that common law, as it is generally practiced and understood in the New England states, be, and is hereby established as the common law of this state.

Be it further enacted by the authority aforesaid, that the constitution of this state, as established by general convention held at Windsor, July and December 1777 together with and agreeable to such alterations and additions as shall be made in such constitution, agreeable to the 44th section in the plan of government shall be forever considered held, and maintained, as part of the laws of this state.

AN ACT DIRECTING JUSTICES OF THE PEACE IN THEIR OFFICE AND DUTY

13 FEB 1779

Be it enacted, and it is hereby enacted, by the representatives of the freemen of the state of Vermont, in general assembly met, and by the authority of the same, that on complaint made to any of the justices of the peace within this state, of any breach of law, committed in the county where such justice lives, he shall grant out his writ, warrant, or summons (as the nature of the case may require) requiring the appearance of the person, so complained of, before him; who shall duly examine into the matter (the delinquent being present); and if, upon examination, such justice does find the matter in demand, or fine, to exceed twenty pounds, or corporal punishment due to the crime with which the party complained of is charged, to exceed ten lashes; then such justice shall bind such offender in recognizance, or send him by mittimus to gaol, as he shall find convenient or necessary, to appear before the next superior or county court, and be dealt with as the law directs.

That in case the justice shall, upon such examination, find the matter in demand, or fine, does not exceed twenty pounds, or corporal punishment due for such offence as the offender is charged with, does not exceed ten lashes, and title of land is not concerned, such justice, with the advice and assistance of one or two other assistants or justices, shall proceed and try such action, and award sentence and execution accordingly.

And in case the justice does find the matter in demand, or fine, does not exceed ten pounds, or corporal punishment as aforesaid does not exceed ten lashes, and title of land is not concerned, as aforesaid, such justice may and shall have a right to try such action, and award sentence and execution accordingly.

Always provided, that such cases shall be tried by jury, if either party require it; of which such justice or justices shall always give information to the parties, before they proceed to trial.

Which jury shall be six freemen of the neighbourhood, qualified, impannelled and sworn, who shall find the matter in issue with damages, according to law and evidence; and the justice or justices thereon shall make and declare sentence.

AN ACT CONCERNING ABATEMENT AND AMENDMENT OF WRITS, JUDGMENTS, ETC.

23 FEB 1779

Be it enacted, and it is hereby enacted, by the representatives of the freemen of the state of Vermont, in general assembly met, and by the authority of the same, that all writs, processes, declarations, indictments, pleas, answers, replications, and entries in the several courts of justice within this state, shall be in the english tongue, and no other.—

And that no summons, process, writ, warrant, or other proceedings in court or course of justice, shall be abated, arrested, or reversed for any kind of circumstantial error of mistake, where the parties and the cause may be rightly understood and intended by the court; or through defect, or want of form only, and the judges, or justice, on motion made in court, may order amendment thereof.

AN ACT AGAINST, AND FOR THE PUNISHMENT OF ADULTERY

18 FEB 1779

Be it enacted, and it is hereby enacted, by the representatives of the freemen of the state of Vermont, in general assembly met, and by the authority of the same, that whosoever shall commit adultery with a married woman, or one betrothed to another man, both of them shall be severely punished by whipping on the naked body not exceeding thirty-nine stripes, and stigmatized, or burnt on the forehead with the letter A, on a hot iron; and each of them shall wear the capital letter A, on the back of their outside garment, of a different colour, in fair view, during their abode in this state. And as often as such convicted person shall be seen without such letter, and be thereof convicted before an assistant or justice of the peace in this state, shall be whipped on the naked body, not exceeding ten stripes.

AN ACT AGAINST POLYGAMY

19 FEB 1779

Whereas the violation of the marriage covenant is contrary to the command of God, and destructive to families:

Be it enacted, and it is hereby enacted, by the representatives of the freemen of the state of Vermont, in general assembly met, and by the authority of the same, that if any person or persons in this state being married, or who shall hereafter marry, do at any time presume to marry any other person, the former or other husband or wife being alive, and not by law divorced; or shall continue to live together so married, that then every such offender shall suffer and be punished as in case of adultery; and such marriage shall be, and is hereby declared to be null and void—which offenders shall be tried in the county where they shall be apprehended.

AN ACT FOR THE PUNISHMENT OF LASCIVIOUS CARRIAGE AND BEHAVIOUR

19 FEB 1779

For the preventing of lascivious carriage and behaviour—against, and for the punishment of which (in regard of the variety of circumstances) particular and express laws cannot be easily suited and made. Therefore,

Be it enacted, and it is hereby enacted, by the representatives of the freemen of the state of Vermont, in general assembly met, and by the authority of the same, that the several and respective county courts within this state, shall be, and are hereby impowered and directed, to proceed against and punish such persons as shall be guilty of lascivious carriage and behaviour, either by imposing a fine on them, or by committing them to the house of correction, or by inflicting corporal punishment on them, according to the nature and aggravation of the offence, according to the discretion of such court; that such reasonable and exemplary punishment may be inflicted on such offender in that kind, that others may hear or fear.

AN ACT FOR THE PUNISHMENT OF INCEST, AND FOR PREVENTING INCESTUOUS MARRIAGES

18 FEB 1779

Be it enacted, and it is hereby enacted, by the representatives of the freemen of the state of Vermont, in general assembly met, and by the authority of the same, that no man shall marry any woman within the degrees of kindred hereafter named in this act; that is to say, no man shall marry his grandfather's wife, wife's grandmother, father's sister, mother's sister, wife's mother's sister, father's wife, wife's mother, daughter, son's daughter, daughter's daughter, son's son's wife, daughter's son's wife, wife's son's daughter, wife's daughter's daughter, brother's daughter, sister's daughter, brother's son's wife, sister's son's wife.

And if any man shall hereafter marry, or have carnal copulation with any woman who is within the degrees before recited in this act, every such marriage shall be null and void; and all children that shall hereafter be born of such incestuous marriages or copulation, shall be forever disabled to inherit by descent, or by being generally named in any deed or will, by father or mother.

That every man and woman who shall marry, or carnally know each other, being within any of the degrees before mentioned in this act, and shall be convicted thereof before any superior court in this state, shall be set upon the gallows, the space of one hour, with a rope about their neck, and the other end cast over the gallows; and in that way from thence to the common gaol, shall be severely whipped, not exceeding thirty nine stripes each.

Also, every person so offending, shall for ever after wear a capital letter I, of two inches long, and proportionable bigness, cut out in cloth of a contrary colour to their clothes, and sewed upon their garments, on the outside of their arm, or on their back, in open view.

And if any person or persons, convicted and sentenced as aforesaid for such offence, shall at any time be found without their letter so worn, during their abode in this state, they shall, by warrant from any one assistant or justice of the peace, be forthwith apprehended, and ordered to be publicly whipped, not exceeding fifteen stripes, and from time to time, or as often as they shall so offend.

AN ACT FOR THE PUNISHMENT OF RAPE

19 FEB 1779

Be it enacted, and it is hereby enacted by the representatives of the freemen of the state of Vermont, in general assembly met, and by the authority of the same, that if any man shall forcibly, and without consent, ravish any woman, or maid, by committing carnal copulation with her against her consent, he shall be put to death.

Provided complaint and prosecution be made forthwith, upon the rape; and that the woman, in time of distress, did make an out-cry on the occasion.

AN ACT REGULATING OF MARRIAGES
15 FEB 1779

Be it enacted, and it is hereby enacted, by the representatives of the freemen of the state of Vermont, in general assembly met, and by the authority of the same, that no man or woman shall be joined together in marriage, before the purpose or intention of such marriage has been published in the respective towns where the persons do ordinarily belong or reside, by the town clerk, or clerks of such town or towns, at least eight days before such marriage is consummated; nor shall any such persons be joined together, before they arrive to lawful age; that is to say, a male person to the age of twenty one years, and a female person to the age of eighteen years, without leave first obtained from the parents (if living), or the master or masters, or guardians of such person.

Any person that shall presume to join any man or woman together in marriage, before he is certified that such purpose of marriage has been published as aforesaid, and if minors, without consent as aforesaid, shall forfeit and pay to the treasurer of the county where the offence is committed, the sum of fifty pounds, to be recovered by bill, plaint, or information.

And that no person whatsoever in this state, other than the governor, deputy governor, members of the council, judges of superior and inferior courts, justices of the peace in their respective counties, settled ministers of the gospel in their respective towns, and during the time of his or their ministry in such town or towns, shall join any person in marriage, on penalty of forfeiting the sum of twenty pounds, to be recovered and appropriated as aforesaid, and suffer imprisonment not exceeding twelve months.

AN ACT TO PREVENT THE TAKING AND USING BOATS AND CANOES, WITHOUT LEAVE
19 FEB 1779

Whereas the taking and using of boats and canoes, without liberty, is too frequently practiced, to the damage of the owners thereof.

Which to prevent,

Be it enacted, and it is hereby enacted, by the representatives of

the freemen of the state of Vermont, in general assembly met, and by the authority of the same, that whosoever shall take and use any kind of boats or canoes, other than such as shall be taken up going adrift, and loose from any shore, or found when driven away and lost, without liberty from the owner or owners thereof, shall, for every such offence, forfeit and pay to the owner or owners thereof double the damage he or they shall sustain by his or their boat or canoe's being taken and used as aforesaid, to be covered by bill, plaint, or information.

AN ACT FOR ENABLING COMMUNITIES TO MAINTAIN, RECOVER, AND DEFEND THEIR COMMON RIGHTS, ESTATES AND INTERESTS

19 FEB 1779

Be it enacted, and it is hereby enacted by the representatives of the freemen of the state of Vermont, in general assembly met, and by the authority of the same, that it shall and may be lawful for all and every town, village, precinct, trustees for schools, proprietors of commons or undivided lands, grants, and other estates and interests, and all other lawful societies and communities whatsoever, to sue, commence, and prosecute any suits or actions, for the maintaining, recovery, or defence of their grants, interest and estates, in any court proper to try the same; and to appear either by themselves, agents, or attornies: and in like manner to defend in all such suits and actions as shall be brought or commenced against them.

And when any such town, village, precinct, trustees, proprietors, or society, as aforesaid, shall be sued, it shall be sufficient notice for them to appear and answer, to leave a true copy of the writ or summons containing such suit or action, with their clerk, or other principal member, inhabitant or proprietor, twelve days before the sitting of the court where the case is to be heard as in other actions is provided.

AN ACT AGAINST HIGH TREASON

13 FEB 1779

Be it enacted, and it is hereby enacted, by the representatives of the freemen of the state of Vermont, in general assembly met, and by the authority of the same, that if any person or persons belonging to, or residing within this state, and under the protection of its laws, shall levy war against the state or government thereof; or knowingly and willingly shall aid or assist any enemies at open war against this state, or the United States of America, by joining their armies, or by enlisting, or procuring or persuading others to enlist for that purpose; or by furnishing such enemies with arms, or ammunition, provision, or any other articles for their aid or comfort; or by carrying on a treacherous correspondence with them; or shall form, or be any way concerned in forming any combination, plot, or conspiracy, for betraying this state, or the United States, into the hands, or power of any enemy; or shall give, or attempt to give or send any intelligence to the enemies of this state for that purpose; every person so offending, and being thereof convicted, shall suffer death, and his estate shall be confiscated.

And be it further enacted by the authority aforesaid, that if any person or persons shall endeavour to join the enemies of this state, or of the United States; or use their influence to persuade or induce any person or persons to join, aid, comfort, or assist them, in any way or manner whatsoever; or shall have knowledge of any person or persons endeavoring, or using their influence aforesaid, and shall conceal the same, shall be punished by fine, according to the nature of his offence, and shall be imprisoned, at the judgment of the superior court, in any of the gaols in this state, not exceeding ten years.

AN ACT FOR ESTABLISHING COUNTY LINES

FEB 1779

Be it enacted, and it is hereby enacted, by the representatives of the freemen of the state of Vermont, in general assembly met, and by the authority of the same, that the tract of land in the hereafter described limits, as well the lands that are, as those that are not appropriated, shall be and remain one entire county, and known by the name of the county of Bennington, viz.

Beginning at the southwest corner of the town of Pownal, thence northerly in the west lines of the towns of Pownal, Bennington, Shaftsbury, Arlington, Sandgate, Rupert, Pawlet, and Wells, to the southwest corner of Poultney; thence northerly on the west line of said Poultney, to the center of a small river, commonly called and known by the name of Poultney River; thence down the center of said river, into the head of East Bay; thence down said bay, through the center of the deepest channel of the same, into South Bay; thence down said bay, through the center of the deepest channel of the same, into Lake Champlain; thence down said lake through the center of the deepest channel of the same, to the south line of the province of Quebec, being the west line of this state; thence east in the south line of the province of Quebec, fifty miles, being the north line of this state; thence southerly to the northeast corner of Worcester, then southerly on the easterly lines of the towns of Worcester, Middlesex, and Berlin to the southeast corner thereof; thence on a straight line to the northwest corner of Tunbridge; thence on the westerly line of Tunbridge to the southwest corner thereof; thence in a straight line to the northwesterly corner of Barnard; thence in the westerly line of Barnard and Bridgewater, to the southwesterly corner thereof; thence southerly in a straight line to the northeast corner of Shrewsbury, thence on the easterly line of Shrewsbury, to the southeasterly corner thereof; thence west to the northeast corner of Wallingford; thence southerly on the easterly lines of Wallingford, Harwich, Brumley, Winhall, and Stratton, to the southeasterly corner of the latter; thence southerly to the northwest corner of Draper; thence southerly in the west lines of Draper and Cumberland, to the north line of the Massachusetts Bay; thence westerly on the line of the Massachusetts Bay, to the southwest corner of Pownal aforesaid, being the south line of this state.

Be it further enacted by the authority aforesaid, that the tract of land in the hereafter described limits, as well the lands that are, as those that are not appropriated, shall be and remain one entire county, and known by the name of the county of Cumberland, viz.

Beginning at the southeast corner of the county of Bennington, in the north line of the state of the Massachusetts Bay; thence east in said line to Connecticut River, being the south line of this state; thence up said river as it tends to the south line of the province of Quebec, being the east line of this state; thence west in the south line of the province of Quebec, to the northeast corner of the county of Bennington, being the north line of this state; thence southerly in the east line of the county of Bennington, to the southeast corner thereof.

AN ACT DIRECTING LISTERS IN THEIR OFFICE AND DUTY

13 FEB 1779

Be it enacted, and it is hereby enacted, by the representatives of the freemen of the state of Vermont in general assembly met, and by the authority of the same, that the listers in the several towns in this state, being sworn to the faithful discharge of their office, shall by themselves, or one or more deputed by them, some time in the month of May annually, warn all the inhabitants proper to be listed, in their towns or precincts, or leave notice at their houses, or usual places of abode, to give in to them their respective lists.

And the said inhabitants being so warned, shall give in to the listers, in writing, a true account of all their listable polls, and all their rateable estate, being their property or belonging to them, on the twentieth of June following, at or before the tenth day of July following particularly mentioning therein all such things as are in this act hereafter expressly valued, signed with their names, or marks; which accounts the said listers shall accept, adding thereto according to their best judgment, a value for all things hereafter mentioned in this act to be listed, that are not particularly valued, and make the whole into one general list.

And that every person or persons, having any lands or real estate proper to be rated, in any other town than where such person dwells, shall give in to the listers of such towns where such estate doth lie; a true list thereof, in manner as before mentioned, without any warning given by the listers of the town where such estate is liable to be rated as aforesaid, or be liable to be fourfolded.

That the listers shall return the sum total of the list unto the general assembly in October annually, with a certificate from the assistant, justice, or town clerk, before whom the said listers were sworn, that they were sworn to the faithful discharge of their office, some time before the first day of May preceding.

And every lister who shall neglect carrying or sending by one of the representatives to the general assembly, the sum total, and certification aforesaid, shall forfeit and pay to the treasurer of this state the sum of ten pounds.

That if no sum total be returned from any town, or there be no such certificate, such town shall be doomed by and at the discretion of the assembly.

That the listers after the tenth of August annually, shall, and they are hereby required, carefully to inspect the said list, until the twenty-fifth of the succeeding September, and to add four-fold for all the polls and rateable estate they shall find left out of the list by any person or persons, the property whereof did belong to such person or persons on the twentieth of June preceding; and if any doubt shall arise thereon the said estate shall be adjudged or reputed the property of the person assessed for the same, unless he can show it to have been the property of some other person on the said twentieth of June; and also add to the said lists four-fold for the whole rateable estate and polls of all such persons as have given in no lists, as a penalty on said persons for their neglect; who shall pay rates for the same, according to their fourfold assessments.

And one half of all sums arising upon such additions, shall, by the constables, or collectors of rates, be paid to said listers, as a reward for their trouble; and the other half shall be for the use for which such rates are made.

And the said listers shall add the sum total of such additions and four-folds, to the sum total before-mentioned, and transmit the same to the assembly, with such additions, on pain of paying the before-mentioned penalty.

That the said listers shall annually, some time in the month of October, deliver the lists of the polls and rateable estate of the inhabitants of their town, by them made, to the clerk of the town, taking his receipt for the same, upon penalty of paying five pounds each lister so neglecting, to the treasurer of the town; to be recovered by bill, plaint, or information.

That when, and so often as any person or persons are overcharged in their lists, it shall be the duty of the listers to grant relief, in such cases only where the estate shall appear not to have belonged to the person on the twentieth day of June preceding; or that it was not left out by him through his neglect or wilfulness, but from sufficient grounds to think it was lost; and that so soon as he was sensible of his duty therein, he did offer his said estate (bona fide) to be entered in the public list, by said lister or listers; and in case the listers do refuse to grant such relief, upon application of the aggrieved party, an assistant, or justice of the peace, with two of the selectmen of the town, may consider the case, and grant such relief as they shall judge just, and agreeable to this act; first notifying two or more of the listers to attend, and show cause (if any they have) why such relief should not be granted.

That if any of the listers in the respective towns, do neglect, within the time ordered by law, to demand of any person or persons within their precinct, their list as aforesaid; in every such case, such listers are hereby required, at any time before the 20th of September next following, to demand such lists of every person so neglected.

And if any person, of whom such list is demanded as aforesaid, shall neglect to bring in a true list of his estate, unto the lister so demanding the same, within five days after the demand, that then such lister shall make up a list for the person so neglecting, according to the best of his judgment, and return the same to the general assembly; and all persons shall be accordingly assessed, in the several rates to be made on such lists.

Be it enacted by the authority aforesaid, that all male persons in the several towns in this state, from sixteen years old to sixty (ministers of the gospel, the president and tutors of the college, annual school masters, and students of the college, until the expiration of the time for their taking their second degree, excepted), shall be set in the list each person at six pounds.

And all rateable estate shall be set in the list as follows, viz.

Every ox or steer, of four years old and upwards, at four pounds each.

Each steer or heifer, of three years old, and each cow, three pounds.

Each steer, or heifer, of two years old, two pounds.

Each steer and heifer, of one year old, one pound.

Each horse or mare, of three years old upward, three pounds.

All horse kind, of two years old, two pounds each.

All horse kind, of one year old, one pound each.

All swine, of one year old or upward, one pound each.

Every person having money on hand, or due to them over and above all debts charged thereon, shall put the same in the annual list, at the rate of six for every hundred pounds; and in case the listers shall suspect any person has not given in the full sum of money on hand, or due as aforesaid, the listers are hereby impowered to call such person or persons before them, there to give in such lists on oath; and either of said listers are impowered to administer such oath.

That all lands within this state, after being improved one year, either for pasture, plowing, or mowing, or stocked with grass, and within inclosure, shall be set in the list at ten shillings per acre.

That all horse kind, or other creatures, rateable by law, that are put upon any farm in this state, remote from the town where the owner dwells, and under the care, occupancy and improvement of a tenant, shall be put into the list of the polls and rateable estate of such tenant, in the town or peculiar where such farm lies. And in all other cases, all horse kind, and other creatures, rateable by law, shall be put into the list of the polls and rateable estate of the owners thereof, in the towns where they dwell.

And all peculiars, or lands not as yet laid within the bounds of any town, those lands, with the persons and estates thereupon, shall be assessed by the rates of the next town unto it; the measure or estimation to be by the distance of the meeting house or center.

That the ministers of the gospel that now are, or hereafter may be settled in this state, and the president of the college (during the continuance of their public service in the gospel ministry, and presidency), shall have all their estate lying in the same town where they dwell, exempted.

As also shall all lands in this state, sequestered, or improved for schools, and other pious uses, be exempted.

Be it further enacted by the authority aforesaid, that all allowed attornies at law in this commonwealth, shall be set in the annual list for their faculty, the least practitioner fifty pounds, and the others in proportion, according to their practice; to be assessed at the discretion of the listers of the respective towns where said attornies live, during their practice as such.

All tradesmen, traders, and artificers shall be rated in the list proportionable to their gains and returns; in like manner all warehouses, shops, workhouses, and mills, where the owners have particular improvement or advantage thereof, according to the best judgment and discretion of the listers.

Such persons as are disabled by sickness, lameness, or other infirmities shall be exempted.

That the listers chosen in the respective towns, shall take the oath provided in the constitution of this state, for such officers.

And for enabling the said listers to recover their part of the fourfold assessments, out of the hands of the officers collecting the same,

Be it further enacted by the authority aforesaid, that when any constable or collector of rates, shall neglect or refuse to make payment to the listers of any such sum or sums of money, as shall be come due to them from such constables or collectors, on account of such four-fold assessments, it shall be lawful for such listers to make application to the next assistant, or justice of the peace, who shall be, and is hereby impowered, to grant a writ of scire facias against such constable or collector, to show cause (if any he hath), why execution shall not be granted against him for such sum, or sums, with the necessary charges: and if such constable, or collector do not appear according to such scire facias, before such assistant, justice of the peace, or county court, according to the value of the action, and show sufficient cause why execution shall not be granted as aforesaid; such assistant, justice, or county court, shall grant out execution in due form of law, to levy on the goods and chattels of said constable or collector, for such sum or sums, so neglected to be paid, and the necessary charges; and for want of such estate, to take the person, and retain the same until satisfaction be made, and the money, so collected, be paid to the said listers.

AN ACT CONSTITUTING AND ESTABLISHING ONE SUPERIOR COURT IN THE STATE OF VERMONT

13 FEB 1779

Be it enacted, and it is hereby enacted, by the representatives of the freemen of the state of Vermont, in general assembly met, and by the authority of the same, that one superior court, consisting of five judges, be and is hereby constituted in this state, held and kept for the year ensuing, at the times and places hereafter mentioned, by one chief judge, and four other judges; to be appointed and commissioned for that purpose; any three of whom shall have power to hold said court: which court shall have cognizance of all pleas of the state, that relate to life, limb or other corporal punishment: also fines, banishment and divorce; and shall have power to hear and determine the same by jury, or otherwise according to law, and award execution accordingly. And shall have cognizance of all pleas in causes or actions between party and party, or between this state and any of the subjects of this or the other states, whether the same do concern or relate to murder, treason, burglary, theft, robbery, riot, gaol-breaking, rescuing prisoners, impeding the authority of this state in the execution of their office; also trespass, damage, fraud or cheat; either by appeal, review, writ of error, scire facias, indictment, complaint, or otherwise as the law directs; and the same to try by jury, or otherwise, as aforesaid, and therein proceed to judgment, and award execution thereon accordingly.

That this court shall not have cognizance of any action where the matter in demand does not exceed twenty pounds, or the fine does not exceed twelve pounds, except by appeal.

That this court shall have no power to try any action or title of land, for the year ensuing; any clause in this or any other act of the legislature of this state to the contrary notwithstanding.

That when, and so often as it shall happen, that by reason of the necessary absence of, or just exception against, any of the judges of the said superior court, there shall not be a sufficient number of them to hold said court, or try any cause, the vacancy shall be supplied by any of the counsellors of this state.

That any one or two of the judges of said court, being at the time and place for opening of said court, shall have full power to open and adjourn the same.

That the judges of the said court shall have full power to appoint and swear a clerk for said court; who shall be, and is hereby impowered to grant executions on judgments rendered in said court, and to act and do all things proper for him as a clerk of said court, in the execution of said office, according to the rules, orders, and directions of said court, and according to law.

That the chief judge, or in his absence any three of the other judges, shall be, and they are hereby impowered to call a special court upon any extraordinary occasion.

That the times and places for holding the superior court of judicature for the year ensuing, shall be as follows; that is to say,

Within and for the county of Bennington, at Bennington, on the second Thursday of December next.

Within and for the county of Cumberland, at Westminster, on the second Thursday of March next.

Within and for the county of Bennington, at Rutland, on the second Thursday of June next.

Within and for the county of Cumberland, at Newbury, on the second Thursday of September next.

Be it further enacted by the authority aforesaid, that all actions that are entered in any of the special courts in this state, which remain untried shall be transferred as they now stand, from the said special courts into the superior court, at the first sitting of said court in the county where such actions are now entered.

AN ACT TO PREVENT RIOTS, DISORDERS, AND CONTEMPT OF AUTHORITY, WITHIN THIS STATE, AND FOR PUNISHING THE SAME

FEB 1779

Whereas breaking open gaols, rescuing prisoners, &c. are much to the damage of civil society,

Which to prevent,

Be it enacted, and it is hereby enacted, by the representatives of the freemen of the state of Vermont, in general assembly met, and by the authority of the same, that if any person, or persons, shall impede or hinder any officers, judicial or executive, civil or military, under the authority of this state, in the execution of his office, on conviction thereof before the superior court of this state, he or they shall be whipped on the naked back, not exceeding one hundred lashes for the first offence, and pay all costs and damages that shall accrue from such disorder, beside cost of prosecution: and for want of estate to pay said costs, damages &c. the offender may be bound in service to any subject of this state, for such time as shall be judged by said court to be sufficient to pay costs, damages, &c. And said court are hereby authorized to bind said delinquent.

Be it further enacted by the authority aforesaid, that if any person shall be guilty of a second offence of the like nature, and shall be convicted thereof, he shall be branded with the letter C on the forehead, and shall be whipped on the naked back, not exceeding one hundred lashes; to be repeated every time of conviction.

Be it further enacted by the authority aforesaid, that if any person or persons, either directly or indirectly, shall break open, or aid or assist in breaking open, any goal, or place of confinement, wherein any prisoner or prisoners may be confined by the authority of this state, on conviction thereof, he or they shall be whipped on the naked back, not exceeding one hundred lashes, and be branded on the forehead with the letter B, and pay a fine, not exceeding one hundred pounds, and all costs and damages that may accrue from such disorders, together with cost of prosecution; and for want of estate to pay said costs and damages, the offender may be bound in service as aforesaid.

That the superior court, before the dismission of such delinquent, may call on him to give bonds, in surety, not exceeding three thousand pounds, for his good behaviour: and in case such delinquent shall refuse to give such surety, said court are hereby impowered to confine such delinquent in any of the goals of this state.

AN ACT DIRECTING PROCEEDINGS AGAINST FORCIBLE ENTRY AND DETAINER

13 FEB 1779

Be it enacted, and it is hereby enacted by the representatives of the freemen of the state of Vermont, in general assembly met, and by the authority of the same, that upon complaint made to any one or more assistants or justices of the peace, of any forcible entry made in any house, lands, tenements, or other possessions, lying within the county where such assistant or assistants, justice or justices reside; or of any wrongful detainer of any such houses, lands, tenements, or other possessions, by force, or strong hands, that is to say, by or with such violent words or actions as have a natural tendency to affright and terrify;

every such assistant or assistants, justice or justices, within convenient time, at the cost of the party aggrieved, shall go to the place where the said force is, taking with him or them the sheriff of the county (if need be), to aid and assist said authority; and any of the people of the county, shall attend the said assistant or assistants, justice or justices, to assist him or them to arrest such offenders (when thereunto called) upon pain of imprisonment for a term not exceeding one month, and of paying a fine of twenty shillings to the treasury of the county.

And that two assistants, or two justices, or one assistant and one justice, shall have authority to enquire by oath, of the people of the same county, as well as of them that make such forcible entry, or hold and detain the same by force and strong hand: and if it be found on such enquiry, that a forcible entry hath been made into houses, lands, tenements, or other possessions, that the same are held by force; then such assistants, or justices, shall cause the same houses, lands, tenements, or other possessions, to be re-seized, and the party to be put into possession thereof, who in such manner was put or held out of the same.

And in such cases, where the nature of the facts are cognizable before such authority, the said authority shall also tax a bill of cost against such persons as before them shall be convicted of forcible entry, or detainer.

And in case the person complained of is found not guilty, cost shall be taxed against the complainant, and execution thereon granted accordingly.

And to the end that enquiry may be made, as aforesaid,

Be it enacted by the authority aforesaid, that such assistants or justices shall make out their warrants or precepts, directed to the sheriff of the same county, or his deputy, commanding him, in the name of the freemen of this state, to cause to come before them eighteen sufficient and indifferent persons, dwelling near unto the houses, lands, tenements, or other possessions, so entered upon, or held as aforesaid, whereof fourteen shall be sworn well & truly to enquire of such forcible entry, or detainer, and to return a true verdict, according to their evidence.

And if the sheriff shall make default, in not executing such warrant or precept, to him directed, he shall be fined or amerced in the sum of five pounds, for every default.

And every juror, legally summoned, making his default by non-appearance, shall pay a fine of twenty shillings.

That when it shall so happen, that the sheriff is either a party, or stands in the relation of a father or son, by nature or marriage, or of a brother in the like kind, uncle or nephew, landlord or tenant to either of the parties; either of the constables of the town where the facts are said to be done, not being interested, or related as aforesaid, shall have in those cases, all the powers and authority that the sheriffs, in this act, are vested with; and shall be under the same regulations, and in case of default, liable to the same penalties.

And that any assistant, or assistants, justice, or justices, holding such court of enquiry, may impose a fine on every such offender, not exceeding twenty shillings; and demand bonds of such offender or offenders, for their good behaviour, until the next county court in that county, there to appear; and on such offender refusing or neglecting to give such bonds, they may commit such offender to prison, until he or they do comply with the judgment.

And if the offence be aggravated by any open or high-handed breach of peace, or otherwise, the county court may increase the fine according to the aggravation, or circumstances of the offence.

All fines arising by virtue of this act, to be to and for the use of the county treasury.

And the party aggrieved shall recover treble damages, and costs of suit, by action of trespass against the offender or offenders, if it be found by verdict, or in any other manner by due form of law, that he or they entered into his house, lands, tenements, or other possessions, by force.

Provided always, that this act shall not extend to any person or persons who have had the occupation, or have been in the quiet possession of any houses, lands, tenements, or other possessions, for the space of three whole years next before, and his or their estate or estates therein, is not ended or determined, anything to the contrary in this act notwithstanding.

AN ACT FOR RELIEVING AND ORDERING IDIOTS, IMPOTENT, DISTRACTED AND IDLE PERSONS

16 FEB 1779

Be it enacted, and it is hereby enacted, by the representatives of the freemen of the state of Vermont, in general assembly met, and by the authority of the same, that when and so often as it shall happen, that any person or persons shall be naturally wanting of understanding, so as to be uncapable to provide for themselves; or, by the providence of God, by age, sickness, or otherwise, become poor and impotent, or unable to provide for themselves, and having no estate wherewithal they may be supported; then they, and every of them, shall be provided for and supported by such of their relations as stand in the line or degree of fathers or mothers, grandfather or grandmother, children or grand-children, if they are of sufficient ability to do the same; which sufficient relations shall provide such support and maintenance in such manner and proportion as the county court in that county where such idiot, dis-tracted, poor or impotent person dwells, shall judge just and reasonable, whether such sufficient relations dwell in the same or another county. And the said courts are hereby fully authorized, upon application to them made either by the selectmen of the town, or any one or more of such relations, to order the same accordingly.

And if any of such relations who shall be by such court assessed, or ordered to pay any certain sum or sums, for the purpose aforesaid, shall neglect to do the same, or give sufficient security to abide by and fulfill the judgment of the court, the said court may award execution quarterly against such persons respectively, for levying so much as they are re-spectively assessed, to be delivered into the hands of the complainant or complainants respectively, for the purpose aforesaid.

But if such idiot, distracted, or impotent person, have any estate, the county court of that county where they dwell, may order and dispose thereof in such manner as they shall judge best, for and toward the support of the persons; as also the persons themselves, to any proper work or service, he, she, or they may be capable of performing, at the direction of the selectmen; or the selectmen may appoint and impower some meet person, a conservator to take care of, and oversee such idiots, distracted, and impotent persons, and their estates, for their support; who shall be accountable to said selectmen for their management of said trust, when thereto ordered by said selectmen.

And if the estate of such idiot, distracted or impotent person, con-sist of houses or lands, the general assembly (upon application to them made) may license and authorize the selectmen of the same town, or some other meet person to make sale of such houses or lands, or so much thereof as the assembly shall think fit to order, to and for the use, relief and benefit of such impotent person, the produce thereof on sale to be secured and employed for the purpose aforesaid, so long as such person shall live; or until he or she be capable of providing and taking care of him or herself; and the overplus (if any there be) in case of restoration, to and for the use of the person; and in case of death, to and for the use of the next and right heirs of such person.

That if such idiot, distracted, poor and impotent persons have not estate (the income whereof being improved, or disposed of, as aforesaid) sufficient for their support, and no relations appear to provide for them, or that stand in so near a degree that they may be compelled thereto; in every such case the selectmen, or overseers of the poor of the town or peculiar where such person is by law an inhabitant, be, and are hereby impowered and required to take effectual care, and make necessary provision, for the relief, support and safety of such person, at the charge of the town or place where he or she of right belongs. And if they belong to no town or place in this or the other American states, then at the cost of this state.

Be it further enacted by the authority aforesaid, that the selectmen for the time being, in the several towns in this state, shall from time to time, diligently inspect into the affairs, and management, of all persons in their town, whether householders or others; and if they shall find any person or persons that are likely to be reduced to want, by idleness, mismanagement or bad husbandry, that then such selectmen may appoint an overseer to advise, direct, and order such persons in the management of their business, for such time or times as they shall think proper: a certificate of which appointment shall be set upon the sign-post, and a copy thereof lodged in the town clerk's office, by such select-men, forthwith; and thereupon no such person, while under such appointment, shall be able to make any bargain, or contract, without the consent of such overseer, that shall be valid in law. And if such measures do not prove sufficient to reform such person, then the selectmen may, and they are hereby directed to make application to the next assistant, or justice of the peace, and inform him thereof; which assistant, or justice, is hereby directed and impowered, at the request of the selectmen, to issue forth his warrant to the sheriff, his deputy, or either of the constables of that town, commanding him to take the body of such person, and bring him before such authority, in order that such person may be examined concerning his idleness or mismanagement, and be dealt with according to this act.

And in case such person, who shall be informed against, shall abscond, so that he can not be taken; then the officer shall serve such warrant, by leaving a true attested copy thereof at the usual or last place of his abode; and after the proceedings above directed to, the selectmen (if no sufficient reason be offered to the contrary) shall, by and with the advice of said assistant, or justice (and having such advice are hereby authorized to), take such person, and his family, if any he hath, into and under their care; and such person, and family, assign, bind, or dispose of in service, as they shall judge best.

And when the selectmen shall have taken into their care any such person, and disposed of him as aforesaid; or in case of his absconding, as aforesaid, being proceeded against as aforesaid, the selectmen are hereby authorized, and fully impowered, by and with the advice of such assistant or justice, to take into their custody all the lands, goods, chattels, and credits of such persons, and the same dispose of, improve and manage for the best good and advantage of such person, or his heirs.

Always provided, that no selectmen shall sell the lands of such idle, or mismanaging, or poor person, without the order of the general assembly.

And the selectmen shall publish their doings with and on such estate taken by them, as aforesaid, by forthwith setting up a certification thereof, under the hands of such authority and selectmen, at some public place in the town, and lodge a true copy thereof in the town clerk's office in said town; and shall also, within ten days after the taking of such estate, make a true and perfect inventory of all and singular the goods, chattels and credits, of such person, as shall come into their hands, with a just estimate of the true value of every article thereof, by the appraisement of two indifferent freeholders under oath, being thereunto appointed and sworn by said authority; which inventory, so taken, shall be lodged in the town clerk's office of that town.

And if any person or persons shall detain, or withhold from such selectmen, any estate, lands or credits, belonging to such idle, mismanaging, or poor person, the said selectmen are hereby impowered to demand and recover the same by action, or other lawful means; which being recovered and received by such selectmen, shall be inventoried, and improved as aforesaid.

And the said selectmen shall take care to pay out of such estate, the just debts due from such persons.

And if any person or persons shall be aggrieved with the doings of such selectmen, in any such case, they may apply and complain to the next county court in that county, for relief; who are hereby impowered to afford such relief, as, on hearing the case, they shall think convenient and just, and give orders therefor, and put the same in execution.

And all such persons, who shall be taken, and whose estates shall be taken and disposed of, according to this act, shall be disabled to make any contract, act, or deed, that shall be binding upon their persons or estates, as minors under guardians by law are, until by their industry, good management, and application to business, they shall obtain a certificate, under the hands of such selectmen and authority, that they are released and their estate put into their own hands and improvement.

AN ACT FOR FORMING AND REGULATING THE MILITIA; AND FOR ENCOURAGEMENT OF MILITARY SKILL, FOR THE BETTER DEFENCE OF THIS STATE

16 FEB 1779

Be it enacted, and it is hereby enacted, by the representatives of the freemen of the state of Vermont, in general assembly met, and by the authority of the same, that the governor of this state, for the time being, shall be captain general and commander in chief; and the deputy governor for the time being, shall be major general, of and over all the military forces within the same.

That all the military companies in this state, shall be formed into regiments, as followeth viz.

That the military companies in the several towns included in the limits hereafter described viz.

Beginning on the west bank of Connecticut River, where the same enters into the state of the Massachusetts-Bay; from thence up said river to the northeast corner of the township of Westminster; thence west by the needle of the compass, to the county line; thence southerly on said line until it comes to the north line of the Massachusetts-Bay aforesaid; from thence easterly on said line, to the place of beginning, be and are hereby made and declared to be one entire and distinct regiment; and shall be distinguished and called by the name of the first regiment.

The military companies in the several towns and gores included in the limits hereafter described, viz.

Beginning at the south-west corner of the township of Pownal; from thence northerly in the line of this state, to the north-west corner of Arlington; thence east a parallel line, until it strikes the county line; thence southerly on said county line, until it comes to the north line of the state of Massachusetts-Bay; thence westerly on said Massachusetts line to the place of beginning, be, and is hereby made and declared to be one entire and distinct regiment; and shall be distinguished and called by the name of the second regiment.

The military companies in the several townships and gores included in the limits hereafter described, viz.

Beginning at the northeast corner of the township of Westminster. on Connecticut River, and running northerly up said river, to the southeast corner of the township of Norwich; thence westerly on the southerly lines of the towns of Norwich and Sharon, and to continue the same course to the county line; thence southerly on said line, until it comes to the northwest corner of the first regiment; thence easterly on said line, to the place of beginning, be, and is hereby made and declared to be one entire and distinct regiment; and shall be distinguished and called by the name of the third regiment.

The military companies in the several townships and gores included in the limits hereafter described, viz.

Beginning at the southeast corner of the township of Norwich, on the west bank of Connecticut River; thence running northerly on said river, until it comes to the forty-fifth degree of northern latitude; thence west on said line, until it comes to the county line; thence southerly on said county line, until it comes to the northwest corner of the third regiment; thence easterly on the north line of said third regiment, to the place of beginning, be and is hereby made and declared to be one entire and distinct regiment; and shall be distinguished and called by the name of the fourth regiment.

The military companies in the several townships and gores included in the limits hereafter described, viz.

Beginning at the northeast corner of the second regiment; from thence running northerly on the county line, until it comes to the forty-fifth degree of north latitude; thence running west on Canada line, until it comes to Lake Champlain; then turning southerly on the west line of this state, until it comes to the northwest corner of the second regiment; thence running easterly with the north line of the second regiment, until it comes to the first mentioned bounds, be and is hereby made and declared to be one entire and distinct regiment; and shall be distinguished and called by the name of the fifth regiment.

That where, by the aforesaid division, or by any division which shall be hereafter made, it shall so happen that any of the said military companies shall be divided, and put part into one regiment, and part into another regiment; in such case, such company or companies shall belong to that regiment, to which the major part of the company doth belong.

That there shall be in each regiment, from time to time, appointed by the soldiery and freemen within the same, a colonel, lieutenant colonel, and major, who shall be commissioned by the governor of this state, for the time being.

That the colonel, or officers commanding in each regiment, as often as he shall see cause, shall require the captain, or chief officers of each company in his regiment, to meet at such time and place as he shall appoint, to confer with them, and give in charge such orders as shall by them, or the major part of them, be judged meet, for the better ordering military affairs, and promoting military skill and discipline in said regiment.

And the said colonel, lieutenant colonel, and major of each regiment, are hereby impowered to dignify the several companies belonging to their respective regiments, calling to their assistance the commissioned officers of the respective companies of said regiment.

And be it further enacted by the authority aforesaid, that all male persons, from sixteen years of age to fifty, shall bear arms, and duly attend all musters, and military exercise of the respective troops and companies, where they are inlisted, or do belong, except ministers of the gospel, counsellors, justices of the peace, the secretary, judges of probate, and superior and inferior courts, the president, tutors, and students at collegiate schools, masters of arts, allowed physicians and surgeons, representatives or deputies for the time being, schoolmasters, attornies at law, one miller to each gristmill, sheriffs and constables for the time being, constant jurymen, tanners who make it their constant business, lamed persons, or others disabled in body, producing a certificate thereof from two able physicians or surgeons, to the acceptance of the two chief officers of the company whereto the person seeking dismission appertains, or the chief officers of the regiment to which such company belongs.

That every listed soldier and other householder, shall always be provided with, and have in constant readiness, a well fixed firelock, the barrel not less than three feet and a half long, or other good firearms, to the satisfaction of the commissioned officers of the company to which he doth belong, or in the limits of which he dwells; a good sword, cutlass, tomahawk or bayonet; a worm, and priming wire, fit for each gun; a cartouch box or powder and bullet pouch; one pound of good powder, four pounds of bullets for his gun, and six good flints; on penalty of eighteen shillings, for want of such arms and ammunition as is hereby required, and six shillings for each defect; and like sum for every four weeks he shall remain unprovided: that each company shall chuse some suitable person to be clerk, who shall be sworn to the faithful discharge of his office, before some counsellor or justice of the peace, which oath shall be administered in the words following, viz.

You .... do solemnly swear by the ever-living God, that you will faithfully execute the office of clerk of the military company of foot, commanded by captain .... until another shall be chosen and sworn in your room; and will do equal right and justice to all men, to the best of your judgment and abilities, according to law. So help you God.

And every clerk so chosen and sworn, shall give his attendance in the field, with his sword by his side, on every of the muster or training days, by his captain or chief officer appointed, to call over the roll of the soldiers, and to take notice of their defects, by their absence or otherwise.

And every such clerk shall take an exact list of all the soldiers within his limits, twice in every year at least, and deliver to the captain or commanding officer of the company of which he is clerk, a true copy of such list twice in every year if thereto required; and also deliver a true and exact account of the number of officers and soldiers contained in his list, to the colonel or chief officer of the regiment to which said company belongs, attested by him as clerk, sometime in the month of April annually and oftener if by such chief officer required; on penalty of forfeiting the sum of ten pounds for every such neglect, to the use of the company to which he belongs; which fine shall be levied by distress and sale of the offenders goods, by warrant from the chief officer of said company, directed to the constable of the town in which said clerk dwells.

And every such clerk is hereby authorized and required to execute all lawful warrants, by his superior officers to him directed, and for the levying any fine or fines on delinquents, together with necessary charges arising thereon; being by virtue of such warrant as fully impowered thereto as constables are in other cases, and shall have the same fees, and shall account for such fines to the chief officer of the company whereto he belongs.

That the colonel or chief officer of each regiment, shall be, and is hereby impowered and authorized, upon any alarm, invasion, or notice of the appearance of an enemy, either by water or land, to assemble in military array, and put in warlike posture, the whole militia of the regiment under his command, or such part of them as he shall think needful; and being so alarmed, to lead, conduct, and employ them, as well within the regiment whereto they belong, as in any other adjacent place in this state; for the assisting, securing and relieving, any of the subjects of the united and independent states of America, or their forts, towns, or places, that shall be assaulted by any enemy, or in danger thereof; and with them, by force of arms to encounter, repel, pursue, kill and destroy such enemy, or any of them, by any fitting ways, enterprizes or means whatsoever.

And the colonel, or chief officer of any regiment, so taking to arms, or leading forth any party of men, shall forthwith post away the intelligence, and occasion thereof to the captain general or commander in chief for the time being, and to the commanding officer of the northern department for the time being; and shall attend and observe such directions and orders as he shall receive from time to time, from him the said captain general.

That when any town or place in this State shall be assaulted, attacked, or set upon by Indians, or any other enemy, it shall be lawful for, and in the power of the chief commissioned officer or officers of the company or companies, in such place so assaulted, attacked, or set upon, to call forth all such soldiers under his or their command, and to martial, order, and dispose them in the best manner, to defend the place so beset; and to encounter, repel, pursue, and destroy the enemy; and, if need so require, to assist a neighbour town, when assaulted or set upon as aforesaid: and in case any officer or soldier shall refuse to muster, and march, according to orders given him for the purposes aforesaid, by his superior officer; such officer shall be cashired, and forfeit and pay to the treasurer of the town where such officer belongs, a sum in proportion to the wages such officer, so neglecting, would be entitled to for such service, with the soldier; who is, for such neglect, by this act, to pay a fine of eighteen pounds, to be applied for the purpose of employing soldiers in the service of this and the United States; and to be recovered by bill, plaint, or information, in any court proper to try the same.

And whereas, for the speedy and effectual defence of this and the United States of America, to raise men on sudden emergencies, and for particular services, by detaching part of the militia for that purpose:—

Wherefore, that the same, when ordered by the general assembly, or the governor and council, in the recess of the assembly, may be rendered effectual,

Be it enacted by the authority aforesaid, that whenever the general assembly, or the governor and council as aforesaid, shall resolve or order that any certain number or proportion of effective men shall be detached, or draughted out of the respective regiments of militia in this state, or any of them, for any particular service, or to be in readiness therefor on a sudden emergency, according as the general assembly, or governor and council shall judge proper; and that if in consequence and pursuance of such resolve or order, any captain, or chief officer of any company, shall cause his company to be warned to assemble and muster at such time and place as he shall appoint, which he is directed to do when required by his superior officer to detach or draught any part thereof, for the purpose aforesaid; every soldier belonging to such company, being duly warned, shall appear, and attend such muster according to such warning; and for neglect thereof, shall forfeit and pay to the treasurer of the town where he dwells, the sum of twelve pounds, to be recovered by bill, plaint, or information in any court proper to try same.

And if any soldier shall in any manner be duly and legally detached or draughted, for the purpose and service or services aforesaid, and shall neglect or refuse reasonably to muster, join to, or proceed with the troops he is appointed to serve with (being duly noticed thereof), he shall forfeit and pay the sum of eighteen pounds, to be recovered as aforesaid and to be applied for the purpose of employing soldier or soldiers, to perform such service: and for want of goods or estate to answer the same, shall be disposed of in service to any subject of this or the United States of America, to satisfy the same: any law, usage, or custom, in any wise heretofore to the contrary notwithstanding.

And be it further enacted by the authority aforesaid, that if at any time it shall appear to the captain, and other commissioned officer or officers of any company, that the following method is more convenient, he may and shall have a right to proceed accordingly, that is to say,

The captain, or commanding officer, shall, with the advice of his under officers, make a roll of all the men's names that he has a right to command, and then divide them into as many divisions as he has orders to draught or detach men, always having reference to those who have done most in the present war, as well as the estates of men; and when it shall so happen that the divisions or classes cannot be equal in number, such officer, with the advice of his under officers then present shall make all such classes as near equal as possible, by connecting men of interest, poor men, and those that have been at most expence in the present war, together in one class.

Then such commanding officer shall make out a list of each person's name that is connected in one class, and give such list to some one man in each class, ordering each class to furnish one man, appointing a time and place for such men to meet, in order to muster or march to the place they may be ordered to.

And in case any such class shall refuse or neglect to furnish a man, as aforesaid, then such officer shall immediately hire one man for every class so neglecting or refusing, as cheap as may be, pledging the faith of this state for the payment of such sum.

And such captain, or commanding officer so hiring man or men, for any class or classes, with the advice of as many of his under officers as may be convenient, shall make out each man's proportion of the cost of hiring as aforesaid (always having particular regard to those that have done most in this war, as well as the estates of persons), and issue his warrant thereon to his clerk, or some other meet person, directing him to take of the goods and chattels of such persons, in such proportion as his warrant shall direct, as also for the cost; and such clerk or other meet person, shall sell such goods or chattels at public vendue, and return to the captain or commanding officer the money which his warrant shall direct; which shall be disposed of to pay the engagement of the captain or commanding officer, to the soldier who engages or does the service; and the cost being paid, the overplus, if any there be, shall be repaid to the owner of the goods or chattels so sold.

And every person authorized by any captain, or commanding officer of any company of the militia of this state, to serve such warrant, is hereby authorized, and fully impowered, if he should at any time meet with opposition in the execution of his warrant, to command a sufficient number of the militia to his assistance; and all persons are hereby directed to assist such person in the execution of his warrant.

And be it further enacted by the authority aforesaid, that if any general officer shall at any time receive orders from the captain general, or commander in chief, requesting him to call together any regiment or regiments of militia within this state, or any part or parts of such regiment or regiments and to march them for the immediate defence of this, or the United States of America, agreeable to such orders, and shall neglect or refuse to put the same in execution, agreeable thereto, shall forfeit and pay to the treasurer of this state, the sum of three hundred pounds, to be recovered in the manner aforesaid.

And in case any field or other officer, commanding any regiment of militia within this state, shall refuse or neglect to put in immediate execution, any order or orders he may receive from the captain general, or from the general officer to whom any such order had been previously issued by the captain general, for the purposes aforesaid; such officer shall, for such refusal or neglect, forfeit and pay to the public treasurer of this state, two hundred pounds, to be recovered as aforesaid.

And in case any captain or other commanding officer of any company of militia within this state, shall refuse or neglect to put in immediate execution, any orders he may receive from any of his superior officers for the purposes aforesaid; or in case any such captain, or other commissioned officer of any such company of militia, who may be nominated, and to whose lot it of course falls to take the command of any number of soldiers so detached or draughted from the company or companies of the regiment to which such officer does belong, shall neglect or refuse to perform such service, shall, for such neglect or refusal, be cashiered, and suffer the penalty as aforesaid for a commissioned officer; and the next commissioned officer to whose lot it shall in course fall, shall forthwith take such command; and said officer so neglecting or refusing to perform his tour in the service, thereto required for his commanding officer, shall be reduced to the ranks; and that if any commissioned officer of any military company, shall lay down his place, or give in his commission without liberty from the captain general; and if any sergeant, clerk or corporal of such company, shall lay down his place without liberty from the colonel or chief officer of the regiment whereto such sergeant, clerk or corporal doth belong; every such officer shall be listed in the roll of the company in the limits whereof he resides, and do all duties and services as private sentinels are by law required to do: that all such persons that are not fifty years of age, who have been sergeants of the foot, in any company within this state, or such as have sustained such office in any war, who shall dwell in the limits of any other company than that in which they have sustained such office, shall be, and are hereby freed from doing duty as private sentinels, and shall be required only to be present, to attend the exercise in such place or office as they have before served in. And if any such officer shall refuse or neglect to be present on days of exercise when required and to attend the duty of his office, he shall be liable to the same fine as others who sustain the same office in any particular company are liable to; and all commissioned officers of the like kind shall be excused from attending.

That all fines, penalties and forfeitures, arising by virtue of this act, or any breach thereof, shall be levied on the goods and chattels of the respective delinquents, if they be not minors; and on the goods or chattels of the parents, masters or guardians of such delinquents as are minors; and shall be for the use of the respective companies to which such person or persons fined do belong (except such fines as are otherwise disposed of in this act).

And every person chosen by any company for their drummer, or fifer, upon his accepting said service shall provide himself a good drum, or fife, and constantly attend service when required, on penalty of ten shillings fine for each day's neglect; to be levied by warrant from the two chief officers of the company to which such drummer of fifer doth belong.

Be it further enacted by the authority aforesaid, that in any town in this State, where there are thirty able bodied men, or more that are freed by the laws of this state from doing duty in the militia companies formed in said towns, on account of age or commissions, etc., that it shall and may be lawful for them to form themselves into a military company, choosing for said company one captain, one lieutenant, and one ensign, who shall be commissioned by the governor of this state, and under the command of the field officers of the regiment where they live, and to which they belong.

Be it further enacted by the authority aforesaid, that where there be twenty or more of the before described persons inclining as aforesaid, it shall and may be lawful for them to form themselves into a military company, choosing one captain, and one lieutenant, to be commissioned and commanded as aforesaid.

Be it further enacted by the authority aforesaid, that where there are two towns lying and joining together, where either of the before mentioned numbers of the before mentioned persons are inclined to form themselves into such company, under such regulations as before mentioned, it shall and may be lawful, and they shall be commissioned and commanded as aforesaid.

Be it further enacted by the authority aforesaid that each and every person in this state who are by law exempted from doing military duty (ministers of the gospel, president, tutors and students in college only excepted), and do not comply with the preceding paragraph of this act, as to forming into a military company, shall be under the command of the military officers within their respective towns, with respect to doing their proportion in the present war.

AN ACT IMPOWERING COLLECTORS TO COLLECT RATES

20 FEB 1779

Be it enacted, and it is hereby enacted by the representatives of the freemen of the state of Vermont, in general assembly met, and by the authority of the same, that whensoever any town, society or other community, which by law are or shall be enabled and authorized to grant and levy any rate, or tax, for the answering or defraying the necessary changes and expences thereof, shall in any of their lawful meetings, agree upon and grant a rate or tax, to be levied upon such town, society, or other community, for any of the purposes for which by law they are or shall be impowered to grant such rate or tax, they shall choose some meet person to be collector of such rates or taxes; and the selectmen, or a committee appointed for that purpose, shall take proper care that such rates be accordingly made for the assessment of the several persons to be taxed, and deliver the same to such collector.

And upon application made to some assistant, or justice of the peace, such assistant or justice, is hereby authorized and directed to grant a warrant for the collecting such rate or tax; which warrant shall be directed to such collector appointed to collect the same, requiring and impowering him to gather and collect such rate or tax, according to the grant thereof made as aforesaid.

And that all such collectors, authorized and directed to gather any rates or taxes whatsoever, duly laid and assessed on any of the inhabitants of this State, shall have full power and authority to collect the same, according to such warrant as shall be given them; and shall have the same power and authority to command assistance in the execution of their office (when need shall require), as is by law given to a sheriff or constable, in the execution of their office: and all persons are hereby required to yield due obedience thereunto.

Provided always, such collector show and read his warrant or authority to the persons whose assistance is commanded.

AN ACT FOR THE ORDERING AND DISPOSING OF TRANSIENT PERSONS

15 FEB 1779

Be it enacted, and it is hereby enacted by the representatives of the freemen of the state of Vermont, in general assembly met, and by the authority of the same, that the selectmen of each respective town in this state, shall be and are hereby authorized and impowered to warn any transient person (residing in such town that is not of a quiet and peaceable behaviour, or is in their opinion like to be chargeable to such town) to depart out of such town, except such person does obtain a vote of the inhabitants of such town in legal town meeting, to remain in such town; and if any such person or persons being so warned, do not leave such town within twenty days after such warning, then one or more of said selectmen may make application to an assistant or justice of the peace, who is hereby impowered to issue his warrant to the sheriff or constable to take such person or persons, and transport him or them, to the next town towards the place where such person was last an inhabitant, in the same manner to be transported to the place where such person or persons were inhabitants last, or in the same way out of this state, if he be not an inhabitant thereof; and all such expence shall be paid by the person or persons so warned, if of ability, but if he is not of ability, to be paid by such town.

Provided always that no person shall be subject to such warning, after he or she has lived in such town one year.

Be it further enacted by the authority aforesaid, that if any transient person or persons shall be taken sick or lame, in any town in this state: whoever shall keep any such person or persons (if such transient, sick or lame person or persons be not of sufficient ability), shall defray all such expence, until complaint thereof be by him made to the selectmen of such town; after which such selectmen shall provide for such transient, sick, or lame person, according to law.

AN ACT FOR THE DUE OBSERVATION AND KEEPING THE FIRST DAY OF THE WEEK AS THE SABBATH, OR LORD'S DAY; AND FOR PUNISHING DISORDERS AND PROFANENESS ON THE SAME

23 FEB 1779

Be it enacted, and it is hereby enacted, by the representatives of the freemen of the state of Vermont, in general assembly met, and by the authority of the same, that no tradesman, artificer, labourer, or other person whatsoever, shall, upon land or water, do or exercise any labour, business, or work, of their ordinary callings, or any kind whatsoever (works of necessity and mercy only excepted), nor use any game, sport, play, or recreation, on the lord's day, or day of public fasting, and Thanksgiving, on pain that every person so offending, and being convicted thereof before an assistant or justice of the peace, shall for every such offence, forfeit not exceeding a sum of ten pounds, as the nature of the offence may require.

That whatsoever person shall be guilty of any rude, profane, or unlawful behaviour on the Lord's day either in words or actions, by clamorous discourse, or by shouting, hallooing, screaming, running, riding, dancing, jumping, blowing of horns, or any such like rude or unlawful words or actions, in any house or place so near to, or in any public meeting house for divine worship, that those who meet there may be disturbed by such rude and profane behaviour, and being convicted, shall incur the penalty of forty shillings for every such offence, and be whipped on the naked back, not exceeding ten stripes, nor less than five.

That no person shall drive a team, or droves of any kind, or travel on said day (except it be on business that concerns the present war, or by some adversity they are belated, and forced to lodge in the woods, wilderness or highways the night before, and in such case to travel no farther than the next inn, or place of shelter, on that day), upon penalty of forfeiting a sum not exceeding ten pounds, as the nature of the offence may require.

Nor shall any person go from his or her place of abode on the Lord's day, unless to or from the public worship of God, attended, or to be attended upon by such person, or unless it be on some work or business of necessity or mercy then to be done or attended upon, on penalty of paying a fine, not exceeding five pounds for every such offence.

Nor shall any person or persons keep or stay at the outside of the meeting house, during the time of public worship (there being convenient room in the house) nor unnecessarily withdraw themselves from the public worship to go without doors, nor profane the time by playing, or profanely talking, on the penalty of paying a fine, not exceeding three pounds, for every such offence, as the nature of the offence may require.

That if any number of persons shall convene and meet together in company or companies, in the street or elsewhere, on the evening next before or after the Lord's day, and be thereof convicted, shall pay a fine, not exceeding three pounds, or sit in the stocks, not exceeding two hours.

Always provided that this act shall not be taken or construed to hinder the meetings of such persons upon any religious occasions.

Provided also, that all presentments or informations against any person or persons, for being guilty of any of the before-mentioned offences, be made within one month after the commission thereof.

That the grandjurymen, and tythingmen, and constables of each town, shall carefully inspect the behaviour of all persons on the Sabbath, or Lord's day, and due presentment make of any profanation of the worship of God, on the Lord's day, or on any day of public fast or Thanksgiving, and of every breach of Sabbath which they, or any of them, shall see or discover any person to be guilty of, to the next assistant, or justice of the peace; who is hereby impowered to proceed therein, according as the nature of the offence requires.

That each grand juryman, tything man, or constable, shall be allowed six shillings per day, for each day he spends in prosecuting such offenders, to be paid by the person offending, or the parent, or guardian, or master of such person when he is under age; and all fines imposed for the breach of this act on minors, shall be paid by the parents, guardians, or masters, if any be; otherwise, such minors to be disposed of in service, to answer the same; and upon refusal, or neglect of payment of such fines, and charges of prosecution, the offender may be committed, unless he be a minor, in which case, execution for the fines and charges shall go forth against his parent, guardian, or master, after the expiration of one month next after such conviction of such minor, and not sooner.

Provided, no person or persons prosecuted on this act, shall be charged with more than for one person prosecuting him for such offence.

That whatever person shall be convicted of any profanation of the Lord's day, or of any disturbances of any congregation, allowed for, as attending on such worship, and shall, being fined for such offence, neglect or refuse to pay the same, or present estate for that purpose, the court, assistant, or justice of the peace, before whom the conviction is had, may sentence such offender to be publicly whipped, not exceeding twenty stripes, respect being had to the nature and aggravation of the offence.

But if any children, or servants, not of the age of discretion, shall be convicted of such profanation or disturbance, they shall be punished therefor by their parents, or guardians, or masters giving them due correction in the presence of some officer, if the authority so appoint, and in no other way; and if such parent, guardian, or master, shall refuse or neglect to give such due correction, that every such parent, guardian or master, shall incur the penalty of ten shillings.

And that no delinquent, on this act, shall be allowed any appeal or review.

And all and every assistant, justice of the peace, constable, grand juryman, and tything man, are hereby required to take effectual care, and endeavour that this act, in all the particulars thereof, be duly observed; as also to restrain all persons from unnecessary walking in the streets, or fields, swimming in the water, keeping open their shops, or following their secular occasions or recreations in the evening preceding the Lord's day, or on said day, or evening following.

AN ACT RELATING TO BRIEFS

17 FEB 1779

Be it enacted, and it is hereby enacted by the representatives of the freemen of the state of Vermont, in general assembly met, and by the authority of the same, that no briefs, craving the charitable contributions of the people in any of the towns or plantations in this state, shall be read or attended in any of the said towns or plantations, unless it have the allowance of the governor and council, and by them directed into what towns or congregations it shall pass (except it be on some special occasion, for any distressed or afflicted person of their own inhabitants), upon penalty of the forfeiture of five pounds for every person that shall read and publish any such brief, not allowed and directed as aforesaid; to be recovered by bill, plaint, or information, in any court of record: one third of which penalty or forfeiture shall be to him that shall inform and prosecute to effect, and the other two thirds to the town treasurer where such offence is committed.

AN ACT FOR THE SECURITY OF THIS STATE

20 FEB 1779

Be it enacted, and it is hereby enacted by the representatives of the freemen of the state of Vermont, in general assembly met, and by the authority of the same, that all securities to this state shall be to the treasurer, in the name and behalf of the general assembly, and lodged in his office; except securities from the treasurer to the state, which shall be given to the secretary, in the name and behalf of the general assembly, and lodged in his office. And all suits that shall be commenced against this state, shall be against the treasurer, in the name and behalf of the general assembly; and all suits that shall be commenced in favour of this state, shall be in the name of the treasurer, in behalf of the assembly.

And be it further enacted by the authority aforesaid, that the treasurer general and trustees of the loan office, shall provide two sufficient sureties; each to bind themselves with the treasurer and trustee of the loan office, in the penal sum of ten thousand pounds for the security of this state, to be lodged in the secretary's office.

AN ACT FOR THE REGULATING AND STATING FEES

17 FEB 1779 (REPEALED PAGE 221)

Be it enacted, and it is hereby enacted by the representatives of the freemen of the state of Vermont, in general assembly met, and by the authority of the same, that the fees of the several courts and officers shall be as follows, viz.

Superior Court's Fees

	£	S	D
Each judge, per day	1	10	0
For trying each action	2	2	0
For each of the jurymen, per day	0	15	0
For judgment on default	0	18	0

Clerk's Fees

For entering each action	0	1	6
Attachments or summonses each	0	3	0
Execution	0	6	0
For licence to each tavern keeper	0	6	0

Assistant's or Justice's Fees

Attachments or summonses each	0	3	0
When bond is given	0	4	6
A subpoena	0	2	0
Entry and trial of an action	0	12	0
An execution	0	6	0
Each warrant for criminals	0	6	0
Bond for appeal	0	3	0
Copy for evidence	0	2	0
Copy of a judgment	0	3	0
Every recognizance	0	3	0
Judgment on confession or default	0	6	0
Affidavits taken out of court each	0	3	0
Taking the acknowledgment of a deed, mortgage, or other instrument	0	3	0

Courts of Probate Fees

	£	S	D
For granting administration	0	9	0
For receiving, and probate of every will and inventory, of fifty pounds	0	12	0
To the clerk	0	4	6
Receiving and probate of every will and inventory above fifty pounds	0	18	0
To the clerk	0	6	0
Each quietas, or acquittance	0	6	0
To the clerk	0	3	0
Recording every will, and inventory, of fifty pounds, or under	0	15	0
Recording every will, and inventory, above fifty pounds, and not exceeding one hundred	0	18	0
Also one shilling and six pence after the first hundred; and half so much for a copy of the same.			
For making out a commission, receiving and examining the claims of the creditors to insolvent estates, and regulating the same	0	3	0
For each page of twenty eight lines, and ten words in a line	0	3	0
For entering an order upon administrator to pay out the estate unto the several creditors, returned by the commissioners	0	3	0
Allowing of accounts, selling and dividing intestate estates	0	9	0
Appointing guardians and taking bond	0	6	0
Each bond for administration	0	6	0
Each letter of administration	0	6	0
Each citation	0	2	0

Secretary's Fees

	£	S	D
For recording laws and orders of public concernment in the state records each	0	6	0
Affixing the state seal	0	3	0
Each military commission	0	6	0
Each commission for a justice of the peace	0	6	0
Each commission for judge of probate	0	6	0
Each petition to the assembly	0	6	0

Sheriff's and Constable's Fees

	£	S	D
Serving every summons	0	2	0
If a copy	0	3	0
Serving attachment	0	3	0
Bail bond	0	4	0
For levying every execution, not exceeding five pounds	0	12	0
For levying every execution above five, & not exceeding ten pounds	0	18	0
For levying every execution, not exceeding twenty pounds	1	10	0
For levying every execution, not exceeding forty pounds	2	5	0
For any greater sum than forty pounds, shall be allowed after the rate of two shillings more on every twenty pounds, above the sum of forty pounds, which shall be levied by the said execution: and the above fees on execution, shall be taken in the same currency that is to be levied by each respective execution.			
Attending at a justice's court, when obliged to attend, for each action tried	0	6	0
Each mile travel out, at	0	1	6
Sheriff attending the general assembly, superior or county court per day	1	4	0
Constable per day for like service	0	18	0
Fees for plaintiff and defendant attending any court, per day	0	9	0
Witnesses attending any court, per day	0	12	0
Travel for plaintiff, defendant, or evidence to any court, per mile	0	1	0

Town Clerk's Fees

For recording a deed	0	6	0
For a copy of a deed	0	6	0
For a survey bill	0	3	0
For recording a marriage	0	1	6
For recording a birth or death	0	1	0
County Surveyor's fees per day	1	4	0

AN ACT TO ADMIT QUAKERS AFFIRMATION

20 FEB 1779

Whereas a considerable number of the good people of this state bearing the denomination of Quakers, being satisfied with the constitution of this state, yet cannot be qualified as freemen, by reason of the oath or affirmation not being adapted to the rules of their church:

Be it enacted, and it is hereby enacted, by the representatives of the freemen of the state of Vermont, in general assembly met, and by the authority of the same, that the following affirmation be established for those people that call themselves Quakers.

I .... solemnly affirm and declare, that whenever I am called to give any vote or suffrage touching any matter that concerns the state of Vermont, I will do it so as in my conscience I shall judge will most conduce to the best good of the same, as established by constitution, without fear or favour of any man, on the penalty of perjury.

AN ACT REGULATING THE PAYMENT AND DISPOSAL OF FEES, FINES, AND PENALTIES

17 FEB 1779

Be it enacted, and it is hereby enacted, by the representatives of the freemen of the state of Vermont, in general assembly met, and by the authority of the same, that every person that shall at any time be fined for the breach of any penal law, or for other just cause, shall forthwith pay the fine or penalty imposed upon him, or give in good and sufficient security speedily to do the same, or shall be imprisoned, or bound out and kept in service until it be paid. And no warrant or distress for levying of fines and penalties, shall be sent out after the expiration of one year after conviction of the delinquent. That all fees paid for trial of any matter or cause in the general court, and in the superior court (the secretary and clerk's fees excepted), and all fines, forfeitures and penalties imposed on any person or persons, by either of the said courts, for any matter of delinquency, shall be and belong to the state treasury, for the defraying the public charges of this state.

And all fees paid for the trial of any matter or cause in the respective county courts in this state (the clerk's fees excepted) and all forfeitures, fines and penalties, imposed on any person or persons, for any matter of delinquency, by any of the said county courts, shall be and belong to the treasury of the said county courts, to defray the charges of the county courts, and other county charges.

And all such fines, forfeitures, and penalties, as shall by the judgment of any assistant or justice of the peace, be imposed on any person or persons, for any matter of delinquency, shall be and belong to the treasury of the town where such judgment is given.

Always provided, that where any such fines, forfeitures or penalties, are or shall be otherwise ordered, by any express law of the state, they shall be disposed of according to the order of such law; any thing before in this act to the contrary notwithstanding.

AN ACT FOR REGULATING GAOLS AND GAOLERS

17 FEB 1779

Be it enacted, and it is hereby enacted, by the representatives of the freemen of the state of Vermont, in general assembly met, and by the authority of the same, that there shall be kept and maintained in good and sufficient repair, a common gaol in every head or county town in this state, the whole charge of building, when there shall be occasion, and of keeping such gaols, shall be by the county to which the same belongs. And that the assistants and justices of the peace, in the several counties, shall have full power, and they are hereby impowered to tax the inhabitants of their respective counties for building, repairing and furnishing the said gaols as need shall require; and from time to time to order, direct, and take care of the building, and keeping in repair the said gaols.

That all and every person or persons whatsoever, that shall be committed to the common gaol within any county in this state, by lawful authority, for any offence and misdemeanor, having means and ability thereunto, shall bear their own reasonable charge for conveying or sending them to the said gaol; and also the charge of such as shall be appointed to guard them thither; and also of their support while in gaol before they are discharged; and the estate of such person shall be subjected to the payment of such charge; and for want of estate, they may be disposed of in service to answer the same, according to the law, entitled "an act concerning delinquents": unless they shall be freed from the payment of said charge, agreeable to the direction of the law as aforesaid.

That all prisoners shall be permitted to provide, and send for their necessary food, from whence they please; and use such bedding, and linen, and other necessaries, as they think fit, without their being purloined, detained, or their paying for the same. Neither shall any keeper of a common gaol demand of them greater fees for their commitment, discharge, or chamber room, than what is allowed by law.

And if any keeper of a common gaol shall do, or cause to be done, to any prisoner that is committed to his custody, any wrong, or injury, contrary to the intent of this act, he shall pay treble damages to the party aggrieved, and also such fine as the county court of that county wherein the offence is committed, upon information or complaint to them made, shall (considering all circumstances) impose upon him.

AN ACT RELATING TO GUARDIANS AND MINORS

17 FEB 1779

Be it enacted, and it is hereby enacted by the representatives of the freemen of the state of Vermont, in general assembly met, and by the authority of the same, that when, and so often as there shall be occasion, the courts of probate in the several districts in this state, shall be, and they are hereby impowered to allow of guardians, who shall be chosen by minors of age by law for choosing of guardians; and to appoint guardians for such as shall be within that age. And that when it shall so happen, that there shall be any minor of age for the choosing a guardian, who hath neither father, guardian, nor master; then each and every of the judges of the said courts of probates, within whose district such minor lives or resides shall notify such minor to appear before him and elect some meet person to be his or her guardian; which being done, the same may be allowed, as aforesaid. And upon refusal or neglect to make such election, such judge shall appoint, and the respective judges aforesaid are hereby impowered to appoint a guardian for such minor neglecting or refusing as aforesaid. And the power and authority of such guardian shall be as good and effectual, to all intents and purposes, as if first elected by such minor, and thereupon allowed as aforesaid.

And every judge of probate, on his allowing or appointing any guardian as aforesaid, shall take sufficient security of all such guardians, for the faithful discharge of their trust, according to law; and oblige them to render their account of their guardianship to the court, or minor when such minor shall arrive at full age, or at such other time as the said court of probate, upon complaint to them made, shall see cause to appoint.

AN ACT FOR PREVENTING WRONG BY IMPRESSES

17 FEB 1779

Be it enacted, and it is hereby enacted by the representatives of the freemen of the state of Vermont, in general assembly met, and by the authority of the same, that no person shall be compelled to do any work or service for the public, unless it be by warrant from authority, and he have reasonable allowance therefor. Nor shall any man's horse, cattle, or goods, of what kind soever, be impressed, or taken for any public use or service, unless it be by virtue of such warrant, nor without such reasonable satisfaction: and if such horse, cattle, or goods perish, or suffer damage in such service, the owner shall be duly recompensed.

AN ACT REGULATING MILLS AND MILLERS

17 FEB 1779

Be it enacted, and it is hereby enacted, by the representatives of the freemen of the state of Vermont, in general assembly met, and by the authority of the same, that each miller in this state, or the owners of grist mills, shall be allowed two quarts out of each bushel of Indian corn he grinds; and for English grain, two quarts out of each bushel, and one pint for bolting; except malt, out of each bushel of which he grinds, he shall have one quart, & no more.

And if any miller shall presume to take or receive a greater toll, or fee for grinding, than is herein allowed, he shall forfeit and pay the sum of ten shillings, for each time he shall be convicted of the breach of this act; one half whereof shall be to the complainer, who shall prosecute the same to effect, and the other half to the treasury of the town where the offence shall be committed.

And that there shall be provided for every grist mill within this state, by the owners of such mills, sealed measures, viz. one of a pint, one of a quart, and one of two quarts, for their toll measures, with an instrument to strike the said measures, which shall be stricken when toll is taken of all grain that is brought to the mill stricken measure, to be ground there.

AN ACT TO ENCOURAGE THE DESTROYING WOLVES AND PANTHERS

17 FEB 1779

Be it enacted, and it is hereby enacted, by the representatives of the freemen of the state of Vermont, in general assembly met, and by

the authority of the same, that if any person shall kill and destroy any grown wolf, or wolves, or panther, within the bounds of this state, he shall have eight pounds paid out of the public treasury; and half so much for every wolf's whelp that sucks which he shall kill and destroy; the head or heads of every such wolf, whelp, or panther, being first brought to the selectmen, or constables of such town wherein such creatures are killed; which selectmen, or constables, shall cut off both ears from such head or heads.

And for preventing frauds in obtaining bills on the treasury for the killing the aforesaid creatures.

Be it enacted by the authority aforesaid, that the selectmen and constables within the respective towns in this state, shall (when the head of any wolf, panther, or whelp, is by any person brought to them, in order to obtain a certificate for the same) strictly examine the said person or persons, how he or they obtained the head or heads of such wolf or wolves, panther or whelp; and whether they were taken and killed within the bounds of this state.

And to prevent fraud being done by one person to another respecting the matters aforesaid.

Be it further enacted by the authority aforesaid, that if any person shall take a wolf out of any pit made to catch wolves in, or out of any trap, thereby to defraud the owner of the pit or trap of his due, every such person shall pay to the owner or owners of the pit or trap, the sum of eight pounds for every such offence, and be whipped on the naked back, according to the direction of the authority into whose cognizance it shall come, not exceeding ten stripes.

AN ACT FOR PRESERVING DUE ORDER IN TOWN-MEETINGS, SOCIETY MEETINGS, AND IN THE MEETINGS OF OTHER COMMUNITIES; AND FOR PREVENTING TUMULTS THEREIN

17 FEB 1779

Be it enacted, and it is hereby enacted by the representatives of the freemen of the state of Vermont, in general assembly met, and by the authority of the same, that when any town, society, or proprietor's meeting or the meeting of any other community is lawfully assembled, if any person or persons whatsover, shall in any such meeting, or assembly, by tumultuous noise, quarreling, or by any unlawful act, disturb such meeting or hinder the members thereof from proceeding in an orderly and peaceable manner to the choice of their moderator, or after the choice of such moderator, shall vilify or abuse him, or interrupt him in the discharge of his trust; or after he has commanded silence in such meeting, shall speak in the meeting, to the disturbance of the business of the meeting, without the moderator's leave first had and obtained (unless it be to ask reasonable liberty to speak), such person or persons, so offending in any of the particulars above mentioned, contrary to the intent of this act, shall, for every such offence, forfeit and pay a fine of twenty shillings, to the treasurer of the town where such offence is committed.

All offences against this act, to be heard and determined before any one councillor, or justice of the peace, unless the offence be aggravated by some notorious breach of peace; in which case the offender shall be bound over by such assistant or justice, to the next county court, to answer for such offence: which court may impose such fine as the aggravation of the offence, in their judgment deserves, not exceeding fifteen pounds. And that no such meeting shall be adjourned, but by the major part of the members present.

AN ACT FOR RESTRAINING SWINE FROM GOING AT LARGE

17 FEB 1779

Be it enacted, and it is hereby enacted, by the representatives of the freemen of the state of Vermont, in general assembly met, and by the authority of the same, that no swine shall be allowed to run at large on the highways or commons in this state: and if any person or persons shall allow their swine to run at large in the highways or common aforesaid, it shall be the duty of the hayward, in the several towns in this state (and it shall be lawful for any other person or persons), to impound such swine; and the owner or owners of such swine, shall pay the poundage thereof, by law allowed, before they are released out of pound.

Always provided, that every town in this state shall have liberty to agree otherwise in their own precincts, respecting the swine in such town.

Provided nevertheless, that if the swine (of such town so agreeing), shall at any time come within the bounds of any other town, they shall, in all respects, be under the regulations of this act, as fully as if no such agreement had been made; unless such other town, whereinto such swine shall come, as aforesaid, shall also agree as aforesaid.

AN ACT FOR THE PUNISHMENT OF THEFT

17 FEB 1779

Be it enacted, and it is hereby enacted, by the representatives of the freemen of the state of Vermont, in general assembly met, and by the authority of the same, that whosoever shall steal, or purloin any money, or chattels, and be thereof convicted, by confession, or other sufficient evidence, every such offender shall forfeit and pay treble the value of the money, goods, or chattels, so stolen, or purloined, unto the owner or owners thereof; and be further punished by fine, at the discretion of the court, assistant, or justice, that hath cognizance of such offence, not exceeding ten pounds.

And if the value of the money, goods, or chattels, so stolen, amount to the sum of six pounds, such offender, stealing the same to that value, shall, besides the aforesaid forfeiture, be further punished by whipping, not exceeding thirty nine stripes for one offence.

And if any such offender be unable to make restitution, and pay such threefold damages, such offender shall make satisfaction by service; and the prosecutor shall be, and is hereby impowered to dispose of such offender in service, to any subject of this state, for such time as he shall be assigned to such prosecutor by the court, assistant, or justice, before whom the prosecution shall be.

And if any person or persons shall conceal any theft, or receive any stolen goods, knowing them to be such, every such person so concealing, or receiving shall suffer, and be punished, as he or they who commit the theft.

And that every assistant, and justice of the peace, in the county where such offence is committed, or where the offender is apprehended, is hereby authorized and impowered to hear and determine all offences against this act.

Provided, the value of the money, goods, or chattels stolen, do not exceed the sum of ten pounds; any law, usage, or custom, to the contrary notwithstanding.

AN ACT FOR APPOINTING COUNTY SURVEYORS IN THE COUNTIES; AND FOR DIRECTING AND REGULATING THEM IN THE EXECUTION OF THEIR OFFICE

17 FEB 1779

Be it enacted, and it is hereby enacted, by the representatives of the freemen of the state of Vermont, in general assembly met, and by

the authority of the same, that there shall be appointed by the general assembly, from time to time, as there shall be occasion, one or more persons in each county in this state, to be public or county surveyors, or surveyors for laying out of lands, and for the running of the bounds of lands already laid out, according to their original grants, as need shall require; and for the running of lines, and other services proper for a surveyor to do; who shall be sufficiently skilled in the surveyor's art, and be furnished with instruments suitable and sufficient for that service. And being appointed and qualified as aforesaid, shall have full power and authority to execute said office in the respective counties for which they are or shall be appointed.

That when, and so often as any county surveyor shall be employed in laying out any grants of land, renewing boundaries that are lost, or running any line, or doing any service in his office, and there be occasion for carrying the chain to measure the lines; that the men employed to carry the chain, shall take the oath by law appointed for them; which oath such surveyor is hereby fully impowered to administer to such chain-men as he calls to his assistance, as aforesaid.

That when a county surveyor is called out to run any line between adjoining proprietors, and that in order to find the course from boundary to boundary, he is obliged to run a random line to find the certain and true course, and in so doing runs on the land of adjoining proprietors; such surveyors shall not be deemed guilty of trespass in so running such random line, but may lawfully do the same.

Provided he do the said service in either the months of March, April, October or November.

Be it further enacted by the authority aforesaid, that if any person or persons shall, by any way or means, oppose, hinder, or interrupt any county surveyor, in the due execution of his office; or shall, by any way or means, oppose, hinder or interrupt any committee appointed by the general assembly, to run, fix or ascertain the bounds or lines between particular townships, or proprietors, or for other business; or any other person by them employed to assist in the running and fixing any such line, or doing any other business such committee are appointed to do; every such offender shall incur the penalty of five pounds, and be bound to his good behaviour, with one or more sureties, at the discretion of the court that hath cognizance of such offence; the one moiety of which penalty to be paid to the treasurer of the county wherein the offence is committed, and the other moiety to the person who shall prosecute the same to effect.

AN ACT FOR REGULATING THE ELECTION OF GOVERNOR, DEPUTY GOVERNOR, COUNCIL AND TREASURER

17 FEB 1779

Be it enacted, and it is hereby enacted, by the representatives of the freemen of the state of Vermont, in general assembly met, and by the authority of the same, that the constables in the several towns in this state, without further order, shall, by themselves, or some person deputed by them, warn all the freemen in their respective towns to meet together at some suitable place by them appointed in said town, on the first Tuesday of September annually, at nine of the clock in the morning, at which time shall be read the freeman's oath, and the last paragraph of this act, against disorderly voting; who then shall proceed first to choose representatives to attend the general assembly for the year ensuing, on the second Thursday of the succeeding October: Then the freemen shall proceed to bring in to the constable present, the name of him whom they would choose to be governor for the year ensuing, fairly written on a piece of paper; which the said constable shall receive, and in the presence of the freemen, seal up the same in a piece of paper, and write on the outside of the paper so sealed, the name of the town, and then add these words, viz. votes for the governor—in like manner for the deputy governor, and treasurer. Then said constable shall call upon the freemen to give in their votes for twelve assistants or councillors, for the year ensuing, with their names fairly written; which votes shall be counted and sorted by said constable, who shall then make a proper list, on one sheet or piece of paper, of the names of the several persons voted for; with the number of votes for each person affixed to his name; which paper shall be sealed up by said constable, in the presence of the freemen, and wrote on the outside, the name of the town, and then these words, viz. votes for assistants, or councillors, and delivered to one of the representatives chosen for said town to attend the general assembly, who shall deliver the same to said assembly.

And at the opening of the general assembly, there shall be a committee appointed out of the council and assembly, who, after being duly sworn to the faithful discharge of their trust, shall proceed to receive, sort, and count the votes for the governor, and declare the person who has the major part of the votes to be governor for the year ensuing: and if there be no choice made, then the council and general assembly, by their joint ballot, shall make choice of a governor; and the deputy governor and treasurer shall be chosen in like manner.

Then said committee shall proceed to receive, sort and count the votes for the councillors, and the twelve highest in nomination shall be declared to be chosen councillors or assistants for the year ensuing.

And be it further enacted, by the authority aforesaid, that if any constable shall refuse or neglect to attend such order as aforesaid (annually), he shall forfeit and pay to the treasury of the town, the sum of five pounds, for every such neglect.

And if no constable be present at such freemen's meeting, an assistant, justice of the peace, or one or more of the selectmen of said town, shall supply the place of the constable.

Be it further enacted by the authority aforesaid, that every man of the full age of twenty one years, having resided in this state for the space of one year next before the election of representatives, and is of a quiet and peaceable behaviour, and will take the following oath (or affirmation) shall be intitled to all the privileges of a freeman of this state, viz.

"You .... solemnly swear by the ever living God (or affirm in presence of Almighty God) that whenever you are called to give your vote of suffrage, touching any matter that concerns the state of Vermont, you will do it so as in your conscience you shall judge will most conduce to the best good of the same, as established by the constitution, without fear or favour of any man."

Be it further enacted by the authority aforesaid, that no person shall be admitted to take the freeman's oath, until they have obtained the approbation of the selectmen of the town signifying that they are qualified according to this act; which oath any one assistant, justice of the peace, or town clerk in their absence, is hereby impowered to administer.

And all such persons, admitted and sworn as aforesaid, shall be freemen of this corporation, and their names shall be enrolled in the roll of freemen, in the town clerk's office of that town, wherein they are admitted as aforesaid.

And that if any freeman of this corporation shall walk scandalously, or commit any scandalous offence, it shall be in the power of the superior court in this state, on complaint thereof to them made, to disenfranchise such freeman; who shall stand disenfranchised, until, by his good behaviour, the said superior court shall see cause to restore him to his franchisement or freedom again; which the said court is impowered to do.

And if any person that is not a freeman of this state, admitted and sworn according to law, shall presume to vote, or give in his proxy, in the election of any of the members of the general assembly, governor, or deputy governor, treasurer, or councillor; or if any freeman shall put in more than one vote or proxy for one person, in the same election to one office, he shall pay a fine of five pounds to the treasurer of the town where such offence is committed.

AN ACT DIRECTING TOWN CLERKS IN THEIR OFFICE AND DUTY

17 FEB 1779

Be it enacted, and it is hereby enacted, by the representatives of the freemen of the state of Vermont, in general assembly met, and by the authority of the same, that the town clerk, or register, in every town in this state, shall record all marriages, births, and deaths, of persons in their towns; and that all parents, masters, executors, and administrators respectively, shall bring in to the clerk of the town to which they belong, the names of such persons belonging to them that shall be born, or die; also, that every new married man shall bring the time of his marriage, sufficiently proved, either by certificate from him that married him, or by other legal proof, to the clerk, within one month after such marriage, birth or death; and every person so neglecting, shall forfeit the sum of four shillings; and for every month after the said first month, four shillings.

And the clerks of every town shall, as far as they can come at, give in an account of all such neglects to the grand jury, who shall make presentment thereof to the next assistant, or justice of the peace: which forfeitures shall be paid to the town treasurer.

Be it further enacted, by the authority aforesaid, that there shall be a suitable book or books for registering kept in each town in this state (at the cost of the town), with an index or alphabet to the same; in which book or books, the town clerk shall record every man's house and lands, granted and measured out to him, with the bounds and quantities of the same, and date the time of his entering all such records.

And the town clerk in each town shall keep the town book or books, in their respective towns, and shall truly enter in the said book or books, all votes of the said town, grants, or conveyances of lands, choice of town officers, and other town acts and matters upon his oath (except when at any town meeting he shall necessarily be absent); and shall grant copies of the same, as need shall require, for reasonable satisfaction.

AN ACT DESCRIBING THE PROBATE DISTRICTS

17 FEB 1779

Be it enacted, and it is hereby enacted, by the representatives of the freemen of the state of Vermont, in general assembly met, and by the authority of the same, that this state shall be divided into seven districts, and in each district there shall be a court of probate of wills held, consisting of one judge, who shall appoint his clerk; and said districts to be divided in the following manner, viz.

All the towns south of the north line of Shaftsbury, extending east the same course to the east line of the county of Bennington, be one entire and distinct district, known by the name of the district of Bennington.

Then beginning at the northwest corner of the district of Bennington; thence running northwardly with the north line of the state, until it comes to the northwest corner of Pawlet; thence running easterly with the north line of said Pawlet, extending the same course to the county line aforesaid, shall be one entire district, and known by the name of the district of Manchester.

Then beginning at the northwest corner of the district of Manchester, and running northerly with the line of the state until it comes to the forty-fifth degree of north lattitude; thence running easterly on Canada line to the county line aforesaid, shall be one entire district, and known by the name of the district of Rutland.

Then beginning at the northeast corner of Putney, and running westerly on the north line of the same tier of towns to the county line; then running south until it comes to the south line of this state; thence running easterly until it comes to the bank of Connecticut River; thence running northerly on the bank of said river until it comes to the place of beginning, shall be one entire district, and known by the name of the district of Guilford.

Then beginning at the northeast corner of the district of Guilford, running northerly on the bank of the river until it comes to the northeast corner of Weathersfield; thence running westerly until it comes to the county line; then running southerly until it comes to the northwest corner of the district of Guilford, shall be one entire district, and known by the name of the district of Rockingham.

Then beginning at the northeast corner of the district of Rockingham, and running northerly on the bank of the river until it comes to the northeast corner of Norwich; thence running westerly to the county line; thence running southerly until it comes to the northwest corner of Rockingham, shall be one entire district, and known by the name of the district of Windsor.

Then beginning at the northeast corner of the district of Windsor, and running northerly on the bank of said river until it comes to the latitude of forty-five; thence running westerly to the county line; thence running southerly until it comes to the northwest corner of the district of Windsor, shall be one entire district, known by the name of the district of Barnet.

AN ACT FOR LAYING OUT AND ALTERING HIGHWAYS

24 FEB 1779

Be it enacted, and it is hereby enacted, by the representatives of the freemen of the state of Vermont, in general assembly met, and by the authority of the same, that where a new highway, or common road from town to town, or place to place, shall be found necessary, and where old highways with more conveniency may be turned or altered, that upon any person or persons making application, the selectmen of each town respectively, be, and are hereby impowered by themselves or others whom they shall appoint, to lay out or cause to be laid out such roads, and likewise private ways for such town only as shall be thought necessary, so as no damage is done to any particular person in his land or property, without due recompence be made by the town, as the selectmen and the parties interested may agree; but if such owners or proprietors shall not be satisfied with what the selectmen offer by way of recompence for their damage they have liberty of making application to one assistant or justice of the peace, who is hereby impowered to grant a summons to the sheriff of the county, or constable of such town, to cause to appear before him, not more than seven, or less than three freeholders, who being sworn, shall appraise the damages, and make final order thereon: and if it be found there were no grounds of complaint, the complainer shall pay all charges arising thereby.

That if any person, being summoned to serve as aforesaid, shall neglect to attend the same, he shall incur the penalty of twenty shillings to the town treasurer where such person dwells, to be recovered by bill, plaint, or information.

Be it further enacted by the authority aforesaid, that the selectmen aforesaid shall make, or cause to be made, a true survey of all such roads or highways, which shall be recorded in the town clerk's office in their respective towns.

Always provided, that the cost arising by surveying and laying out all roads, together with all damages that shall be found due to the owner of said lands, be, and is hereby ordered to be paid out of the town treasury of the town wherein such road lieth.

Be it further enacted by the authority aforesaid, that where allowance is made for highways, in or adjoining any lot of land, that the owner shall not be intitled to any damages, but the roads to be laid as above.

AN ACT FOR MAKING AND REPAIRING PUBLIC HIGHWAYS

19 FEB 1779

Be it enacted, and it is hereby enacted, by the representatives of the freemen of the state of Vermont, in general assembly met, and by the authority of the same, that there shall be to the amount of four days work to each male person from sixteen years old to sixty (except ministers of the gospel improved within their respective towns), for making and repairing highways, in the following manner, viz., the selectmen of each town shall make a rate on the list of the polls and rateable estate of each town, to the amount of four days to each person as aforesaid, at eighteen shillings per day, and deliver the same, or a copy thereof, to each surveyor within the respective towns, who shall warn the inhabitants of their respective towns to work at highways to the amount of their rates, at eighteen shillings per day, between the fifteenth day of May and the fifteenth day of June, and between the fifteenth day of September and fifteenth day of October annually.

And if any person or persons shall refuse or neglect to do their proportion of their respective rates, according to the warning, they shall forfeit and pay thirty shillings in lieu of every day's work they neglect to perform, provided they have three days warning.

Be it further enacted by the authority aforesaid, that the surveyors of highways shall make return of all the persons so neglecting, their names, and number of days within six days after such neglect, to the next assistant, or justice of the peace: and if the said person or persons doth not, within six days next after such return, show sufficient reason why he did not comply with the order of such surveyor, then the said assistant, or justice of the peace, shall grant his warrant against the goods or chattels of such delinquent or delinquents, directed to the sheriff, his deputy, or constable of the town where the delinquents dwell, to collect the forfeitures, together with additional cost; which money shall be delivered to such surveyor, to be by him laid out for the purpose of making and repairing highways: such goods or chattels shall be, by said officer, sold at public vendue, after having been posted at least ten days before such sale; and the overplus, if any there be, to be returned to the owner.

And that the surveyors shall have power to order out such number of persons as they shall think proper, to mend the roads, on any extraordinary occasion, at anytime; and the pay therefor shall be deducted out of such person's rates who shall do such labour.

AN ACT FOR THE REGULATING FERRIES AND FERRIAGES WITHIN THIS STATE

20 FEB 1779

Whereas it has been found by experience, that great advantage (of travellers and others) has been taken, by ferry men demanding an unreasonable price for ferrying.

And whereas this assembly cannot so knowingly distinguish between the several rivers, and the several parts of the same river, pond or lake, on account of distance, swiftness of water, number of travellers, etc.

Therefore to prevent such impositions for the future,

Be it enacted, and it is hereby enacted, by the representatives of the freemen of the state of Vermont, in general assembly met, and by the authority of the same, that the magistrates, selectmen, and constables of the several towns where ferries are needed, shall meet before the first day of August annually, at time and place by them agreed on, and appoint proper persons and places for ferries, and provide suitable roads to and from the same; and further regulate the price thereof, according to the profits of such ferries, and the price of labour, to be varied from time to time, as occasion shall require.

And where two or more towns shall border on the same river, pond, or lake, opposite to each other, being within this state,

Be it further enacted, by the authority aforesaid that the magistrates, selectmen, and constables of such towns shall meet together for the purposes, and by the time aforesaid.

And if any person or persons shall violate this act, by demanding any greater sum for ferriage, than that stated by the authority aforesaid, he or they shall, for every such offence, forfeit the sum of fifteen shillings; one half to the informer, and the other half to the town treasurer where such offence is committed, to be recovered by bill, plaint, or information, before any one assistant, or justice of the peace in the county where such offence is committed.

AN ACT FOR THE APPOINTMENT AND REGULATING ATTORNIES

15 FEB 1779

For the well ordering proceedings, and pleas at the bar,

Be it enacted, and it is hereby enacted by the representatives of the freemen of the state of Vermont, in general assembly met, and by the authority of the same, that the superior and county courts in this state, shall appoint, and they are hereby impowered to approve of, nominate and appoint, attornies in this state, as there shall be occasion to plead at the bar; which attornies shall before such court, take the following oath, viz.

You .... swear by the everliving God, that you will do no falsehood, nor consent to any to be done in the court; and if you know of any to be done, you shall give knowledge thereof to the judges, or justices of the court, or some of them, that it may be reformed: you shall not, wittingly and willingly, or knowingly, promote, sue or procure to be sued, any false or unlawful suit, nor give aid or consent to the same: you shall demean yourself in the office of an attorney within the court, according to the best of your learning and discretion, and with all good fidelity, as well to the court, as to the client. So help you God.

The administration and taking of which oath, together with the said appointment, shall be registered by the clerk of said court, and be a sufficient evidence of his admission as an attorney at the bar.

And that no person (except in his own case) shall be admitted to make any plea at the bar, in any superior or county court, but such as are allowed and qualified attornies as aforesaid, except he obtain special liberty from said court.

And whosoever shall transgress the rules of pleading appointed by any court, shall be liable to suffer such fine for every such offence as the said courts shall impose, not exceeding the sum of five pounds.

That in all cases whatsoever, there shall be allowed but one attorney on a side to plead at the bar.

And the fees of such attornies shall be as stated in the table of fees. And the party that shall recover judgment shall have his attorney's fees according to the above regulations, allowed as part of cost of trial.

And be it further enacted by the authority aforesaid, that in each county in this state there shall be one state's attorney, who shall prosecute, manage, and plead, in the county where he is appointed, in all matters proper for and in behalf of this and the United States; which attornies shall be appointed by the respective county courts.

And that the several attornies who shall be allowed and appointed as aforesaid, shall, from time to time be under the directions of the courts before whom they shall plead, who shall and may displace, and wholly suspend, any of said attornies, or fine them, as is before in this act provided.

Be it further enacted, by the authority aforesaid, that no attorney's fees be allowed, or taxed, in any bill of cost in any justices court, anything in this act notwithstanding.

AN ACT FOR THE PUNISHMENT OF DRUNKENNESS

16 FEB 1779

Be it enacted, and it is hereby enacted by the representatives of the freemen of the state of Vermont, in general assembly met, and by the authority of the same, that if any person shall be found drunken, so that he, or she, be thereby bereaved and disabled in the use of his or her speech, gesture, or behaviour, and be thereof convicted, he or she shall forfeit, as a fine, the sum of eight shillings for every such offence to the treasurer of the town where the offence is committed, for the use of the poor therein; and for want of goods whereon to make distress, the offender or offenders, shall sit in the stocks, there to remain not to exceed three hours, nor less than one hour.

AN ACT AGAINST PROFANE SWEARING AND CURSING

16 FEB 1779

Be it enacted, and it is hereby enacted by the representatives of the freemen of the state of Vermont, in general assembly met, and by the authority of the same, that if any person or persons within this state, shall swear profanely, either by the holy name of God, or any other oath; or sinfully and wickedly curse any person or persons; such person so offending, shall upon conviction thereof before one assistant or justice of the peace, forfeit and pay for every such offence, the sum of six shillings. And if such person or persons so convicted, shall not be able, or shall refuse to pay the aforesaid fine, he or they shall sit in the stocks, not exceeding three hours, and not less than one hour, for one offence, and pay cost of prosecution.

AN ACT DIRECTING CONSTABLES IN THEIR OFFICE AND DUTY

19 FEB 1779

Be it enacted, and it is hereby enacted, by the representatives of the freemen of the state of Vermont, in general assembly met, and by the authority of the same, that one constable in each respective town in this state, shall be chosen to levy and gather the state's tax in such town; and it shall be his duty to collect such tax, when properly authorized thereto by the treasurer, and shall also make up his accounts with the treasurer.

Be it further enacted by the authority aforesaid, that every person tendered to any constable of any town in this state, by any constable, or other officer belonging to any of the neighbouring states, with a warrant from any of their authority, shall presently be received, and forthwith convey from constable to constable, by the respective constables in this state, until such person shall be brought unto the place to which he or she is sent, or before some assistant or justice of the peace in this state, who shall dispose of him or them as the justice of the case shall require.

That every constable shall duly receive all hue and cries, and the same diligently pursue to full effect; such as are granted and sent out after capital or criminal offenders at the cost and charge of this state; but such as are taken out by particular persons, in their own cases, at the cost and charge of those who take them out.

That every constable within this state, is hereby authorised, and fully impowered, to put forth pursuits, or hue and cries, after murderers, peace breakers, thieves, robbers, burglars, and any other capital of-fenders, where no magistrate or justice of the peace is near at hand: as also, without warrant, to apprehend such as are overtaken with drink, guilty of profane swearing, sabbath-breaking, lying; also vagrant per-sons, and unreasonable night walkers; provided they be taken and ap-prehended in the fact, either by the sight of the constable, or present immediate information of some others. As also, to make search for all such persons, either on the sabbath, or other days, when there shall be occasion, in taverns, and other suspected places or houses; and those to apprehend, and keep in safe custody, till opportunity serves to bring them before the next assistant or justice of the peace, for further examination, in order to their being proceeded against according to law.

That each and every constable shall have power and authority to serve and execute such lawful precepts, writs, or warrants, as are directed to them from lawful authority, within the town only where he belongs: and shall have the power of water bailiffs in the several respective towns in this state, when and where there shall be occasion for the same.

Provided nevertheless, that when any constable is employed or commanded by any assistant or justice of the peace, to apprehend or arrest any person or persons, he shall not do it without a warrant in writing.

Be it further enacted by the authority aforesaid, that all constables may, and from time to time shall, make diligent search, throughout the limits of their town, upon the Lord's days, and all other times, as oft as they shall be informed, or see cause, for such offenders as shall be tippling in any inn, or house of entertainment, or private house, excessively or unreasonably; and after such as retail strong drink without licence: and also warn all those that frequent public houses, and spend their time there idly, to forbear; and also warn all those that keep such houses, not to suffer any such persons in their houses: and to make due presentment of all breaches of law (coming within their knowledge) to some authority proper to receive the same, once in every month.

And if, upon due information, any constable shall refuse or neglect to make such search, seizure and presentment, and be thereof legally convicted, he shall pay a fine of five shillings to the treasury of the town whereto he belongs.

And the better to enable, and more effectually to oblige, the respective constables to execute their office,

Be it further enacted by the authority aforesaid, that if any person shall refuse, at any time, to assist any constable in the execution of his office, being by him duly thereunto required, he shall forfeit five pounds.

And if it appear that any person shall willfully, obstinately, or contemptuously refuse to assist such constable, as is before expressed, he shall forfeit and pay to the use of the town where the offence is committed, ten pounds: the said offence to be heard and tried by an assistant, or justice of the peace.

And if any constable, or other person upon urgent occasion, shall refuse to use his best endeavors in raising and prosecuting hue and cries, either by foot, or upon horse (if need be), after capital offenders, he shall forfeit the sum of forty shillings to the use aforesaid; and to be determined as aforesaid.

AN ACT AGAINST COUNTERFEITING BILLS OF PUBLIC CREDIT, COINS, OR CURRENCIES; AND EMITTING, AND PASSING BILLS OR NOTES ON PRIVATE CREDIT; AND PREVENT INJUSTICE IN PASSING COUNTERFEIT BILLS

FEB 1779

Be it enacted, and it is hereby enacted, by the representatives of the freemen of the state of Vermont, in general assembly met, and by the authority of the same, that whosoever shall presume to forge, counterfeit, or alter any of the bills of credit of this or the other American States, that now are, or hereafter shall be by law emitted, and established current, either in this or any of the aforesaid states: or that shall utter or put off any such forged, counterfeit, or altered, bills, or coin, knowing them to be such; or that shall counsel, advise, procure, or any ways assist in the forging, counterfeiting, imprinting, stamping, altering or signing of any false, forged, and counterfeit bill or bills, or coins, knowing them to be such; or shall engrave any plate, or make any other instrument to be used for that purpose; every person or persons so offending, being convicted thereof before any of the superior courts in this state shall be punished by having his right ear cut off, and shall be branded with the capital letter C, on a hot iron, and be committed to the work house, there to be confined and kept to work, under the care of a master, and not to depart therefrom without special leave from the assembly of this state, until the day of his death, under the penalty of being severely whipped by order of any court, assistant or justice, and thereupon to be returned to his former confinement and labour. And all the estate of any person offending as aforesaid, shall be forfeited to this state, and may be accordingly seized for that purpose, by order of the court before whom such offender is convicted.

And that such offenders may more effectually be discovered and prosecuted,

Be it further enacted by the authority aforesaid, that whosoever shall make discovery and give information of such vile and wicked practices of making or altering any such bills or coins; or of making any of the instruments aforesaid; or of aiding therein, so that the person or persons guilty thereof be tendered to justice, and convicted; every such informer shall have and receive as a reward for his good service in discovering and informing as aforesaid, the sum of ten pounds.

And the more effectually to prevent the passing such counterfeit, forged, or altered bills, and injustice arising thereby,

Be it further enacted by the authority aforesaid, that when, and so often as it shall happen, that any such false, forged, altered; or counterfeit bill, shall be brought to the treasurer of this state, or offered to him in payment of rates, or to be exchanged, he shall secure them; and he is hereby authorized to seize and retain them, entering on the back thereof the name of the persons in whose possession they were, and then deliver the same into the hands of some authority, to be enquired into.

And every assistant and justice of the peace, is hereby also authorised and impowered to seize and take into his custody every such bill, which he shall see, observe, or have knowledge of, and the same to retain, entering on the backside thereof, the name of the person from whom he took the same; and at his discretion to cause the person from whom he took such bill so lodged with him, to come before him, to be examined in the premises; and to administer an oath to such person or persons, to declare of whom he or they received it; and proceed in his inquiries, in manner aforesaid, after the author of the mischief, as far as such authority's discretion will guide him.

Be it further enacted by the authority aforesaid, that whensoever any person shall be the possessor of any such false or counterfeit bill, he shall (on his discovering it to be such) deliver the same to some assistant, or justice of the peace, and inform him that he concludes the same to be false and counterfeit; and if such assistant or justice shall suppose the same to be false, as aforesaid, he shall take the same, and write the name of the person of whom he received it, on the back of said bill, and that it was delivered to him as a counterfeit bill: and such person that so delivers up such bill, or from whom such bill is taken, in either of the methods aforesaid, may, after such delivery, or taking, go to the person of whom he received the same, and demand of him pay therefor, informing him where such bill is lodged.

And if the person of whom he received said bill, shall refuse or neglect to make him satisfaction therefor, may bring his action for his damage, in not paying him for said bill, or for putting off said bill to him, before any court, assistant, or justice of the peace, proper to try the same, alleging the same to be taken or delivered up as aforesaid. And in the trial of any such case, if the bill be found to be false, forged, or counterfeit, to the satisfaction of the court that tries the same, the said court shall proceed to enquire into the equity of the cause, by examining the parties under oath, and taking any other evidences, as they shall judge just and right; and upon their finding to their satisfaction, that such plaintiff received the same bill of the defendant for a true bill, and shall give judgment for the plaintiff, for his just damages and cost.

Provided always, such bill be delivered up, or taken as aforesaid, before the plaintiff offered the same back to the person of whom he received it.

Provided also, that no person be prosecuted in form as aforesaid, but within one year after he puts off such bill; which fact may be inquired into in form aforesaid.

Be it further enacted, that all and every person that hath at any time had any such bill that shall be taken from the possessor; or shall by the possessor be delivered up as aforesaid, and hath satisfied the person to whom he put off said bill, for the same, shall have like liberty of prosecuting and taking remedy as aforesaid, against the person of whom he received the same.

And that every assistant or justice that shall have such bill in hand, shall at the cost of the party safely convey the same to any court where the same may be wanted in the trial of the case. And that if any court, assistant, or justice, had the possession of such false counterfeit bill the space of one year, he or they shall destroy the same.

And whereas the putting out, and passing of bills, notes, or coins, to be used and improved as a general currency, or medium of trade, or private funds or credit, is an infringement on the right and power of the state, and would greatly depreciate the public credit, and tend to create confusion, injustice, and mischiefs amongst the subjects of this state:—therefore,

Be it further enacted by the authority aforesaid, that if any person, society, number of persons, or company, within this state, shall presume to strike, emit, or put out, any bills of credit, of the nature or tenor of the bills of credit in this state, on any funds or credit of any person or persons, society, or company, to be used and improved as a general currency, or medium of trade, as, and in lieu of money; such person or persons, society, or company, and every of them, shall be subject to the same pains, penalties, and forfeitures, and be punished in the same manner as those are by this act subject to, who shall be convicted of forging or counterfeiting the bills of credit emitted by this state.

And that if any person or persons in this state, shall utter, vend, or pass any bills, notes, or coins, or any other currencies whatsoever, which either have been, or hereafter shall be used as aforesaid, on the fund or credit of any private person or persons, society or company whatsoever, either in this or the neighbouring states; he or they so offending shall forfeit double the sum or value expressed in such bill, note, or other currency; the one half thereof to him or them that shall prosecute the same to effect, and the other half to the town treasurer, when the trial shall be before the county court.

And all grand jurors and constables are hereby required to make presentment of all breaches of this act.

AN ACT FOR AUTHENTICATING DEEDS AND CONVEYANCES

19 FEB 1779

For preventing fraudulent and uncertain sales of houses and lands, and to the intent it may be better known what title or interest persons have in or to such estates as they shall offer to sale,

Be it enacted, and it is hereby enacted by the representatives of the freemen of the state of Vermont, in general assembly met, and by the authority of the same, that henceforth all deeds or conveyances of any houses or lands, within this state, signed and sealed by the parties granting the same, having good and lawful right or authority thereto, and attested by two or more witnesses, and acknowledged by such grantor or grantors, before an assistant or justice of the peace, and recorded at length in the town clerk's records where such houses and lands do lie, shall be valid to pass, without any other act or ceremony in the law whatsoever. And that no bargain, sale, or mortgage, or other conveyance of houses or lands made and executed within this state, shall be valid in law, to hold such houses and lands against any other person or persons but the grantor or grantors, and their heirs only, unless the deed or deeds thereof be acknowledged and recorded in manner as is before expressed.

Provided nevertheless, that when, and so often as it shall happen, that any grantor shall live in parts beyond the sea, or be removed out of this state, or be dead before any deed or conveyance by him or her so made be acknowledged, as aforesaid; or in case the grantor or vendor neglects or refuses to acknowledge, as before mentioned, being thereto required by the grantee or vendee, his, her, or their attorney, executors, administrators, heirs or assigns; in every such case, the proof of such deed, or conveyance made, by the oath of the witnesses, before an assistant, or judge of the superior or county court, shall be esteemed in law equivalent to the party's own acknowledgment thereof.

Be it further enacted by the authority aforesaid, that any mortgagee of any lands or tenements, his or her heirs, executors, or administrators, having received full satisfaction and payment of all such sum or sums of money, shall, at the request of the mortgager, his heirs, executors or administrators, acknowledge and cause such satisfaction and payment to be entered in the margin of the records of such mortgage, and shall sign the same; which shall thereafter for ever discharge, defease and release such mortgager, and perpetually bar all actions to be brought thereupon, in any court of record.

And if such mortgager, his or her heirs, executors, or administrators, shall not, within ten days next after request in that behalf made, and tender of his or their reasonable charges, repair to the records, and there make and sign such acknowledgment as aforesaid, or otherwise sign and seal a discharge of the said mortgage, and release and quit-claim to the estate therein mentioned to be granted, and acknowledge the same before an assistant or justice of the peace, he, she, or they so refusing, shall be liable to make good all damages for want of such discharge or release, to be recovered by action or suit in any court of record: and in case judgment pass against the party so sued, he, she, or they, so cast, shall pay the adverse party treble cost arising upon such suit.

Be it further enacted by the authority aforesaid, that the town clerks in the several towns in this state, shall fairly enter and record at length in their records, all deeds, conveyances, and mortgages of lands, tenements, rents, or other hereditaments lying and being within the town where such clerk's records are kept within this state, made, executed, and acknowledged or received in manner aforesaid, which shall be brought to him to record; and shall on receipt thereof in his office, note thereon the day, month, and year, when he received the same, and the record shall bear date accordingly.

Provided also, that where there are no inhabitants in such town, and consequently no town clerk or register, in every such case, such grants or deeds shall be recorded in the town clerk's record in the next adjoining town; and in case there is no clerk's office in any adjoining town, then such grants or deeds shall be recorded in the records of the county clerk in the county where the lands are, any thing in this act to the contrary notwithstanding.

And be it enacted by the authority aforesaid, that if any town clerk or register within this state, shall neglect to do and perform his duty according to this act, and be thereof convicted, he shall pay a fine of five pounds to the treasurer of the town whereto he belongs, for every such neglect.

Be it further enacted by the authority aforesaid, that any person or persons having signed, sealed, and delivered, a deed or grant of land, or buildings, and shall refuse to acknowledge the same; in such case, the person or persons to whom such deed or grant was made, shall make application to an assistant or justice of the peace (who are hereby authorized to hear and determine the same) for a warrant to bring such person or persons immediately before him, and shew cause, if any there be, why he refuses to acknowledge the said deed or grant; and if it doth not appear to the said assistant or justice of the peace, that the said grantor has just grounds to refuse to acknowledge the same; and he or they still continuing to refuse, the said assistant or justice of the peace, may commit the said grantor or grantors to gaol, there to remain until he or they do acknowledge the said grant or deed.

Provided always, that the party grieved have liberty to appeal from the judgment of said assistant or justice of the peace, unto the next county court in said county; and either party shall be debarred from making any conveyance of said premises in the meantime, or until the matter be determined by said county court.

AN ACT FOR THE PUNISHING OF TRESPASSES IN DIVERS CASES, AND DIRECTING PROCEEDINGS THEREIN

FEB 1779

Be it enacted, and it is hereby enacted by the representatives of the freemen of the state of Vermont, in general assembly met, and by the authority of the same, that no person or persons, shall cut, fell, or destroy, or carry away, any tree or trees, timber, stone, or underwood whatsoever, standing, lying, or growing on the land of any other person or persons within this state, without leave of the owner or owners of such lands, on pain that every such trespass, forfeit and pay to the party or parties injured or trespassed upon, the sum of ten shillings for every tree of one foot over, and for all trees of a greater dimension three times the value thereof, besides ten shillings as aforesaid, and five shillings for every tree or pole under that dimension; which several penalties, forfeitures, and damages, shall and may be recovered by action, bill, plaint or information, upon conviction of the trespasser or trespassers.

Provided always, that no person that is not a resident of the town where the trespass is done, shall be enabled by virtue of this act to prosecute another for trespass done on his unimproved lands, by cutting timber for any public use.

Always provided, that the proprietors of common or undivided lands in the respective towns, may grant liberty for the cutting or felling any tree or trees, or carrying away timber, wood, or underwood, growing or lying on their common or undivided lands, under such regulations and restrictions as they, or the major part of them, shall agree in their legal meeting: and if they shall see cause, may appoint and impower their agents or attornies in their place or stead, to prosecute any person or persons that shall trespass on their undivided lands, contrary to this Act.

And the like power is hereby also given to the inhabitants of the several towns in their respective town meetings, with respect to the timber, wood, or underwood, growing or lying on lands within their township requestered for public uses.

Provided also, and it is hereby enacted, that when the court, assistant or justice, before whom any trial upon this act shall be had, shall be well satisfied that the defendant was guilty through mistake, and that he really believed the timber, stone, or trees, complained of, was, when growing, on his own or some other person's land where he had a right to cut, etc. that in such case the defendant shall be sentenced to pay to the plaintiff only the just value of the timber felled, taken away, or destroyed, and cost of trial, and no more.

Be it further enacted by the authority aforesaid, that if any person or persons shall unlawfully throw down, or leave open any bars, gates, or fence or fences, belonging to, or inclosing any common field, or any lands held in propriety, or common, or belonging to any particular person or persons within this state, shall, for every such trespass, upon conviction thereof, forfeit and pay to the parties injured thereby double damages, and also a sum not exceeding twenty-five shillings, according to the nature and aggravation of the trespass, to be recovered in manner as aforesaid.

Be it further enacted by the authority aforesaid, that every person or persons that shall set fire on any land in this state, that shall run into any common and undivided lands, or towns, commons, or lands belonging to any particular person or persons; such person or persons setting such fire, or that shall be aiding or assisting therein, shall pay and satisfy to the owner or owners of the lands, all damages that shall be done by such fire, except he make it appear that the damage happened by inevitable accident.

That if any person or persons, having their faces blacked, painted, or any ways disguised, shall, either by day or by night, commit any of the trespasses aforesaid; or shall beat or abuse any of the subjects of this or any other of the American States, and be thereof convicted by due course of law; such person or persons so trespassing, shall, over and above the penalties and damages aforesaid, be publicly whipped, not exceeding ten stripes, as the nature of the trespass may require.

That if any horse or other beast, shall trespass in any corn-field, or other inclosure, being fenced in such sort as secures against cows, oxen, calves, and such like cattle, the party or parties trespassed upon, shall procure two able men, of good report and credit, to view and adjudge the harms done, which the owner or owners of the beast or beasts shall satisfy, where known, upon reasonable demand, whether the beasts shall be impounded or not: but if the owner or owners be known, or near residing, as in the same town, or the like notice thereof shall be given to him or them, or left at the place of his or their usual abode, before an estimation be made thereof, to the end he or they, or some other person appointed by him or them, may be present when the judgment is made; the like notice also shall be left for him or them, of the damage charged upon them, that if he or they, shall not approve thereof, he or they may repair to the selectmen, or some of them, who shall, in such case, nominate and appoint two able and indifferent men, to review and adjudge the said harms, which being forthwith discharged and paid, together with the charge of notice, former and latter view, and determination of damages, the first judgment to be void. Provided always, that when damage is done to any person or persons, if it appear to be done or happen by the meer default of him or them to whom the damage is done, it shall be judged no trespass, and no damage shall be given.

AN ACT FOR THE SETTLEMENT OF TESTATE AND INTESTATE ESTATES

19 FEB 1779

Be it enacted, and it is hereby enacted by the representatives of the freemen of the state of Vermont, in general assembly met, and by the authority of the same, that the executor or executors, named by the testator of any last will or testament, or such other person or persons to whom the administration of the estate of persons deceased shall be committed, calling, or taking to him or them, two or more, to whom the deceased person was indebted, or made a legacy; and upon their refusal, or absence, two other honest persons being next of kin to the person so dying; or (on their default or absence) two or more honest neighbours, friends to the deceased, and in their presence, and by their discretion, being under oath, shall make or cause to be made, a true and perfect inventory of all the estate of the person deceased, as well moveable as not moveable, whatsoever, and the same shall cause to be indented: whereof the one part, by the said executor or executors, administrator or administrators, upon his or their oath, or oaths, to be taken before the court which hath power to take probate of wills and testaments, granting administration, and the like, shall be by him or them delivered to the said court of probate, and the other part to be and remain with the said executor, executors, administrator or administrators. That if any executor or executors of the will of any person deceased, knowing of his or their being so named and appointed, shall not, within the space of thirty days next after the decease of the testator, cause such will to be proved, and recorded in the register's office of that district where the deceased person last dwelt; or present the said will, and declare his or their refusal of the executorship; every executor so neglecting of his or her trust and duty in that behalf (without just excuse made and accepted for such delay) shall forfeit the sum of five pounds per month, from and after the expiration of the thirty days, until he or they shall cause probate of such will to be made, or present the same as aforesaid.

And upon any such refusal of the executor or executors, the court of probate shall commit administration of the estate of the deceased, with the will, unto the widow, or next of kin to the deceased; and upon their refusal, to one or more of the principal creditors, as the court shall think fit.

And if the executor or executors of any last will and testament, brought for probate in any of the courts of probates in this state, shall not, within the space of two months next after the probate of such last will and testament, cause such inventory to be made, as aforesaid, and the same to be exhibited in the register's office of the same court of probate where the said will was accepted and recorded; every executor so neglecting his or her trust, in that case (without just excuse made to the judge of said court, and accepted for such delay) shall forfeit the sum of five pounds per month, from and after the said two months are expired, until he or they shall inventory the said estate, and exhibit the said inventory as aforesaid.

Every such forfeiture, as well for not causing the will to be proved, etc. as for not exhibiting an inventory, as aforesaid, shall be and belong, one moiety thereof to the town treasury of that town where the deceased last dwelt, for the use of the said town; and the other moiety to him or them who shall inform or sue for the same, and prosecute to full effect—to be recovered by action or information, in the county where the testator last dwelt.

And if any person or persons shall alienate or embezzle any of the goods or chattels of any person deceased, before he or they have taken out letters of administration, and exhibited a true inventory of all the known estate of the said deceased; all and every such person or persons so acting, shall stand chargeable, and be liable to the actions of the creditors, and other persons grieved, as being executors in their own wrong.

And the court of probates shall cause a citation to be made out to the widow, or next of kin; and upon their neglect of appearance, or refusal, may commit administration of any such estate, to some one or more of the chief creditors, if accepted by him or them; or others, as the said court shall think fit, upon their refusal.

And for preventing fraud in concealing any part of the estate of any person deceased,

Be it further enacted by the authority aforesaid, that if any person or persons in this state, shall have in his or their custody or possession, any goods or chattels belonging to the estate of any deceased person; or any bills, bonds, accounts, or such other things as may tend to disclose such estate; and upon demand of the same made by the executor or administrator of such estate, shall refuse to make delivery, or give a satisfying account thereof to the said executor or administrator; it shall be in the power of the next assistant, or justice of the peace, upon complaint thereof made to him by the said executor or administrator, to issue a warrant to some fit person, to apprehend such offender, and to bring him or her before such assistant or justice of the peace, who may bind such person, with sufficient sureties, to appear before the next court of probates; and the said court shall be, and is hereby impowered to examine such offender or offenders, under his or their oaths, upon such interrogatories touching such goods, chattels, bills, bonds, accounts, and other things, tending to disclose the estate aforesaid, as the said court shall think meet: and that if therein the offender or offenders shall refuse to be examined upon oath, or to answer fully to every interrogatory to such person or persons to be administered or put by the said court of probate, it shall be lawful for the said court to commit every such offender to the common gaol, there to remain until such person shall better conform.

Be it enacted by the authority aforesaid that if any of the creditors or legatees of the deceased, are aggrieved by the appraisement of the estate made by the administrator, or the persons by him appointed, they may have relief by application to the court of probates that granted administration; which court is hereby impowered and required to appoint twelve good and lawful men of the neighbourhood, and to swear them to make a new appraisement of such estate, at the true value and worth thereof, in common estimation, according to the best of their skill; and the administrator shall be accountable for such estate, according to the appraisement thereof made by the said twelve men; and if he make payment of debts or legacies therewith, or any part thereof, the creditors or legatees shall have such estate at the value stated by such appraisers.

Provided, said application be made to such court within three months after the inventory of such estate be exhibited into the registry of the said court, and not after.

Be it further enacted by the authority aforesaid, that when, and so often as, it shall happen, that any person dies intestate, administration of such intestate's estate shall be granted to the widow, or next of kin to the intestate, or both, as the court of probate shall judge fit; and on granting administration upon the estates of intestates, or other whomsoever, the court of probate granting such administration, shall take sufficient bond, with sureties, of such person or persons to whom administration is granted as aforesaid, for a faithful discharge of that work: which bond shall be conditioned according to the form hereafter in this act directed. And the court of probates may and shall proceed to call such administrator or administrators to account for, and touching the estate of such deceased person, whether intestate or other.

And whereas the lands and real estates of persons dying intestate, in this state, by ancient and immemorial custom, and common consent of the people, have descended to and among the children or next of kin of such intestate, as heirs of such intestate; and the same by order of the courts of probates, have generally been divided to and among such heirs, in common with the chattels or moveable estate; and the estates, real and personal, of persons dying intestate, have, ever since the first settlement of this country, been divided among, and settled upon the heirs of such intestates.

And whereas, according to the ancient practice, it is necessary that the real as well as the personal estate be divided by the same court, in order to make a just division of the whole estate; which, by two different courts, proceeding in different methods, and by different rules, cannot be effected.

And whereas, in the courts of common pleas, in the usual manner of proceeding, no such division can be made; but in order thereto, it is necessary that the proceedings therein be in a more summary way.

And whereas, for the more certain, speedy, and just settlement of such estates, according to the said ancient law and custom, it is expedient that some general rules of division, and methods of proceeding, should be established by act of this assembly:—Therefore,

Be it further enacted by the authority aforesaid, that the courts of probates (debts, funeral, and other just expences of all sorts, being by said court first allowed), shall, and are hereby fully impowered, to order and make a just division and distribution of the surplussage, or remaining goods and estate of any such intestate, as well real as personal, in manner following, that is to say—one third part of the personal estate to the wife of the intestate (if any be) forever, besides her dower, or thirds, in the houses and lands during life, where such wife shall not be otherwise endowed before marriage; and all the residue and remainder of the real and personal estate, by equal portions to and among the children, and such as shall legally represent them (if any of them be dead), other than such children who shall have any estate by settlement of the intestate in his lifetime, equal to the other shares: children advanced by settlement or portions not equal to the other shares, to have so much of the surplussage as shall make the estates of all to be equal: and the same shall be so divided, as that the male heirs shall have their parts in the real estate, so far as the estate will allow; and where there are no sons, the daughters shall inherit as coparceners.

And the division of the estate shall be made by three sufficient freeholders upon oath, or any two of them, to be appointed by the said court of probate, unless all the parties interested in any estate, being legally capable to act, shall mutually agree upon a division among themselves, and present the same in writing, under their hands and seals; in which case, such agreement shall be accepted and allowed for a settlement of such estate, and be accounted valid in law, being acknowledged by the parties subscribing before the said court of probates, and put upon record.

Provided nevertheless, that when any estate in houses and lands cannot be divided among the children, without prejudice to, or spoiling of the whole, being so represented and made to appear unto the said court of probates, the said court may order the whole to the eldest son, if he accept it, or to any other of the sons successively (upon his refusal), he to whom it shall be ordered, paying to the other children of the deceased, their equal and proportionable parts or shares of the true value of such houses and lands, upon a just appraisement thereof, to be made by three sufficient freeholders upon oath, to be appointed and sworn as aforesaid; or giving good security to pay the same in some convenient time, as the said court of probate shall limit, making reasonable allowance in the interest, not exceeding six per centum per annum.

And if any of the children happen to die before he or she come of age, or be married; the portion of such child deceased shall be equally divided among the survivors.

And in case there be no children, nor any legal representatives of them, then one moiety of the personal estate shall be allotted to the wife of the intestate forever, and one third of the real estate for the term of life; the residue both of the real and personal estate equally to every of the next of kin of the intestate, in equal degree, and those who legally represent them: no representatives to be admitted among collaterals, after brother's and sister's children.

And if there be no wife, all shall be divided and distributed among the children.

And if there be no child, to the next of kin to the intestate, in equal degree, and their legal representatives as aforesaid.

And every one to whom any share or part shall be allotted, shall give bond with sureties before the said court of probates (if debts afterwards be made to appear), to refund, and pay back to the administrator, his or her rates, or part thereof, and of the administrator's charges.

And the widow's thirds, or dower, in the real estate, at the expiration of her term, to be also divided as aforesaid, if the same then remain undivided.

Always provided, and it is hereby enacted, that if any person be aggrieved at any order, sentence, or decree, of any court of probates, made for the settlement and distribution of any intestate estate, or at any other order, sentence, decree, or denial, that shall at any time be made and given by the said court of probates, referring to the approbation and allowance of any will, grant of administration, or other matters; such person may appeal therefrom to the superior court, provided they give security, and enter and prosecute such appeals, within the times limited for that purpose, as is provided and directed in the law regulating such appeals.

Be it further enacted, by the authority aforesaid, that every court of probate shall, upon granting administration upon the estate of any deceased person, take bond, with sufficient surety or sureties, to the judge of said court, and his successors in that office, with this condition, viz,

The condition of this obligation is such, that if the above bounden A.B., administrator of all and singular the goods, chattels, credits, and estate, of C.D. deceased do make, or cause to be made, a true and perfect inventory of all and singular the goods, chattels, credits, and estate of the said deceased, which have or shall come to the hands, possession or knowledge of the said A.B. or into the hands or possession of any person or persons for him; and the same so made, do exhibit, or cause to be exhibited, into the registry of the said court of probates, in the district of .... at or before the .... day of .... next ensuing; and the same goods, chattels, credits, and estate, and all other the goods, chattels, credits, and estate, of the said deceased, at the time of his death, which at any time after shall come into the hands or possession of the said A.B. or into the hands or possession of any other person or persons for him; do well and truly administer according to law. And further, do make, or cause to be made, a true and just account of his said administration, at or before the .... day of .... And all the rest, and residue of the said goods, chattels, credits, and estate, which shall be found remaining upon the said administrator's account, the same being first examined and allowed by the said court of probates, shall deliver, and pay unto such person or persons respectively, as the said court of probates, by their decree, or sentence, pursuant to the true intent and meaning of the law, shall limit and appoint: and if it shall hereafter appear that any last will and testament was made by the said deceased, and the executor, or executors, therein named, do exhibit the same into the said court, making request to have it allowed and approved accordingly: if the said A.B. being thereunto required, do render and deliver the said letters of administration (approbation of such testament being first had and made) in the said court, then this obligation to be void, and of none effect; or else to remain in full force and virtue.

And be it further enacted, by the authority aforesaid, that all sales and alienations of houses and lands (belonging to the estate left by any deceased person) made by the administrator or administrators of such estate, shall be void, and of none effect; unless such sales and alienations shall be made by the allowance and order of the general assembly of this state, or by the judge finding the estate insolvent.

And all such houses and buildings as appertain to the estate of any person deceased, shall be kept and maintained in tenantable repair, by the revenue of the lands belonging to such estate; and shall, in such repair, be delivered to the heirs, or legatees, at the time of the division or distribution thereof—extraordinary casualties excepted.

Be it further enacted by the authority aforesaid, that whensoever the estate of any person deceased shall be insufficient to pay the just debts charged upon the same, such estate shall be disposed of by the administrator, in the best way and manner, as the judge shall order, and the produce thereof divided and distributed to the creditors, in proportion to the sums respectively owing to them, so far as the estate will extend; saving the debts due to this state, and for the last sickness, and necessary funeral charges of the deceased, are to be first paid.

And the executor, or administrator, appointed to administer on such insolvent estate, before payment be made to any person (except as before excepted), shall represent the condition and cricumstances thereof to the judge of probate, who shall nominate and appoint two or more fit and indifferent persons commissioners, who shall be sworn to a true and faithful performance of their trust; who shall then proceed to appoint times and places to sit and examine the claims on such estate, and publish the same, by setting up or posting notifications thereof in some public place in the town where such deceased person last resided, and also in the two next county towns. And the said judge shall allow two, six, twelve, or eighteen months (as the circumstances of the estate may require) for the creditors to bring in their claims, and prove their debts: at the end of which limited time, such commissioners shall make their report, and present a list of the claims unto the said judge, who shall order them a meet recompence for their trouble, out of such estate.

And the debts due to this state, and for the last sickness, necessary funeral charges, and cost of settlement, being subducted, the judge shall also order the remainder to be divided to the other creditors that shall have made out and evidenced their claims as aforesaid, in due proportion as aforesaid; saving to the widow (if any be) such household goods as in this act hereafter are allowed her, and her dower during life; which shall also be sold by the administrator immediately, with the incumbrance of the widow having the use thereof during her life.

Provided always, that notwithstanding the report of any such commissioners, or allowances thereof made by the court of probate, it shall and may be lawful to and for the executors or administrators aforesaid, to contest the proof of any debt at the common law. And no process in law (except for debts due to this state, and for sickness, and funeral charges) shall be admitted or allowed against the executors or administrators of any insolvent estate, so long as the same shall be depending as aforesaid.

And whatsoever creditor shall not make out his or her claim with such commissioners, before the full expiration of the time set and limited for that purpose, as aforesaid; such creditor shall forever after be debarred of his or her debt, unless he or she can shew or find some other or further estate of the deceased, not before discovered and put into the inventory.

And be it further enacted by the authority aforesaid, that when it shall happen the personal estate of a deceased intestate, leaving a widow, is not sufficient for the payment of the debts of the said deceased, besides such household goods as are necessary for the support of life, and are exempted from execution in the law, intitled, "An act for directing and regulating the levying and serving executions"; in such cases, the court of probate that grants administration of the estate of the deceased, shall order unto the widow of the said deceased, such necessary household goods as are expressed in said act, for use during life.

AN ACT CONCERNING SUDDEN AND UNTIMELY DEATHS

20 FEB 1779

Be it enacted, and it is hereby enacted, by the representatives of the freemen of the state of Vermont, in general assembly met, and by the authority of the same, that when, and so often as, any person shall come to any sudden, untimely, or unnatural death, or be found dead in this state, the manner of whose death is not known; the next assistant, or justice of the peace, or in their absence the constable of the town, shall forthwith summon a jury of twelve able and discreet men, who shall be sworn by such officer to enquire of the cause, and of the manner of such person's death; and shall present, upon oath, a true verdict thereof, under their hands, unto some near assistant, or justice of the peace, who shall return the same to the next superior court in the same county.

And if any man, summoned to serve as a juror, to enquire as aforesaid, shall refuse or neglect, to appear and attend that service, according to such summons, he shall forfeit the sum of ten shillings for every such neglect, to the use of the treasury of the town whereto he belongs; to be levied by warrant from any assistant, or justice of the peace, before whom such juror shall be convicted of such refusal or neglect.

AN ACT FOR THE PRESERVATION OF DEER

20 FEB 1779

Be it enacted, and it is hereby enacted by the representatives of the freemen of the state of Vermont, in general assembly met, and by the authority of the same, that no person or persons whatsoever, within this state, at anytime between the tenth of January and the tenth of June next following, in each year, annually, forever hereafter, shall any ways whatsoever, kill or destroy, directly or indirectly, any buck, doe, or fawn, on pain that every such person so offending, and being thereof convicted, shall forfeit and pay for every such offence, the sum of fifteen pounds; the one moiety thereof to the person or persons that shall prosecute the same to effect, and the other moiety to the treasury of the town in which the conviction is made.

And if any person or persons, so convicted, shall be unable to satisfy such judgment, such offender shall be by the assistant or justice of the peace before whom the offender is convicted, put to, and assigned in service, to the complainer, or some other meet person, a sufficient term of time for the answering such judgment.

Any one assistant, or justice of the peace, shall hear and determine any offences committed against this act.

And the more effectually to detect such offences,

It is further enacted by the authority aforesaid, that if any venison, skin or skins, of any buck, doe, or fawn, newly killed, shall at any time wherein the killing thereof is by this act prohibited, be found with, or in possession of any person or persons whatsoever; such person or persons shall be held and accounted guilty of killing deer, contrary to the intent of this act, as fully as if it was proved against such persons by sufficient witness, viva voce; unless such person or persons do bring forth, or make proof who was the person or persons that killed or sold the same; or unless such person can satisfy the judge, before whom the case is tried, that he or they were not the killers, but that the venison, skin or skins were thrust into his or their custody or possession, by some other person, to insnare him or them: in either of which cases, they shall not incur the penalty aforesaid.

That it shall and may be lawful for any person, on just cause of suspicion, of the breach of this act, by killing any buck, doe, or fawn, as aforesaid, to take out a search, from the next assistant, or justice of the peace, as in ordinary cases of lost or stolen goods, or the like, to search for venison or skins, that such offenders may be detected.

And the grand jurymen, and constables, in the respective towns, are hereby strictly required to make diligent inquiry after, and present- ment or information make, of all breaches of this act; who, upon their prosecution thereof, shall have the same reward as other informers by this act are intitled to.

AN ACT FOR REGULATING AND AUDITING THE PUBLIC ACCOUNTS

20 FEB 1779

For preventing of inconveniences in the public accounts, and that no arrears in the state accounts be standing out after the year be expired,

Be it enacted, and it is hereby enacted, by the representatives of the freemen of the state of Vermont, in general assembly met, and by the authority of the same, that male persons shall by this assembly be ap- pointed annually in October, to make up and audit the state's accounts with the treasurer of the state; which accounts shall be audited and per- fected before the next sitting of the general assembly. And all such persons as shall be appointed to audit said accounts, shall, before their entering upon that service, take the oath provided by law for such auditors.

And the treasurer is hereby obliged to make himself debtor for the several sums due from every of the towns in this state, and also for all fines belonging to the state treasury; and so for the whole rate or sum total arising by bringing the several particular sums into one entire sum; and to bring in credit (according to law) until he shall consum- mate and perfect the state accounts as aforesaid. And this the said treas- urer shall do annually, on the penalty of twenty pounds to be forfeited to the public treasury for every month after such session annually, that he shall neglect to make up and perfect said accounts, and pay according to the order of this assembly, such sum or sums as remain due.

And the treasurer of each respective county in this state, shall an- nually, make himself debtor for all fines and other monies belonging to the county whereof he is treasurer, and also make a fair account of his payments, how he hath disposed of them. And the accounts of each county treasurer shall be annually audited and perfected by the judge and justices of the county courts respectively, and their respective treas- urers.

And be it further enacted, by the authority aforesaid, that the secretary of the state shall annually give an account to the treasurer of the state, of all the fines due to the public treasury, that the same may be gathered and improved for the use of the state; and a copy thereof shall by the secretary also be yearly transmitted to the auditors when they shall audit the treasurer's accounts.

AN ACT FOR PREVENTING AND PUNISHING RIOTS AND RIOTERS

22 FEB 1779

Be it enacted, and it is hereby enacted, by the representatives of the freemen of the state of Vermont, in general assembly met, and by the authority of the same, that when three persons, or more, shall come or assemble themselves together to the intent to do any unlawful act with force and violence, against the person of another, as to kill, beat, or otherwise to hurt; or against his possession, or goods, as to break open, or to pull down, an house, building, or fence, wrongfully; or to cut or take away corn, grass, wood, or other goods, wrongfully; or to do any other unlawful act with force or violence against the peace, or to the manifest terror of the people; and being required or commanded by any of the civil authority, by proclamation to be made in the form herein after directed, shall not disperse themselves, and peaceably depart to their habitations or lawful business; or being so assembled as aforesaid, shall do any unlawful act against the person, possessions or goods of any man; or against the public interest in any particular, in manner as aforesaid and be thereof convicted before the county or superior court, in the county where this law shall be transgressed and broken, shall be punished by fine, not exceeding for each person, the sum of two hundred pounds; imprisonment, not exceeding six months; or by whipping not exceeding forty stripes: and the number convicted shall pay all damage to the aggrieved party, as shall arise by such disorder, together with cost. And whensoever it shall so happen, that there be a number who transgress this law, and one or more of them is unable to pay the damage and cost, the damage and cost shall be paid by the persons who are offenders with them, and are of ability to pay the same.

Any, or all of the aforesaid punishments, at the discretion of the court that hath cognizance of such offence, as the nature and circumstances of the fact shall require.

That the order and form of the proclamation before mentioned, shall be as followeth,—That is to say,—the person authorized by this act, shall, among, or as near as he or they can safely come to said rioters, with a loud voice command, or cause to be commanded, silence to be whilst proclamation is making; and after that shall openly, and with a loud voice, make proclamation in these words, or like in effect, viz.

In the name of the freemen of this state, I command all persons, being assembled, immediately to disperse themselves, and depart to their habitations, or to their lawful business, upon the pains contained in the law of this state, intitled, "An act for preventing and punishing riots and rioters".

And every assistant, justice of the peace, sheriff, under sheriff, selectman, or constable, within their respective jurisdictions, are hereby authorised, impowered, and required, on notice or knowledge of such unlawful and riotous assembly, to resort to the place where such assembly shall be, and there make proclamation as aforesaid.

Be it further enacted by the authority aforesaid, that if such persons so unlawfully assembled, or any three or more of them, after proclamation made as aforesaid, shall continue together, and not disperse themselves; that then it shall and may be lawful to and for every assistant, justice of the peace, sheriff, under sheriff, selectman or constable, where such riotous assembly shall be, and to and for such other person or persons as shall be commanded to be assisting to such assistant, justice of the peace, sheriff, under sheriff, selectman, or constable, who are hereby authorised and impowered to command all the inhabitants of this state, to be assisting them therein, to seize and apprehend, and they are hereby required to seize and apprehend such persons, so unlawfully and riotously continuing together, after proclamation made as aforesaid; and forthwith to carry the persons, so apprehended, before some assistant, justice of the peace, in order to their being proceeded against according to law.

And if any of the persons so unlawfully and riotously assembled, shall happen to be killed, maimed or hurt, in dispersing, or apprehending, or in endeavoring to disperse or apprehend them, by reason of their resisting the persons so dispersing, or endeavoring to disperse or apprehend them; that then every such assistant, justice of the peace, sheriff, under sheriff, selectman or constable, and all and singular the persons, being aiding and assisting to them, or any of them, shall be freed, discharged, and indemnified, from any bill, complaint, indictment, or action, that may be commenced against him or them, on that account.

Be it further enacted by the authority aforesaid, that if any person or persons do or shall forcibly, wilfully, and knowingly, oppose, obstruct, or in any manner wilfully and knowingly oppose, let, hinder, or hurt, any person or persons that shall begin or attempt to proclaim according to the proclamation hereby directed to be made, whereby such proclamation shall not be made, and be thereof convicted by due course of law, shall forfeit or suffer in manner and form as aforesaid.

And that all and every such person or persons so being unlawfully and riotously assembled, to the number of three as aforesaid, or more, to whom proclamation should or ought to have been made, if the same had not been hindered as aforesaid, shall likewise, in case they, or any of them, to the number of three, or more, shall continue together, and not immediately disperse themselves after such let, or hindrance so made, having knowledge of such let or hindrance so made, and be thereof convicted by due course of law, shall forfeit, suffer, or be punished, in manner and form as aforesaid.

Provided always, that no person or persons be punished by virtue of this act, unless prosecution be commenced within six months after the offence is committed.

AN ACT FOR APPOINTING OF SHERIFFS; AND FOR IMPOWERING AND REGULATING THEM IN THE EXECUTION OF THEIR OFFICE

16 FEB 1779

Be it enacted, and it is hereby enacted, by the representatives of the freemen of the state of Vermont, in general assembly met, and by the authority of the same, that there shall be a sheriff appointed, according to the constitution, and duly qualified to execute the sheriff's office in each of the counties in this state, who shall become bound before the governor and council, with two sufficient sureties, freeholders in this state, by a recognizance in the sum of two thousand pounds, for the faithful administration and discharge of said office, and for the answering all such damages as any person or persons shall sustain by any unfaithfulness or neglect in the same; and before he executes said office, shall, before the governor, or in his absence the deputy governor, take the oaths required by law to be taken by such as execute the said office; and shall receive a warrant or commission from the governor, or in his absence the deputy governor, expressing him to be elected and qualified as aforesaid, authorising him to execute said office. And every person being so commissioned, shall be accounted lawful sheriff of the county for which he is appointed and shall have full power and authority to serve and execute all lawful writs within their respective counties to them directed, coming from lawful authority: and shall have and execute the power of water bailiffs, which is hereby annexed to the sheriff's office.

And also shall have full power, within their respective counties to conserve the peace, and to suppress, with force and strong hand, when the necessity of the case shall so require, all tumults, riots, routs, and other unlawful assemblies; and to apprehend, without warrant, all such as they shall find so as aforesaid, appearing in the disturbance of the peace, who may, as the cause after examination thereinto shall require, bind over such offenders to the next county court in that county wherein the offence is committed; which court, upon conviction, shall punish them, and every of them, agreeable to an act of assembly for preventing and punishing riots and rioters.

That the sheriffs aforesaid, shall have full power to command suitable persons within their respective counties, such number of them as they shall judge needful to assist them in the execution of their office in every branch thereof. And whosoever being of age and ability, and being so commanded, shall neglect or refuse to yield his assistance to any sheriff in the execution of his office, and be thereof convicted before the county court of that county, shall pay a fine of twelve pounds, and charges of prosecution.

And each and every constable in this state shall, within their respective towns, have power equal to what is hereby given to sheriffs, in their respective counties.

And in case great opposition shall be made against any sheriff, in executing lawful writs, or in serving lawful writs and processes; or in case there be a suspicion that such great opposition will be made; such sheriff is hereby authorised, by and with the advice of two assistants, or one assistant and one justice of the peace, and of such other assistants and justices as may be present, to raise the militia of the county, or so many of them as they may judge needful, for the removing all opposition out of the way; and shall proceed therein, and be indemnified, as is provided by the law, intitled, "An act for preventing and punishing riots and rioters."

And all military officer and soldier, are hereby commanded to yield obedience to the sheriff's commands, in such cases, on the pains and penalties hereafter mentioned.

That if any commissioned officers, or soldiers, belonging to the militia of this state, shall neglect or refuse to obey the command of the sheriff under the regulations aforesaid, and be thereof convicted before the county court, such officer shall pay a fine of thirty pounds; and every such soldier shall pay a fine of twelve pounds; and the charges which shall arise, and the damages which shall be sustained upon such an occasion, shall be paid and satisfied out of the estates of him or them who are the occasion of it; and in case no estate, or not sufficient to answer the said charges and damages can be found, it shall be paid out of the county treasury where such case shall happen; and for want of money in the treasury of said county, it shall be paid out of the treasury of this state.

And the sheriff is hereby authorised to seize and dispose of a sufficiency of the offenders estate, if to be found, to answer the charges and damages aforesaid.

And the wages of such officers, soldiers, and other persons, commanded to the assistance of the sheriff, shall be thirty shillings per day for a captain, twenty four shillings for a subaltern, and twenty shillings for each sentinel, or other person employed in such service.

And the sheriffs shall have full power to search the houses in their respective counties for any persons they shall have warrants from proper authority to apprehend, in matters of delinquency, or of a criminal nature: and any person who shall refuse the sheriff entrance into his house, or threaten him if he does enter, or abuse him, or his assistants, when he or they do enter the house of any person, although it is by force, on such an occasion, and be thereof convicted before the county court, shall forfeit and pay a fine of one hundred pounds, and all damages that shall arise from such disorder.

And the constables shall have the like power and authority in their respective towns; and persons opposing them shall be subject to the same penalties.

And the sheriffs shall not return that they cannot do execution.

And the more effectually to oblige sheriffs and constables to perform the services of their offices.

Be it further enacted, by the authority aforesaid, that sheriffs and constables shall receive all manner of writs, in any places, or at any times within their counties, or towns, when and wheresoever they shall be tendered to them, and shall execute the same, and make return thereof according to the directions therein given.

And any person may demand of the sheriff or constable to whom he delivers any writ, to give a receipt therefor under his hand, wherein the names of the parties, the sum or thing in demand, the date of the writ, and of its delivery shall be contained; and on his refusal, others present may set their hands as witnesses to such delivery.

And if such sheriff or constable shall not execute the writ, or shall neglect to make return thereof, or make a false or undue return; on complaint thereof made to the court of justice to which it was returnable, the court or justice may enquire thereof by the evidence produced; and if it be found in default, the court or justice may set a suitable fine upon him, and award damages to the party wronged; having respect unto the quantity and quality of the action, and the damages that might have happened to the aggrieved by the delay.

Which process, against such sheriff or constable, shall be sued for not executing any writ of execution, delivered to him to be executed, there shall be no appeal or review allowed in any such case.

Provided, receipt be demanded or received of such officer for such writ of execution at the time of the delivery thereof, as is herein before provided.

Be it further enacted by the authority aforesaid, that whenever any sheriff, or constable, by virtue of any writ of execution, shall seize any goods or chattels, to answer and satisfy such execution, and any person shall appear to receive such goods and chattels in his care, and shall give to such officer a writing, well executed by such person, therein expressing the receipt of such goods and chattels, and thereby promising to redeliver the same to such officer, and shall fail of performing accordingly, and any action shall be brought by such sheriff or constable, against such person on such receipt, there shall be no appeal or review allowed or granted in such case.

And that no sheriff, under sheriff, sheriff's deputy, or constable, shall be allowed to draw, or fill up any writ, complaint, process, or declaration, in any case whatsoever; nor appear in any court as an attorney for or in behalf of any person whatsoever.

And if it shall appear, in any case, that the writ, process, declaration, or complaint, was drawn or filled up by any sheriff, deputy sheriff, or constable (their own cases excepted), the same shall be dismissed, and the plaintiff shall be non-suited, any law, usage, or custom to the contrary notwithstanding.

And all processes, served by any sheriff or constable, shall be by them returned to the courts or justices before which the cases are to be tried, before the time set in the processes for trial.

Be it further enacted by the authority aforesaid, that the sheriffs in each county in this state, be, and they are hereby, impowered to depute, each of them, two meet persons, to act or officiate as under sheriffs; for whose conduct in said office the sheriffs are to be accountable.

AN ACT REGULATING JURIES AND JURORS

22 FEB 1779

Be it enacted, and it is hereby enacted, by the representatives of the freemen of the state of Vermont, in general assembly met, and by the authority of the same, that whensoever any person shall be indicted for treason, felony, or other high-handed misdemeanors, which the superior court shall judge necessary, the sheriff attending such court, being ordered thereto, shall summon twenty-four freeholders of the vicinity for a grand jury, eighteen at least of whom shall be impanelled and sworn to make due inquiry and presentment in the premises, in behalf of the freemen of this state; and if they do find the bill or indictment to be founded on good and sufficient evidence, they shall write on the bill or indictment, a true bill; and if they do not find the bill or indictment to be supported by evidence, they shall write, bill not found; in which case the person or indicted shall be acquitted, otherwise the court shall proceed to trial; and in like manner shall the grand jury proceed with regard to indictments before the county courts: and the grand jury summoned by the sheriff to attend the county court; and for default or non attendance, shall be liable to the like penalty.

Provided always, that where the sheriff is a prosecutor, or stands in the relation of father, son, or brother, by nature or marriage, to the prosecutor, or delinquent, or a party; landlord, or tenant, to the prosecutor, or delinquent, or a party; the court shall order some indifferent person to summon the grand jury.

Be it further enacted by the authority aforesaid, that some convenient time before the sitting of the superior or county court, the clerk of such court shall issue out warrants, directed to the constables of the several towns within the county where such courts are to sit, or so many of them as shall appear to him to be necessary, to summon so many able freeholders as the warrant shall direct, to attend and serve as jurors at said court.

And the jurors to attend the superior or county court, shall be summoned to attend at eight of the clock on the second day of the sitting of such courts.

And the constable shall make timely return of the warrant to the clerk who granted the same, with an indorsement thereon, certifying whom he has summoned for the purpose aforesaid; on pain that every constable neglecting his duty therein, shall forfeit and pay to the county treasury a fine, not exceeding five pounds, at the discretion of the judges of the court; unless such constable shall seasonably make his excuse, to the acceptance of such court.

That if any juror summoned as aforesaid, shall make his default of appearance, according to the directions of such warrant he shall forfeit and pay unto the treasurer of the county wherein he dwells, the sum of thirty shillings; unless the court, before whom the action shall be tried, on hearing the excuses made on his behalf, shall judge them sufficient.

Be it further enacted by the authority aforesaid, that when it shall so happen, that a sufficient number of jurors, summoned as aforesaid, do not appear; or if by reason of challenges, or other just cause, there shall not be a sufficient number of jurors to make up the panel or panels, the court shall order the sheriff to fill up the jury or juries, by summoning a sufficient number of substantial freeholders of the vicinity.

Provided always, that where the sheriff stands in the degrees of relation or connection before recited in the regulations of the grand jury, some constable or indifferent person, shall be ordered to summon the jurors.

And such jury shall be called the petit jury, and shall, in matters of dispute, determine the matter in issue, with the damages; and in matters of criminal nature, shall find the defendant guilty or not guilty, and the judges shall determine the punishment according to law.

Be it further enacted by the authority aforesaid, that whensoever it shall be necessary for a jury to attend a justice's court, in matters of dispute, the parties may mutually agree on the jury, and shall be advised thereto by the magistrate; and upon the refusal or neglect of either party, as also in criminal cases, or matters of delinquency, the following method shall be taken to procure and impanel a jury,—that is to say,

The constable shall write the names of eighteen respectable freemen or freeholders of the vicinity, on eighteen distinct pieces of paper of an equal size and roll each piece up so that the name is not to be seen, and deliver them to the justice, who shall put them into a box, shaking it so that they shall mix together, shall draw out one, which person so drawn shall be one of the jury, unless excepted against, or challenged by either of the parties; and so proceed drawing until he has drawn six that are not excepted against or challenged; or in case the first twelve are challenged or excepted against, and the parties do not agree to make choice as aforesaid, the last six shall be the jury; and the jury shall be summoned by the constable, being thereto required by the justice: which jury shall find the matter in issue, and damages in matters of dispute; and in matters of a criminal nature, or of delinquency, shall find the criminal or delinquent guilty, or not guilty; and the assistant or justice, or assistants and justices, shall determine the punishment according to law.

Provided always, that whenever the constable shall stand in relation or connection before recited in the regulations of the grand jury, some indifferent person shall be ordered to write the names of the eighteen freeholders aforesaid, and do all the duty of the constable prescribed in the foregoing paragraph.

And if any juror drawn and summoned as aforesaid to attend on a justices court, shall make default of appearance, he shall be liable to the same forfeiture as jurors for the superior or county court are in such case, unless he shall make sufficient excuse as in that case.

And when it shall so happen that any one or more of the six jury men, so summoned, can not be had, and the parties will not agree on a person or persons to fill such vacancy, the constable, or person doing the constable duty, shall proceed to write the names of three times the number so wanting, on distinct pieces of paper, and deliver, and draw as before mentioned, and in that way fill such vacancy.

Be it further enacted by the authority aforesaid, that the judge or judges of any court, shall have power, if they judge the jury have not attended to the evidence given in, and the true issue of the case in their verdict, to cause them to return to a second consideration of the case, and shall, for like reason, have power to return them to a third consideration, and no more.

And when the court have committed any case to the consideration of the jury, the jury shall be confined under the care of an officer appointed by the court, until they are agreed on their verdict: and the court may set a suitable fine, not exceeding ten pounds, upon such officer or juryman as shall be disorderly, or neglect or refuse a due attendance of their duties respectively, during their attending such court.

Be it further enacted by the authority aforesaid, that whensoever any person shall be tried for life or limb, he may challenge thirty-five of the petit jury; and in all other cases, twice the number that are to be impanelled, may be challenged.

That all juries shall have power and authority to choose their foreman: which foreman shall declare their judgment or verdict.

AN ACT FOR THE ORDERING AND PRESERVING SHEEP, ETC.

16 FEB 1779

Be it enacted, and it is hereby enacted by the representatives of the freemen of the state of Vermont, in general assembly met, and by the authority of the same, that the inhabitants of the respective towns within this state, at their respective town meetings, shall have power and authority to make necessary acts for the restraining of rams from going at large, and for the securing their sheep from being destroyed by dogs; and for stopping hounds from worrying deer within their towns.

And no damage shall be recovered against any person, for killing any dog or dogs, according to the orders of such town.

And the more effectually to prevent mischiefs being done by dogs to sheep in this state,

Be it further enacted by the authority aforesaid, that when any person or persons, living in any town in this state, shall complain to any one of the selectmen of such town, of damages done among sheep, by their being wounded, worried, or killed by dogs, in the woods, or elsewhere in such town, and shall inform such selectman what and whose dog they suspect did said mischief; such selectman shall consider such complaint, and any other matters that may be offered, to convince him of the reasonableness or unreasonableness of such suspicion; and if he be satisfied there is great suspicion that the dog or dogs complained of have done said mischief, such selectman shall give sentence, that such dog or dogs shall be killed: after which it shall be lawful for any person to kill such dog or dogs.

And if, after such sentence be given (such dog or dogs not being killed), such mischief shall again be done by dogs, the owner of such sheep, worried, wounded or killed by dogs, shall recover all his damages against the owner or owners of such dog or dogs sentenced to be killed as aforesaid; unless, upon trial, the owner or owners of such dog or dogs shall satisfy the court or justice before whom the trial is, that the damages were not done by his or their dog or dogs, sentenced as aforesaid.

Always provided, that the owner or owners of such dog or dogs, be notified of the sentence aforesaid, before the damages sued for was done; and that no prosecution by virtue of this act for such damages be made after six days from the time such damages are done.

AN ACT CONCERNING SURETIES AND SCIRE FACIAS

16 FEB 1779

Be it enacted, and it is hereby enacted, by the representatives of the freemen of the state of Vermont, in general assembly met, and by the authority of the same, that whensoever any person or persons not being freeholders of this state, shall desire or demand of any magistrate or clerk of a court, any writ or process whatsoever, to bring or summons any person or persons to answer before any court in this state, there shall be a sufficient bond given by such person or persons requiring such writ, with good surety or sureties, of substantial freemen and freeholders of this state, to prosecute his or their writ to effect, and to answer all damages, if he, she, or they, make not his, her, or their, plea good; before the executing such bond, no writ or process of any kind shall be granted to such persons.

That where bail is given upon common process for the appearance of the party to answer the suit, every such surety or sureties shall be obliged to satisfy the judgment in case of the principal's avoidance, and the return of non est inventus be legally made on the execution; and the party for whom the judgment is given, may have a writ of scire facias, out of the same court, against such surety or sureties; and in case no just cause be shewn to the contrary, the judgment that was rendered against such principal, shall be affirmed against such surety or sureties, with the additional costs of suit, and execution shall be granted accordingly— unless such surety, at the time of entering final judgment, do bring the principal into court, and move to be discharged; upon which the court shall order the keeper of the gaol, or the officer attending such court, to receive him into custody, that so his body may be taken in execution.

Always provided, that such writ of scire facias be taken out and served upon the surety, within six months after the said final judgment, and not afterwards.

And every surety, of whom such recovery is made, may bring his action for, and shall recover all damages against the principal.

Be it further enacted by the authority aforesaid that when any court, assistant, or justice of the peace, upon trial before him, has given judgment for any sum of money to be paid, and before execution is granted thereon, is removed by death, or otherwise; the party recovering judgment shall have a right, at any time within twelve months after such removal, to bring a scire facias to the superior or county court in the county where such justice did live, or court was held, against the person or persons against whom he has recovered such judgment; and upon his producing the record of the said judgment, or an attested copy thereof, in said court, shall have execution thereon granted to him by said court, for so much of the sum as shall then appear to remain unpaid, and for all the additional cost.

Be it further enacted by the authority aforesaid, that no attachment, or special warrant, to apprehend the body, or attach the goods or chattels of any person, shall be granted by any magistrate, or clerk of court, before the person praying out such warrant or attachment has given sufficient surety or sureties, to the acceptance of such magistrates, or clerk of court, to prosecute his writ to effect, and answer all damages, if he does not make good his plea.

Provided always, that a county or town informing officer, shall not be obliged to give such bonds in the prosecution of criminals or delinquents.

AN ACT REGULATING PROPRIETOR'S MEETINGS

23 FEB 1779

Be it enacted, and it is hereby enacted by the representatives of the freemen of the state of Vermont, in general assembly met, and by the authority of the same, that where lands lie in common, in any township in this state, and a number of the proprietors of such lands, to the amount of at least one sixteenth part, shall make application to any assistant or justice of the peace, who is hereby required to issue his warrant for calling such meeting, setting forth the time, place, and the several other matters and things to be transacted, and the reasons for calling such meeting; which warrant shall be inserted in the *Connecticut Courant* three weeks successively, the last time of which shall be at least twenty days before the convening such meeting.

And such proprietors, when met, shall proceed by ballot to choose a moderator, clerk, and treasurer; and may further proceed to transact any business which may concern the propriety, as the promoting of settlement, and laying out and making division of lands, laying out roads, and any other business whatsoever. And every proprietor shall be allowed to vote in proportion to his interest in such propriety. A proprietor of one original right or share, may have one vote, and so on in proportion as aforesaid.

Always excepted, that no person shall be allowed more than one vote by virtue of a power of attorney.

And the votes and proceedings of such meetings shall be good, and valid in law; provided no proprietor shall be curtailed in the quantity of his land: and such proprietors may adjourn and agree on such mode of convening again as to them may be thought expedient; and such clerk being duly sworn, shall make fair and true entries of all the votes and proceedings of such meeting; from which records, such clerk shall give fair and attested copies of any matter or thing therein contained, when requested thereto by any proprietor, on such proprietor's tendry, of a certain sum, which is hereafter mentioned, to be given for recording survey bills.

The charters of each town, which may or can be procured, shall be recorded in the first pages of the proprietor's book of records: and it shall be the clerk's duty to record all survey bills, provided such survey bills are properly attested by a surveyor, and offered for record.

Such clerks are furthermore directed, on receiving any survey bill as aforesaid to enter it on file as soon as may be, with the date when received to record; and such survey bills which are first recorded, or received to record as aforesaid, shall be valid and good in law, without any regard to the date of such survey bills, or time when such land was surveyed.

Always provided, such survey bill be agreeable to the votes and proceedings of the propriety.

And it shall and may be lawful for any such clerk to take six shillings for recording a survey bill which fills one side of a sheet of paper, and no more; and all other writings and different sized survey bills respecting his office, in the same proportion.

And provided any proprietor's clerk shall neglect or refuse to do his duty as aforesaid, shall, on conviction thereof before an assistant or justice of the peace, pay a fine of ten pounds for every such offence, and all damages which may arise by such neglect or refusal; and one half of such fine shall be paid to the complainant, who shall prosecute to effect, and the remainder to the proprietor's treasurer, for the use of the propriety: and all legal cost shall be paid by such delinquent.

That when any proprietors meeting shall be legally warned, and met, as aforesaid, and provided such propriety shall proceed to run out town lines, or make a division of lands to each proprietor, or lay out or make any road or roads in any town, after such service is actually accomplished and done, then, in such case, it shall and may be lawful for such proprietors, being legally met as aforesaid, to tax such cost to the shares of the lawful owners of the original rights in such townships (the four public rights only excepted) and the proprietors taxing such cost, may appoint a collector, who is hereby directed to publish such tax (as being due to the propriety, that those interested in the same may discharge it) in the *Connecticut Courant,* with the cause why such tax was made, three weeks successively, which cost shall be paid by the proprietors; and in case such tax shall not be paid to such collector, within thirty days after the last time of such publication, it shall and may be lawful for such collector to publish in the *Connecticut Courant,* in manner as aforesaid, the names of the original grantees whose tax remains due, either from them or their assigns or heirs, in order to notify the just claimants to such original rights, that in case they do not pay the same, that a certain necessary proportion of their land will be sold at public vendue, to pay such tax and cost, specifying the time and place of such vendue, which shall not be held under twenty days, or over thirty days, from such latest publication in the *Courant* aforesaid.

And provided there shall then remain any part of such tax unpaid, it shall and may be lawful for such collector to proceed to sell at public vendue, so much of such delinquent's land, beginning first with undivided (if any there be) as to pay such tax, together with cost, including not only the cost of such vendue, but that of the last advertisements. And such collector shall make and execute a deed or deeds, to the purchase or purchasors; which deed or deeds shall be good, and valid in law.

Always provided, that if the proprietor of such land shall appear, and tender to such collector the full sum of money for which such land was sold, with the cost arising thereon, any time before such deed of vendue sale is executed; then such collector shall receive the money, and not execute such deed to the purchaser, but redeliver to him his money.

And such collector shall make return of his doings to the proprietor's clerk, within one month after any such vendue, and remit the money which he may have collected, from time to time, to the treasurer, as often as he may be directed by such propriety; and on neglect of any part of his duty, shall be liable to the same penalties as is in this act before directed for any deficiency in his duty.

And provided there shall be any money remaining, after such tax and cost is fully paid, such overplus money shall be paid to the person or persons which were the rightful owners of such lands as may be sold at the time of such vendue, when called for by those to whom it is due, as explained aforesaid.

Be it further enacted by the authority aforesaid, that such persons as may have been in the continental service, or in captivity, at such time when their lands may have been vendued as aforesaid, shall have a right of redemption to such lands, during one full year after the impediments of soldiery or captivity are removed, by payment or tendry of the same sum of money for which such lands were sold, with the interest of such money at six per cent per annum. And in case any improvement shall have been made on such lands in the meantime, then those persons before described, may make payment or tendry of such sum of money as shall be judged by indifferent persons to be equal to the value of such improvements; and such person or persons shall be reinstated in the fee of their land, any thing in this act to the contrary notwithstanding.

And be it further enacted by the authority aforesaid, that from and after the first day of May, in the year 1779, all proprietors meetings, and vendues, respecting any lands in this state, shall be held in the town or county where such land lieth; and if any proprietors meeting or vendue respecting any lands in this state, shall be held out of the same, or in any other manner than what is warranted by this act, the same shall be null and void.

AN ACT TO PREVENT THE RETURN TO THIS STATE OF CERTAIN PERSONS
THEREIN NAMED, AND OTHERS, WHO HAVE LEFT THIS STATE, OR
EITHER OF THE UNITED STATES, AND JOINED THE ENEMIES THEREOF

26 FEB 1779 (REPEALED PAGE 221)

Whereas Samuel Anderson, Joseph Anderson, Benjamin Anderson, Amos Dunning, Beloved Carpenter, Beriah Buck, Caleb Reynolds Jun., Coonraat Devoe, Adam Deal, Peter Deal, Hendrick Deal, and Daniel Straight, of Pownal; James Brakenridge Jun., of Bennington; John Munroe Esq., Ebenezer Wright, and Abraham Marsh, of Shaftsbury; Elisha Hard, Jeptha Hawley, Philo Hulbert, James Hard, Phineas Hurd, Benajah Benedict, Samuel Adams, Isaac Brisco, Samuel Buck, David Williams, Benjamin Holt, Caleb Henderson, Charles Bennet, and Gideon Adams, of Arlington; Jeremiah French, Andrew French, Samuel Rose, Joseph Lockwood, William Reynolds, Joseph Barker, Date Seelick, and Davis Sturges of Manchester; Col. William Marsh, and Israel Bardsley, of Dorset; Joseph Case, Daniel Scott, and James McDonald, of

Rupert; Barnabas Hough, William Fairfield, Elijah Benedict, David Castle, and Reuben Hawley, of Pawlet; James Moore, Caleb Lewis, John Ward, Joseph Morse, James Floom, John Beach, and Enoch Mallery, of Wells; Silvanus Everts, Gilbert Everts, Oliver Everits, Asa Landon, Charles Griffin, and Daniel Culver, of Castleton; Joshua Bostwick, David Shorey, and Robert Perry, of Rutland; Daniel Marsh, Elijah Osbourn, Hazleton Spencer, John Lee, William Sutton, Daniel Walker, Barnabas Spencer, Amariah How, James Clark, Philip Nichols, Daniel Hill Jun., Simpson Jenny, Solomon Johns, Joseph Lewis, Comfort Curtis, Timothy Hill, of Clarendon; Seth Cook, and Aaron Bull, of Danby; Isaac Ives of Wallingford; Joseph Pringle, John Smith, Ithiel Towner, and Samuel Richardson, of Bridport; Abner Wolcott and Justus Sherwood of New Haven; William White of Cornwall; John Nicholas, of Ferrisburg; Roger Stephens Jun., of Pittsford; Samuel Tiler, and John Gray, of Shelburne; William Powers, of Panton, all in the county of Bennington; Caleb Green, Abisha Howe, Shadrach Ball, of Newfane; Malachi Church, Oliver Church, John Arms, and Oliver Wells, of Brattleborough; John Grant of Chester; Col. James Rogers, of Kent; Timothy Lovell, of Rockingham; Crean Brush, of Westminster; Zadock Wright, and Jonathan Wright, of Hertford; all in the county of Cumberland, and many other persons, have voluntarily left this state, or some of the United States of America, and joined the enemies thereof; thereby not only depriving these states of their personal services, at a time when they ought to have afforded their utmost aid in defending the said states against the invasions of a cruel enemy, but manifesting an inimical disposition to said states, and a design to aid and abet the enemies thereof in their wicked purposes.

And whereas many mischiefs may accrue to this, and the United States, if such persons should again be admitted to reside in this state.

Which to prevent,

Be it enacted, and it is hereby enacted by the representatives of the freemen of the state of Vermont, in general assembly met, and by the authority of the same, that if the said Samuel Anderson, Joseph Anderson, or any of the before mentioned persons, or either of them, or any other person or persons, though not specially named in this act, who have voluntarily left this state, or either of the United States, and joined the enemies thereof, as aforesaid, shall, after the passing this act, voluntarily return to this state, it shall be the duty of the sheriff of the county, his deputy, the constable, selectmen, or grand jurors of the town where such person or persons may presume to come, and they are hereby respectively impowered and directed to apprehend and carry such person or persons before an assistant or justice of the peace; who is hereby required to call to his assistance one or more assistant or justices of the peace; who are hereby directed to give their attendance, according to such requisition; and if upon examination into the matter, the said justices shall find that the person brought before them is any one of the before described persons, they shall order him to be whipped on the naked back, not more than forty, nor less than twenty stripes; which punishment shall be inflicted, and the delinquent shall be ordered to quit this state immediately.

Be it further enacted by the authority aforesaid, that if any person shall continue in this state one month, or shall presume to come again into this state, after such conviction (without liberty first had and obtained therefor from the governor, council, and general assembly), and be convicted thereof before the superior court of this state, he shall be put to death.

Be it further enacted by the authority aforesaid, that if any person shall willingly or wilfully harbour or conceal any of the persons above named or described, after their return to this state, contrary to the design of this act; such person so offending, shall, on conviction thereof before the superior court, forfeit and pay the sum of five hundred pounds, two-thirds thereof to the use of this state, the other third to the use of him or them who shall prosecute the same to effect.

AN ACT REGULATING FISHERIES

23 FEB 1779

Be it enacted, and it is hereby enacted, by the representatives of the freemen of the state of Vermont, in general assembly met, and by the authority of the same, that no weirs, hedges, fish garths, disturbances or incumbrances whatsoever (except dams for necessary mills), shall be set, erected or made, on or across any river in this state.

And if any person or persons whatsoever, shall by weirs, hedges, seines, or any other incumbrance, way, or means whatsoever, obstruct the natural or usual course or passage of the fish in the spring, or proper seasons of the year, up or down any river in this state, the same shall be deemed a common nuisance, and shall or may be pulled down, demolished, and removed as such, by any person or persons whatsoever.

And upon complaint or information thereof made to an assistant or justice of the peace of the same county where such common nuisance is erected as aforesaid, a writ shall be granted to the sheriff or constable, to cause diligent enquiry to be made, for finding the person or persons guilty of such nuisance, and him or them to bring before such authority to be examined in the premises; and if convicted thereof, he or they shall forfeit a sum not exceeding four pounds, one half to the complainer or informer, who shall prosecute the same to effect, the other half to the county treasurer.

And the said authority, before whom such conviction is had, shall thereupon command suitable assistance, at the cost and charges of the person or persons so convicted, to remove such nuisance.

And if any person who shall pull down, remove or demolish any such nuisance, shall be sued therefor, he may plead the general issue to such suit, and give this act in evidence.

AN ACT FOR THE PUNISHMENT OF DIVERS CAPITAL AND OTHER FELONIES

19 FEB 1779

Be it enacted, and it is hereby enacted, by the representatives of the freemen of the state of Vermont, in general assembly met, and by the authority of the same, That if any person shall conspire, or attempt any invasion, insurrection, or public rebellion against this state; or shall treacherously and perfidiously attempt the alteration and subversion of our frame of government, fundamentally established by the constitution of this state, by endeavoring the betraying of the same into the hands of any foreign power, he shall be put to death.

That if any man or woman shall lie with any beast, or brute creature, by carnal copulation: such person shall surely be put to death, and the beast shall be slain and buried.

That if any man lieth with mankind, as he lieth with a woman, both of them have commited abomination; they both shall surely be put to death. Except it appear that one of the parties were forced, or under fifteen years of age; in which case the party forced, or under the age aforesaid, shall not be liable to suffer the said punishment.

That if any person rise up by false witness, wilfully, and of purpose to take away any man's life; such offender shall be put to death.

That if any person, of the age of sixteen years, or upwards, shall wilfully, and of purpose, burn any house, barn, or out-house, to the prejudice or hazard of any person's life, he shall be put to death.—Or if no prejudice or hazard to the life of any person happen thereby, shall suffer such other severe punishment as the superior court shall determine, and also satisfy all damages to the wronged or aggrieved party.

That if any person, on purpose, and of malice forethought, and by lying in wait, shall cut out or disable the tongue, or put out an eye, or eyes, so that the person is hereby made blind; or shall cut off all, or any of the privy members of any person, or shall be aiding or assisting therein, such offender shall be put to death.

That if any person within this state, shall blaspheme the name of God the Father, Son, or Holy Ghost, with direct, express, presumption, and high-handed blasphemy; or shall curse in the like manner; such person shall be put to death.

AN ACT CONCERNING DELINQUENTS

22 FEB 1779

Be it enacted, and it is hereby enacted, by the representatives of the freemen of the state of Vermont, in general assembly met, and by the authority of the same, that whensoever any person shall be complained of, indicted, or in any wise prosecuted for any matter of delinquency, or of a criminal nature, by any other person than a county or town informing officer, and that within the town or county where both the complainer and the person complained of does belong, and such complaint can not be supported; such person so complaining, shall pay the cost arising on such suit.

And whensoever any person shall be complained of, indicted, or in any wise prosecuted, for any matter of delinquencies, or of a criminal nature, by any county or town informing officer, of the county or town where he does belong, and such complaint or indictment cannot be supported, the necessary cost arising on such prosecution, shall be paid out of the treasury into which the fine would have been paid, had the delinquent been fined upon such prosecution.

Be it further enacted by the authority aforesaid, that in all matters of delinquency, or of a criminal nature, where the person complained of, or prosecuted, is convicted, he shall pay cost of such prosecution: and in case such criminal, or delinquent, have not estate to pay such cost, it shall and may be lawful for the court, assistant, or justice, before whom such process shall be, to dispose of such person in service, to any freeman of this corporation, so long a time as shall be necessary to procure money sufficient to answer the charges arising on such prosecution.

But if it shall so happen, that such charges can not be obtained out of the estate or service of any person so convicted, such charges, if the trial be in the superior court, shall be paid out of the state's treasury; and if the trial be in the county court, such charges shall be paid out of the county treasury; and if the trial be in a justice's court, such charges shall be paid out of the treasury of the town where such delinquent lives; or if he has no residence in any town in the county, out of the treasury of the town where the conviction is had; and the court, or justice, shall give order accordingly.

Be it further enacted by the authority aforesaid, that no person shall be twice sentenced for one and the same crime, trespass, or offence.

That if any person or persons, on his examination or trial for delinquency, shall either in words or actions, behave contemptuously or disorderly, it shall be in the power of the court, assistant, or justice, to inflict such punishment on him or them, as they shall judge the nature of the offence may require.

Provided always, that no single minister of justice shall inflict any greater punishment than imprisonment for one month; binding to the peace or good behaviour until the next county court; putting them in the stocks, there to sit not exceeding two hours; or imposing a fine not exceeding four pounds.

And that if any person, who shall be required to appear and give his evidence, in the trial or examination of any delinquent or criminal, shall refuse to appear, or to make oath to declare his knowledge in the case; the court, assistant, or justice of the peace, holding such trial or examination, may apprehend and commit the person so refusing to prison, there to remain at his or her own cost, until they shall give evidence.

Provided always, that such evidence shall not be construed to his prejudice.

And that when any sheriff, deputy sheriff, or constable, shall receive a warrant from any court, assistant, or justice (that hath lawful cognizance of the offence), to do execution of a judgment by them given, against any criminal or delinquent; such officer shall proceed according to the directions of such warrant, to do execution himself, or by some meet person by him to be procured, to the acceptance of the court granting such warrant; & for doing execution as aforesaid, a reasonable satisfaction shall be allowed, which shall be taxed as part of the bill of cost, to be paid by such delinquents.

AN ACT REGULATING THE CHOICE OF TOWN OFFICERS AND
PETIT JURYMEN

18 FEB 1779

Be it enacted, and it is hereby enacted, by the representatives of the freemen of the state of Vermont, in general assembly met, and by the authority of the same, that the selectmen of each town in this state, shall set up a notification at such places as have been or shall be agreed on by the inhabitants, as are by law qualified to vote in such meeting, to meet at the meeting house, or some convenient place by them appointed in such town, giving twelve days notice before the convening of such meeting, which shall be held on some day in the month of March annually, at ten o'clock in the morning.

And it shall be the duty of the inhabitants when met as aforesaid, to proceed to choose a moderator for said meeting, and town clerk or register; then they shall choose a number not exceeding five, to be selectmen, or townsmen, to take care of the prudential affairs of such town; also a town treasurer, one or two constables, listers not exceeding five, collectors of rates, leather sealers, one or more grand jurors, one or more tything men, hay wards, branders of horses, sealers of weights and measures, and every other town officer that the law of this state shall direct.

And the selectmen of each town shall forthwith, after such choice, see that all of the officers be sworn to the faithful discharge of their respective offices, by an assistant or justice of the peace, or in case no such officer be present, by the town clerk, who shall make entry in the records of such officers being chosen & sworn.

Then the selectmen and constable or constables, with the town clerk, and such magistrates as may be present, shall agree upon a number of men that may be thought by them to be their proportion of petit jurymen to attend the superior or county courts the ensuing year; which number shall be chosen by the people present, and shall be discreet freeholders.

And the town clerk shall write the names of the persons so chosen, each on a piece of paper, and put them in a box, provided at the town's cost for that purpose, and kept in his office; and when the constable shall receive any warrant from the clerk of the superior or county court, to summons any number of men for jury men, to attend and serve as such at any of said courts, he shall repair to the town clerk's office, and in his presence, or in case he be absent, in the presence of one of the selectmen of such town, draw out of said box the number his warrant directs him to summon; and having so done, he shall proceed to summons the men for jury men whose names are so drawn, but if any of the men whose names are drawn, are gone from home, or sick, or otherwise unavoidably hindered from attending said court, his name or names shall be returned into the box, and others in their room drawn and summoned as aforesaid.

And in case at any time the number of jury men to be summoned is more than there remains in the box, the constable shall, at his discretion, summon a sufficient number of discreet freeholders to supply such place.

And be it further enacted by the authority aforesaid, that if any person shall be chosen to any of the offices aforesaid in this act, and shall refuse to serve therein, or take the oath required by law, if he be able in person to execute the same, shall forfeit and pay to the treasurer of the town where he does belong, a fine of three pounds, except such person shall make it appear to an assistant or justice of the peace before whom the case shall be tried, that he is oppressed by such choice, or others are unjustly exempted.

AN ACT TO PREVENT NUISANCE IN THE PUBLIC HIGHWAYS

22 FEB 1779

Be it enacted, and it is hereby enacted, by the representatives of the freemen of the state of Vermont, in general assembly met, and by the authority of the same, that if any person shall make any fence across any county road, without first obtaining leave therefor from the county court of said county; or across any town road, without first obtaining leave therefor from the selectmen of said town; it shall and may be lawful for any person or persons to remove, throw down, and destroy such nuisance.

AN ACT TO PREVENT UNSEASONABLE NIGHT WALKING, AND FOR THE PUNISHING OF DISORDERS COMMITTED IN THE NIGHT SEASON

15 FEB 1779

Be it enacted, and it is hereby enacted, by the representatives of the freemen of the state of Vermont, in general assembly met, and by the authority of the same, that if any persons that are under the government of parents, guardians, or masters, or any boarders, or sojourners, shall convene or meet together, or be entertained in any house, without the consent or approbation of their parents, guardians, or masters, after nine o'clock at night, any longer than to discharge the business they are sent about; or shall meet together, and associate themselves in company or companies, in streets, or elsewhere, after the time aforesaid, and shall commit any disorder, or make any rout at any time in the night season; each person so offending shall forfeit twenty shillings for every such offence.

And whereas great disorders and insolence are often committed in the night, by disorderly persons, to the disquiet and hurt of the good people of this state.—For the preventing and punishing whereof,

Be it enacted by the authority aforesaid, that when, and so often as any disorders and damages are done in the night season, that upon complaint speedily made thereof to any court, assistant, or justice of the peace, they are hereby impowered to issue forth a writ or writs for the bringing before him or them any such suspected person or persons, and examine him or them concerning such disorders and damages.

And if such suspected person or persons, upon such examination, can not give a satisfactory account to the authority before whom such examination is had, where he or they were when such disorders & damages complained of were committed and done, and that he or they had no hand in doing the same, he or they shall be liable to pay and answer all such damages as the person or persons complaining, shall have sustained or suffered, as aforesaid; and also such fine or punishment as the court, assistant, or justice, before whom the trial is had, shall see cause to order, not exceeding ten pounds.

AN ACT APPOINTING STOCKS AND SIGN POSTS, TO BE MADE AND MAINTAINED IN THE SEVERAL TOWNS IN THIS STATE

15 FEB 1779

Be it enacted, and it is hereby enacted, by the representatives of the freemen of the state of Vermont, in general assmbly met, and by the authority of the same, that every town in this state shall make and maintain, at their own charge, a good pair of stocks, with a lock and key sufficient to hold and secure such offenders as shall be sentenced to sit therein; which stocks shall be set in the most public place in each respective town.

And in the same place there shall be a sign post erected and set up, at the charge of said town, and maintained in sufficient repair; on which sign post all notifications, warrants etc. shall be set up.

And if any town shall be at any time without a pair of stocks or sign post, as aforesaid, after six months from the publication hereof, the selectmen of such town shall forfeit the sum of twenty shillings to the town treasurer, and so the same sum for every month such town shall be defective thereof; to be heard and determined by one assistant or justice of the peace.

AN ACT CONCERNING THE DOWRY OF WIDOWS

15 FEB 1779

That there may be suitable provision made for the maintenance and comfortable support of widows, after the decease of their husbands.

Be it enacted, and it is hereby enacted by the representatives of the freemen of the state of Vermont, in general assembly met, and by the authority of the same, that every married woman, living with her husband in this state, or absent from him elsewhere, with his consent, or through his mere default, or by inevitable providence, or in case of divorce, where she is the innocent party, that shall not, before marriage, be estated by way of jointure, in some houses, lands, tenements, or hereditaments, for term of life, or with some other estate in lieu thereof, shall immediately upon and after the death of her husband, have right, title, and interest, by way of dower, in and unto one third part of the real estate of her said deceased husband, in houses and lands which he stood possessed of in his own right, at the time of his decease, to be to her during her natural life; the remainder of the estate shall be disposed of according to the will of the deceased; and where there is no will according to law.

Provided always, that this law doth not extend to the widow of those that have or may be guilty of treason.

And for the more easy and speedy ascertaining such right of dower,

It is further enacted by the authority aforesaid, that upon the death of any man possessed of any real estate as aforesaid, which his widow by this act as before expressed, hath a right of dower in, if the person or persons that by law have a right to inherit said estate, do not within sixty days next after the death of such husband, by three sufficient freeholders of the same county, to be appointed by the judge of probate (in whose district the estate doth lie) and sworn for that purpose, set out and ascertain such right of dower; that then such widow may make her complaint to the judge of probate in whose district the estate lieth; which judge shall decree & order that such woman's dowry shall be set out and ascertained by three sufficient freeholders of the county, who shall be sworn faithfully to proceed and act therein accordingly, to their best skill; and the said dowry being set out and ascertained in either of the methods aforesaid, the doings of such freeholders shall be returned to the judge who ordered the dowers to be set out as aforesaid; and upon approbation thereof by the said judge, such dower shall remain fixed and certain, and all persons concerned therein shall be excluded thereby.

And every widow so endowed as aforesaid, shall maintain all such houses, buildings, fences, and inclosures as shall be assigned and set out to her for her dowry, and shall leave the same in good repair.

And if such widow shall not maintain, and keep in good repair, such houses, buildings, fences, and inclosures, as shall be assigned and set out to her, for her dowry as aforesaid, it shall be in the power of the county court in which the estate is, upon application to them made, to deliver so much of the said houses and lands, to the next heir of the same, and for so long a term as in their judgment shall be sufficient, out of the rents or profits thereof to repair such defects; unless such widow will give good security for the leaving such houses, buildings, fences, and inclosures in sufficient repair.

AN ACT CONCERNING WITNESSES TO WILLS

15 FEB 1779

Be it enacted, and it is hereby enacted, by the representatives of the freemen of the state of Vermont, in general assembly met, and by the authority of the same, that no wills or testaments, wherein there shall be any devise or devises of real estate, shall be held good, and allowed for any such devise or devises, if they are not witnessed with three witnesses, all of them signing in the presence of the testator.

AN ACT AGAINST BARRATRY AND COMMON BARRATORS

15 FEB 1779

Be it enacted, and it is hereby enacted, by the representatives of the freemen of the state of Vermont, in general assembly met, and by the authority of the same, that if any person shall be proved and adjudged a common barrator, vexing others with unjust, frequent, and needless suits, he shall pay a fine of twenty pounds into the public treasury of this state, by order of the court before whom he shall be convicted; and before the same court he shall become bound, with two sureties, for his good behaviour (for one year at least), or on refusal, to be committed to prison, there to remain for said time, or till he procures sureties, as aforesaid.

And the court before whom such vexatious suit shall be brought, may and is hereby impowered to reject such suit, giving cost to the adverse party.

AN ACT AGAINST GAMING

15 FEB 1779

Be it enacted, and it is hereby enacted, by the representatives of the freemen of the state of Vermont, in general assembly met, and by the authority of the same, that no tavern keeper, inn keeper, ale house keeper, or victualler, shall have or keep in or about his or their house or houses, out houses, yards, gardens or other places to them belonging, any cards, dice, bowls, shuffle boards, or billiards, or any other unlawful game or sport, within their said houses, for any sum or sums of money, goods, or liquors, on pain of forfeiting the sum of twenty pounds for every such offence, upon due conviction thereof; the said fine to be disposed of, one half to the informer, the other half to the treasurer of the town where such offence is committed.

And every person who shall be convicted of playing at any such games as aforesaid, or any horse racing, on any wager as aforesaid, in any such houses or dependencies, or in any other place in this state, shall forfeit the sum of twenty shillings to be disposed of as aforesaid; and the monies, goods, or chattels so played for and won, if the value thereof be more than twenty shillings, shall be appropriated to the use of the town where such wager was won; and the treasurer of the town where such wager is won, is hereby impowered to sue for the same, before any court proper to try the same.

AN ACT CONCERNING REPLEVINS

15 FEB 1779

Be it enacted, and it is hereby enacted, by the representatives of the freemen of the state of Vermont, in general assembly met, and by

the authority of the same, that every man shall have liberty to replevy his cattle or other goods and chattels, impounded, distrained, attached, seized, or extended (except it be upon execution after judgment, and in paying off fines and rates), provided he put in and give good and sufficient security to prosecute his replevin to effect, and to satisfy and answer such damages, demands, and dues, as the adverse party shall by law recover against him.

AN ACT DIRECTING AND REGULATING THE LEVYING AND SERVING EXECUTIONS

15 FEB 1779

Be it enacted, and it is hereby enacted by the representatives of the freemen of the state of Vermont, in general assembly met and by the authority of the same, that when any judgment is recovered, and execution taken out thereon, the sheriff, or other officer to whom the execution is directed, shall repair to the place of the debtor's usual abode (if within his precinct), and there make demand of the debt or sum due on such execution, with necessary charges; and upon refusal, or neglect of payment of the same, the officer shall levy the execution upon any of the personal or moveable estate of the debtor, except necessary apparel, bedding, tools, arms, implements of his household necessary for upholding life, one yoke of oxen, and one cow.

And the officer shall forthwith draw an account of the particulars of the goods or estate he shall so seize and take, and set up the same on the sign post of the town wherein he shall seize the same; and the officer, with the account of the said goods, shall set up a declaration, that the said goods, so posted are to be sold at the place where posted at an outcry, at the end of twenty days, after naming of the day of the month.

And in case the debtor shall not, within the said twenty days, pay the debt, and all the cost and charges arisen thereon, the officer shall cause a drum to be beat at the sign post, to give notice to customers to come, and shall sell the said goods (or as many of them as shall be necessary) there at an outcry, to the highest bidders, and of the effects thereof shall pay the debt and charges due to the creditors, and satisfy himself for his own fees and charges; and the overplus (if any there be) shall be returned to the owner thereof.

That in case moveable or personal estate of the debtors sufficient to satisfy the debt and charges cannot be found, and the creditors shall not agree or accept to take the debtor's lands, the officer shall levy the execution upon the debtor's body, and him commit to the common gaol in that county in which the execution is levied; where the debtors or delinquent shall remain until he shall pay the debt, and all charges with the officers and prison-keepers fees, or be otherwise discharged by due course of law.

And every officer who shall commit any person to prison, by virtue of a distress or execution, shall deliver a true copy of the writ or execution, signed by such officer to the goaler or prison keeper; which copy so signed and delivered, shall be a sufficient warrant or order to the gaoler to receive such person or persons, and him or them to hold in safe custody, till delivered by a law.

And be it further enacted by the authority aforesaid, that all lands & tenements belonging to any person in his own proper right in fee, shall stand charged with the payment of all just debts owing by such person, as well as his personal estate; and shall be liable to be taken in execution for satisfaction of the same, where the debtor or his attorney shall not expose to view, and tender to the officer, personal estate sufficient to answer the sum mentioned in the execution, with charges; and all executions duly served upon any houses and lands, being returned into the clerk's office of the court out of which the same issued, and there recorded; as also a copy thereof lodged in the town clerk's office in the town where such houses or lands lie (which said clerk shall enter in the town book of records, taking the same fee as allowed for recording deeds), shall make a good title for the party for whom they shall be taken, his heirs and assigns forever.

And that whensoever execution shall be levied upon lands, it shall be in the liberty of the creditor to choose one man, and the debtor another, and the officer a third (if need be), to appraise the land; and if either the debtor or creditor shall refuse or neglect to choose such appraisers, the officer shall chuse one or more, as there may be occasion; which appraisers shall be sworn to appraise the land according to the value thereof.

And be it further enacted by the authority aforesaid, that all executions issuing out of the office of the clerk of the county court, or superior court respectively, and executions granted out by justices of the peace, where by law they have authority to grant the same, may by the said clerk & justice respectively, be directed to any of the officers proper to serve the same, in any of the counties of this state in which the person liveth, or estate whereupon the same is to be served is, at the time of granting the execution; which officers to whom the same is directed, and delivered, shall duly and faithfully serve and return the same according to the direction therein given; which being returned, shall be kept on file in the office out of which the same was issued.

And that all writs of execution shall be made returnable within sixty days, or to the court (in case sixty days are remaining between the date of the execution and the next court), at the election of him that prays it out; and all executions granted by a single minister of justice, shall be returnable in sixty days.

And all constables as well as sheriffs shall have power to serve any writ or execution to them directed, within their own precincts, and not out thereof; that is to say, the sheriff within his county, and the constable within his own town.

AN ACT CONCERNING BASTARDS AND BASTARDY

15 FEB 1779

Be it enacted, and it is hereby enacted, by the representatives of the freemen of the state of Vermont, in general assembly met, and by the authority of the same, that he who is accused by any woman, to be the father of a bastard child, begotten of her body, she continuing constant in such accusation, being examined upon oath, and put to the discovery of the truth, in the time of her travail, shall be adjudged the reputed father of such child, notwithstanding his denial thereof, and shall stand charged with the maintenance thereof, with the assistance of the mother, as the county court of that county in which such child is born, shall order; and give security to perform such order, and also to save the town and place where such child is born, free from charge for its maintenance.

And the said court may commit to prison such reputed father, until he find sureties for the same, unless the proofs, evidence, and pleas, made and produced on the part of the man accused as aforesaid, and other circumstances, be such as the court who have cognizance of the same, shall see reason to judge him innocent, and acquit him thereof; in which case they shall and may otherwise dispose of such child.

And every assistant, or justice of the peace, upon his discretion, may bind to the next county court him that is charged or suspected to have begotten a bastard child; and if the woman be not then delivered, the said county court may order the continuance or removal of his bond, that he may be forth-coming when such child is born.

AN ACT FOR THE ASCERTAINING TOWN-BRANDS, AND PROVIDING AND REGULATING BRANDING AND BRANDERS OF HORSES

15 FEB 1779

Be it enacted, and it is hereby enacted, by the representatives of the state of Vermont, in general assembly met, and by the authority of the same, that each town in this state shall have a town brand, to brand their horses with; which shall be the several letters or figures as are hereafter and hereby directed,—that is to say,

Pownal	P	Halifax	H	Thetford	⊥
Bennington	B	Whitingham	4	Stratford	8
Shaftsbury	S	Wilmington	Y	Fairlee	F
Arlington	A	Dummerston	Z	Mooretown	φ
Sandgate	E	Townshend	T	Corinth	g
Sunderland	2	Westminster	&	Newbury	I
Manchester	M	Rockingham	Я	Leister	L
Dorset	D	Kent	K	Barnet	ꓷ
Rupert	R	Springfield	I	Guildhall	Ⴖ
Pawlet	AE	Chester	Ɔ	Peacham	Ↄ
Danby	I	Addison	X	Cavendish	8
Wells	W	Weathersfield	q	Newfane	Ƨ
Poultney	OE	Windsor	△	Andover	E
Clarendon	C	Hertford	∩	Brumley	ꝛ
Wallingford	6	Woodstock	II	Marlborough	ʎ
Rutland	O	Hartford	ꓔ	Brattleborough	°
Castleton	Q	Pomfret	≏	Hinsdale	d
Pittsford	3	Barnard	7	New Stamford	~~
Neshobe	N	Norwich	V	District of Ira	σ
Cornwall	U	Sharon	ꓷ	Harwich	H
Guilford	G	Royalton	5	Hubbardton	ꓷ

Every of which brands shall be set respectively on every horse and horse kind, on the near or left shoulder.

And the inhabitants of each town shall chuse a suitable person to be a brander of horses in such town; and each brander shall be under oath and shall make an entry of all horse kind by him so branded, with the age and colour, natural and artificial marks, in a book by him kept for that purpose.

And if any such brander shall presume to brand any horse, mare, or colt, that is above one year old, at any other place than at a town pound, or those places appointed by the town for that work (unless he has first received a special order from the selectmen of such town so to do), he shall forfeit and pay the sum of four pounds for every such offence, one half to the complainer, and the other half to the treasury of the town in which he lives.

And if any such brander shall refuse or neglect to brand or record any horse, mare, or colt (except such as he is by law forbidden to brand and enter), presented to him for the same; he shall for every such offence, forfeit and pay the sum of twenty shillings to the person presenting such horse and all damages sustained by such person, by him made to appear, through such brander's neglect.

And be it further enacted by the authority aforesaid, that if any person or persons shall counterfeit any town brand, or cause to be branded any horse, mare, or colt, on the near or left shoulder, with any letter or figure, being the brand of any town in this state, without the knowledge or order of one of the branders of such town (under his hand), he or they so offending shall forfeit the sum of ten pounds for every such offence, one half to the complainer, and the other half to the county treasury.

AN ACT FOR THE PUNISHMENT OF BURGLARY AND ROBBERY

15 FEB 1779

Be it enacted, and it is hereby enacted, by the representatives of the freemen of the state of Vermont, in general assembly met, and by the authority of the same, that whosoever shall commit burglary, by breaking up any dwelling house, or shop, wherein goods, wares and merchandize are kept; or shall rob any person in the field or highway, such person so offending, shall for the first offence be branded on the forehead with the capital letter B; on a hot iron, and have one of his ears nailed to a post and cut off; and also be whipped on the naked body fifteen stripes.

And for the second offence, such person shall be branded as aforesaid, and have his other ear nailed and cut off as aforesaid, and be whipped on the naked body twenty five stripes.

And if such person shall commit the like offence a third time, he shall be put to death, as being incorrigible.

AN ACT FOR THE MARKING OF CATTLE, SWINE &c.

15 FEB 1779

To prevent disputes, and differences that may arise in the owning and claiming of cattle, sheep, and swine, that may be lost or stray away,

Be it enacted, and it is hereby enacted, by the representatives of the freemen of the state of Vermont, in general assembly met, and by the authority of the same, that all the owners of any cattle, sheep, and swine, within this state, shall ear-mark, or brand, all their cattle, sheep, and swine, that are above half a year old; and that they shall cause their several marks to be registered in the town book.

And whatsoever cattle, sheep, or swine, shall be found unmarked, and not branded as aforesaid; the owners thereof shall forfeit and pay three shillings per head, one half whereof shall be to the complainer, and the other half to the town treasury.

AN ACT RELATING TO BILLS OF DIVORCE

15 FEB 1779

Be it enacted, and it is hereby enacted, by the representatives of the freemen of the state of Vermont, in general assembly met, and by the authority of the same, that no bill of divorce shall be granted to man or woman lawfully married, but in case of adultery, or fraudulent contract, or wilful desertion for three years, with total neglect of duty; or in case of seven years absence of one party, not heard of; after due enquiry is made, and the matter certified to the superior court, in which case the other party may be deemed and accounted single and unmarried. And in that case, and in all other cases aforementioned, a bill of divorce may be granted by the superior court to the aggrieved party, who may then lawfully marry, or be married again.

AN ACT TO PREVENT ENCROACHMENTS ON HIGHWAYS, AND ON COMMON AND UNDIVIDED LANDS

15 FEB 1779

Be it enacted, and it is hereby enacted, by the representatives of the freemen of the state of Vermont, in general assembly met, and by the authority of the same, that if any person hath within the space of three years, taken or shall take, any part of any highway, or common, or undivided land into his field or inclosure; or erect any fence thereon, in such manner that the said highway is straightened, and made narrower than before; or any part of the common or undivided land is encroached upon; the selectmen of the town wherein the offence is committed, or a committee appointed by such town for that purpose; or a committee appointed for that end by the proprietors of the common or undivided land encroached upon (which committees such town and proprietors are enabled to appoint), or any three of such proprietors are hereby directed and impowered to give notice or warning to the person or persons so offending, that if he or they, do not cause the said fence or encroachment to be removed, in such convenient time as the said selectmen, committee, or proprietors giving the warning shall set, not exceeding the space of one month after such notice or warning given; the said selectmen, committee, or proprietors, giving such warning, shall cause such fence, or encroachment, to be pulled down and removed.

And if the person or persons warned as aforesaid, do not cause such fence or encroachment to be removed, within the time so to be set and limited as aforesaid; it shall be lawful for the said selectmen, committee, or the said three proprietors, and they are hereby impowered, to remove, or cause the said fence, or encroachment, to be removed.

And if the persons offending as aforesaid, shall commit the like offence, by taking in the same, or a greater or lesser quantity of any highway, common or undivided land, where his fence has been removed as aforesaid; he shall incur the penalty of four pounds for every such offence, as often as he shall commit the same; to be recovered by bill, plaint, action, or information, by the persons who gave the warning, and caused the said fence, or encroachment, to be removed; one half of the penalty to be to the prosecutors, with cost of prosecution; and the other half to the town treasury of the town wherein the offence is committed. In which trials no review nor appeal shall be allowed.

And that every person prosecuted for said offence, shall be deemed guilty thereof, unless he can satisfy the court that hath cognizance thereof, that he did it not himself, not by his order nor consent, cause or procure said offence to be committed.

And be it enacted by the authority aforesaid, that if those, or any of those persons that shall pull down and remove such fence or encroachment, as aforesaid, shall be sued in trespass for so doing, by any person or persons whose fence shall be so pulled down, or removed; such selectmen, committee, or proprietors, who shall pull down and remove said fence, or cause the same to be done, may plead not guilty, and give this act in evidence on the trial.

And if the plaintiff or plaintiffs, in such action, shall not prove that the fence removed, when standing, was well on the bounds of his or their lands, or of their lands for whom the plaintiff or plaintiffs hold the same, and so was not any encroachment, as aforesaid, verdict shall be given in favor of the defendants; in which case, as also in case of non suit, judgment shall be rendered for double costs in favor of the defendants.

AN ACT CONCERNING GRAND JURYMEN

15 FEB 1779

Be it enacted, and it is hereby enacted, by the representatives of the freemen of the state of Vermont, in general assembly met, and by the authority of the same, that every town in this state, on the day of their annual town meeting for electing town officers, shall elect and chuse one or more sober, discreet persons, of their inhabitants, to serve as grand jurors for the ensuing year, who shall be sworn by the next assistant, justice of the peace, or the town clerk.

But in case any person so elected, shall refuse to accept, and take the oath for such officers provided, and serve as aforesaid (unless he render a satisfying reason to the town meeting, or to the authority before whom he shall be called to take the oath, why he ought not to serve, as aforesaid), he, for such refusal, shall incur the penalty of forty shillings; and another person shall be chosen in his room, who shall, upon acceptance, be sworn as aforesaid. And the names of such grand jurors shall, by the clerk of the town, be returned to the clerk of the county court within the same county; and the said clerk of the county court shall, by his writ, summon such a number of the said grand jurors within the said county, as shall be necessary, to attend and serve at the said county courts.

And if any such grand juror so as aforesaid required and summoned to serve on the grand jury, shall neglect or refuse to appear (unless he shall give sufficient reason for his refusal), shall forfeit and pay the sum of thirty shillings.

And all grand jurors shall diligently enquire after, and due presentment make, of all misdemeanors and breaches of law, whereof they have cognizance, whether the same were committed before said grand jurors were chosen and sworn to said office, or afterwards; which presentment they shall seasonably make to the court, or to some assistant or justice of the peace, that the offenders may be dealt with according to law.

And if any grand juryman after he is sworn, shall neglect to make seasonable presentment of any breach of law whereof he hath cognizance, he shall pay a fine of twenty shillings.

All which penalties shall be and belong to the town treasury of the town where such grand juror dwells.

And all grand jurymen shall be allowed fifteen shillings per day for their time of attendance, and six pence per mile for their travel, when they shall be required to give their attendance at the said county court, to be paid out of the county treasury.

And every town in this state that shall neglect or refuse to make choice of grand jurors as aforesaid, shall for every such neglect or refusal, incur the penalty of ten pounds to the treasury of the county wherein such town lieth, to be recovered by bill, plaint, or information.

AN ACT FOR THE PARTITION OF LANDS

15 FEB 1779

Be it enacted, and it is hereby enacted, by the representatives of the freemen of the state of Vermont, in general assembly met, and by the authority of the same, that all persons having or holding, or that shall at any time hereafter have or hold any lands, tenements, or hereditaments as coparceners, joint tenants, or tenants in common, may be compelled by writ of partition, to divide the same, where the partners cannot agree to make partition among themselves.

Provided always, that this act extend not to town commons or sequestered lands.

And be it enacted by the authority aforesaid, that the guardians of all minors shall, and are hereby (with the assistance of such persons as the court of probate shall for that end appoint) fully impowered to make division of any such land, with the surviving partners or tenants, as fully and amply as the original partners and tenants might or could have done. And all such minors, their heirs and assigns, shall be firmly bound and concluded by any such division made by their guardians.

And the several courts of probates are hereby directed, upon the application of such partner, or tenant, or guardian to any minor, to appoint any suitable person to assist such guardian to any minor, to appoint any suitable person to assist such guardians in making division as aforesaid.

And all persons having right in any such lands upon such appointment, shall forthwith come to a division of the same.

AN ACT FOR PREVENTING THE SALES OF REAL ESTATES OF HEIRESSES,
WITHOUT THEIR CONSENT

15 FEB 1779

Be it enacted, and it is hereby enacted, by the representatives of
the freemen of the state of Vermont, in general assembly met, and by
the authority of the same, that any real estate, whereof any woman at
the time of her marriage is seized, as her estate of inheritance, or does
during such coverture become so, either by descent, or otherwise, shall
not be alienable by her husband's deed, without her consent, testified by
her hand and Seal set to such deed, and acknowledged before some
magistrate.

And that all sales, or alienations of such estates, whether absolute
or conditional, which shall hereafter be made without such consent, witnessed and acknowledged as aforesaid, are hereby declared and made
to be ipso facto null and void.

Provided nevertheless, that if any wife at the time of such alienation
of such estate to her belonging, did actually refuse to give her assent
to such Sale made by her husband, that then she shall be understood
and taken to hold the said estate; and neither she nor her heirs shall be
barred from recovery of the same.

AN ACT FOR THE LIMITATION OF PROSECUTIONS IN DIVERS CASES

15 FEB 1779

Be it enacted, and it is hereby enacted, by the representatives of the
freemen of the state of Vermont, in general assembly met, and by the
authority of the same, that no person shall be indicted, prosecuted, informed against, complained of, or compelled to answer before any court,
assistant, or justice of the peace, within this state, for the breach of any
penal law, or for other crimes or misdemeanors, by reason whereof a
forfeiture belongs to any public treasury, unless the indictment, presentment, information, or complaint, be made and exhibited within one year
after the offence is committed.

And every such indictment, presentment, information, and complaint, that is not made and exhibited as aforesaid, within the time
limited for the same, as aforesaid, shall be void and of none effect.

Provided always that this act shall not extend to any capital offence,
nor to any crime that may concern loss of members, or banishment, or
any treachery against this state, nor to any pilfering and theft; anything
contained in this act to the contrary notwithstanding.

AN ACT FOR THE PUNISHMENT OF LYING

15 FEB 1779

Be it enacted, and it is hereby enacted, by the representatives of the freemen of the state of Vermont, in general assembly met, and by the authority of the same, that every person of the age of discretion, which is accounted fourteen years, who shall wittingly and willingly make or publish any lie, which may be pernicious to the public weal, or tend to the damage or injury of any particular person, or to deceive and abuse the people with false news, or reports, and be thereof duly convicted before any court, assistant, or justice of the peace, such person or persons shall be fined for the first offense forty shillings; or if unable to pay the same, then such persons to sit in the stocks not exceeding three hours.

And for the second offence in that kind which such person shall be convicted of, shall be fined double the aforesaid sum; and if unable to pay the same, shall be whipped on the naked body, not exceeding ten stripes.

And for the third offence, double the fine for the second; or if the party be unable to pay the same, then to be whipped not exceeding twenty stripes: and yet if any such person shall offend in that kind, and be legally convicted thereof, such person, either male or female, shall be fined ten shillings each time more than formerly; or if unable to pay such fine, then to be whipped as aforesaid, with five stripes more each time than formerly, but not exceeding thirty-nine stripes at any time.

Provided nevertheless, that no person shall be barred of his just action of slander, or defamation, or otherwise, by any proceeding upon this act.

AN ACT FOR LICENSING AND REGULATING HOUSES OF PUBLIC
ENTERTAINMENT, OR TAVERNS; AND FOR SUPPRESSING
UNLICENSED HOUSES

15 FEB 1779

Be it enacted, and it is hereby enacted, by the representatives of the freemen of the state of Vermont, in general assembly met, and by the authority of the same, that the magistrates, selectmen, constables, and grand jurymen, in the respective towns in his state, shall some time in the month of March annually, nominate the person or persons whom they, or the major part of them, think fit and suitable to keep an house or houses of public entertainment in the said town, for the ensuing year;

which nomination shall be sent by them to the next county court in that county; which court shall grant licenses to the said persons accordingly, to keep an house or houses of public entertainment for the year ensuing, and to no others. Which license shall be in force for one year, and no more.

But if the county court are of the opinion that the number nominated in any town be too great, they shall have liberty to lessen the same; and may also refuse to grant licenses to such persons as they shall, on information and proof made, judge to be wholly unfit and unqualified for such trust, such nomination notwithstanding.

Always provided, such court shall take a bond to the treasurer of the county, in the sum of one hundred pounds, of every such person to whom such license shall be granted, for the due observance of all the laws that are made respecting tavern keepers, or houses of public entertainment.

Be it further enacted by the authority aforesaid, that for the present year, the tavern keepers shall be chosen in the month of June next, and shall be licensed by one assistant and one justice of the peace, or by one judge of the superior court and one justice of the peace, under the same regulations as in future they are to be licensed by the county court, anything in this act to the contrary notwithstanding.

Be it further enacted by the authority aforesaid, that when, and so often as, the authority, selectmen, and grand jurymen, in any town; or where there are no assistant or justice living in any town, the selectmen and grand jurors shall understand that any person in such town is a tavern haunter, or spends his time idly at any such house of entertainment, they, or the major part of them, shall at their discretion cause the names of such tavern haunters to be posted at the door of every tavern in the same town, by setting up a certificate, under their hands, forbidding every tavern keeper in such town, on the penalties contained in this act, to entertain, or suffer any such person or persons therein named, to have or drink any strong liquors, of any kind whatsoever, in or about their houses, until such authority, selectmen, and grand jurors, shall agree to take off such prohibition.

And that if any tavern keeper shall, after such posting of any person's name, and notice thereof given by any of the said selectmen, or grand jurors, suffer or permit any person posted as aforesaid, to drink any rum, wine, or other strong liquor, in or about his house, or in any of the dependences thereof, he shall pay as a fine the sum of three pounds.

And in case the person or persons, warned as aforesaid, shall not, after such warning, leave off and forbear such their evil practices, the authority shall cause such person or persons to appear before them, and demand surety for their well-behaving therein; and in case such person or persons shall not find sureties as aforesaid, then he or they shall each one pay a fine of twenty shillings, or sit in the stocks for the space of two hours, on some public time or season.

And be it further enacted by the authority aforesaid, that the constables & grand jurors in each town shall, and they are hereby required, carefully to inspect all taverns or licensed houses in such town, and make due presentment to the civil authority, of all persons who shall be found transgressing this act, or any part thereof; and also warn all tavern keepers, or persons licensed to keep public houses of entertainment, to observe this act, and all other laws respecting the regulation of licensed houses, and that they do not entertain any inhabitants of the town where they dwell, contrary to law.

And if such officers shall find that such tavern keepers do not observe the laws aforesaid, nor keep due order, then they shall make presentment thereof to the next county court in that county, at their first sitting; and such court shall cause the person so presented, forthwith to appear before them, to answer to such presentment; and if, upon trial, such tavern keeper be found guilty, the court shall enter up judgment for the forfeiture of the bond given, or procured to be given by such person, for his or her due observance of all the laws respecting tavern keepers, and for costs. And such person shall forthwith, before said court, enter into a bond of two hundred pounds, in the tenor of the former bond; which shall also be prosecuted in like manner, in case of a forfeiture.

And that whensoever a presentment is made as aforesaid, it shall be inserted that the person presented, had been warned as aforesaid, by such constable or grand jurymen, such presentment shall be sufficient evidence that such warning was given; and the officers making such presentment, shall be ordered by said court to attend the trial, and be allowed to give evidence for the proof of the disorders complained of; and shall by said court be allowed a meet recompence for their trouble and charge.

Be it further enacted by the authority aforesaid, that no tavern keeper or licensed person, as aforesaid, to keep a public house of entertainment, shall be allowed to bring any action against any person whatsoever, to recover of such person any sum or sums of money, or any other thing whatsoever, for any kind or quantity of drink sold to such person, and drank in such house, unless the same be brought within three days after such sale and drinking.

And whereas divers disorderly persons oftentimes take upon them, and presume to sell strong liquors by retail in small quantities, without licence; and to keep tippling houses, to the promoting of tippling, drunkenness, idleness, and many other immoralities; and to the great prejudice of persons orderly licensed, and under the regulations of law, for the entertainment of travellers and others legally and orderly requiring the same.

Which to prevent,

Be it further enacted by the authority aforesaid, that no person or persons whatsoever, dwelling in this state (except such as have licence as aforesaid), shall be an innholder, taverner, or seller of wine, beer, ale, cider, rum, or any other strong liquors, publickly or privately, by a less quantity than a quart of wine, rum, or other such like strong liquors, or a quart of metheglin, cider, beer, or such like drink, and that delivered and carried away all at one time, on the penalty of forfeiting and paying the sum of three pounds for the first offense, and the sum of six pounds for the second offence, and so double for every breach of this act he shall be convicted of; which fines shall be disposed of, half to him that complains and prosecutes the same to effect, and the other half to the town treasury.

And it is especially recommended to those who keep licensed houses, to prosecute the breach of this paragraph of this act.

And when any person shall be duly convicted of keeping a tippling house, or of selling strong beer, ale, cider, perry, metheglin, wine, rum, or mixed drink, or any strong drink whatsoever, by retail in small quantities, as aforesaid, without licence first had, as aforesaid, for the same, and shall be unable to satisfy the fine imposed by law for such transgression, together with the charge of prosecution; or shall not pay such fine and charge, and likewise give bond for the good behaviour, if it be a second conviction, within the space of twenty-four hours next after sentence declared; it shall and may be lawful for two justices of the peace, or the court before whom the conviction shall be, to order such offender to be publickly whipped on the naked body not less than ten, nor exceeding fifteen stripes for one offence; and to restrain the offender in prison, till such fine and charges are paid, or the corporal punishment be inflicted.

And that the oath of one credible witness shall be sufficient to convict any person of retailing strong liquors as aforesaid, contrary to this act; unless the person shall, in open court, positively and plainly assert and declare, that he is not guilty of the fact charged upon him.

And be it further enacted by the authority aforesaid, that the grand jurymen in the respective towns in this state, shall from time to time, make diligent search and enquiry after all persons who are reputed to sell or vend strong liquor by retail, in small quantities as aforesaid, without licence as aforesaid obtained, and make presentment of all such persons to the next assistant or justice of the peace; which assistant or justice shall, by a proper warrant, order such person or persons so presented, to appear before him, and cause him or them to give bond with a surety to the value of ten pounds, that he or they, will not sell or vend any strong drink by retail in small quantities as aforesaid, without licence first had and obtained, and be of good behaviour until the next county court in that county; and also appear before the said court and take up said bond, unless said court shall see cause to continue the same; which the court may do if they judge proper.

And if any such person or persons shall refuse to become bound as aforesaid, the authority before whom he or they shall be brought, shall by mittimus commit such person or persons to the common gaol in that county, there to remain at his or their own charge, till he or they will give bond as aforesaid.

And that if any such person or persons giving bond as aforesaid, shall at anytime after the giving such bond, be presented to the county court of that county by the grand jurors, on suspicion of retailing strong drink in small quantities, without licence as aforesaid, such presentment shall be taken by the court to be sufficient evidence against the person so presented, to convict him, her, or them, of the forfeiture of such bonds or recognizance, unless he or she shall be acquitted by a jury of twelve freeholders of the neighbourhood, declaring upon their oath, that they believe such person is not guilty; which jury, the party at his desire and charge, may have the liberty of.

AN ACT AGAINST FORGERY

15 FEB 1779

Be it enacted, and it is hereby enacted, by the representatives of the freemen of the state of Vermont, in general assembly met, and by the authority of the same, that if any person or persons shall willingly and falsely forge and make, or cause to be forged, or made; or shall aid, abet, help, or assist, in the falsely forging and making any false deed, conveyance, will, testament, bond, bill, receipt, release, acquittance, letter of attorney, or any other writing to prevent equity and justice; such person or persons being thereof duly convicted, shall stand in the pillory three several days of public meeting, not exceeding two hours each day, and render and pay to the party or parties injured thereby, double damages, to be recovered by action founded on this act; and shall also be rendered incapable, and be disenabled to give any evidence or verdict in any court, or before any magistrate or justice of the peace.

AN ACT AGAINST FRAUDULENT CONVEYANCES

15 FEB 1779

Be it enacted, and it is hereby enacted, by the representatives of the freemen of the state of Vermont, in general assembly met, and by the authority of the same, that all fraudulent and deceitful conveyances of lands, tenements, hereditaments, goods or chattels; and all such bonds, suits, judgments, executions, or contracts, made to avoid any debt or duty of others, shall (as against the party or parties only whose debt or duty is so endeavored to be avoided, their heirs, executors, or assigns) be utterly void, any pretence, of feigned consideration notwithstanding.

And every of the parties to such a fraudulent conveyance, bond, suit, judgment, execution, or contract, who being privy thereunto, that shall wittingly justify the same to be done bona fide, and upon consideration; or shall alien and assign any lands, leases, goods, or chattels, so to them conveyed as aforesaid, shall forfeit one year's value of the lands, lease, rents, common, or other profits out of the same; and the whole value of the goods and chattels, and also so much money as shall be contained in such covenous bond or contract, and being thereof convicted, shall also suffer half a year's imprisonment without bail:—which above forfeiture shall be equally divided between the party grieved, and the county treasurer; except the purchaser make it appear by two witnesses, that the contract or bargain was made bona fide, and on good consideration, before any seizure made by the creditor or officer of the estate so conveyed; and that it was without any design of fraud, to defeat the creditor of his just dues.

AN ACT FOR PREVENTING AND SUPPRESSING OF LOTTERIES

15 FEB 1779

Be it enacted, and it is hereby enacted, by the representatives of the freemen of the state of Vermont, in general assembly met, and by the authority of the same, that whosoever shall presume, without special liberty from the general assembly, to set up any lottery for the sale of goods, lands, or tenements; or to sell, put off, or vend any parcel, parcels, or quantity of lands, goods, or monies, or other things whatsoever, by way of lottery; or shall, by wagers, shooting, or any other such like way or exercise whatsoever, offer to sell, vend, put off, or dispose of any goods, monies, or other things, collected or exposed to be run at such adventure; or set up notifications to entice people to bring in and deposit or risque their money or credit, for carrying on the designs aforesaid, and be duly convicted thereof, before any court or authority proper to try the same, shall forfeit the value of such goods, or monies, or things so exposed, or proposed to be exposed to sale, or drawn for; the one half to him that shall prosecute the same to effect and the other half to the county treasury of the county where the offence is committed.

And all grand jurors, and others ordered by law to make presentment of breaches of law, are directed (when no informer or prosecutor appears) to make presentment of the breaches of this act.

AN ACT FOR THE PUNISHMENT OF MANSLAUGHTER

15 FEB 1779

Be it enacted, and it is hereby enacted, by the representatives of the state of Vermont, in general assembly met, and by the authority of the same, that whatsoever person shall be guilty of the crime of manslaughter, or the wilful killing another person, without malice aforethought, and be thereof legally convicted, by confession or verdict, before any of the superior courts of this state, shall forfeit to the public treasury of this state, all the goods and chattels which to him or her belonged at the time of committing the said crimes, and be further punished by whipping on the naked body, and be stigmatized, or burnt on the hand with the letter M, on a hot iron; and shall also be forever disabled in the law from giving verdict or evidence in any court in this state.

Provided nevertheless, that if any person, in the just and necessary defence of his life, or the life of any other, shall kill any person attempting to rob or murther, in the field or highway, or to break into any dwelling house, if he conceives he cannot, with safety of his own person, otherwise take the felon or assailant, or bring him to trial, he shall be holden guiltless.

AN ACT FOR THE PUNISHMENT OF MURDER

15 FEB 1779

Be it enacted, and it is hereby enacted, by the representatives of the freemen of the state of Vermont, in general assembly met, and by the authority of the same, that if any person shall commit any wilful murder, upon malice, hatred, or cruelty, not in a man's just and necessary defence, nor by accident against his will; or shall slay or kill another through guile, either by poisoning, or other such devilish practices, he shall be put to death.

And whereas, many lewd women, that have been delivered of bastard children, to avoid their shame, and to escape punishment, do secretly bury, or conceal the death of their children; and after, if the child be found dead, the said women do alledge that the said child was born dead, whereas it falleth out sometimes (although hardly it is to be proved) that the said child or children were murdered by the said women their lewd mothers, or by their assent or procurement:

Be it therefore further enacted by the authority aforesaid, that if any woman be delivered of any issue of her body, male or female, which, if it were born alive, would be a bastard; and that she endeavored privately, either by drowning, or secret burying thereof, or any other way, either by herself, or by the procuring of others so to conceal the death thereof, that it may not come to light whether it was born alive or not, but be concealed; in every such case, the mother so offending shall be accounted guilty of murder, and shall suffer death therefor, as in case of murder:—except such mother can make proof by one witness (at least) that such child was born dead.

AN ACT AGAINST BREAKING THE PEACE

15 FEB 1779

Be it enacted, and it is hereby enacted, by the representatives of the freemen of the state of Vermont, in general assembly met, and by the authority of the same, that whosoever shall disturb or break the peace, by tumultuous and offensive carriages, threatening, traducing, quarrelling, challenging, assaulting, beating, or striking any other person; such person or persons, so offending shall be liable to pay to the party hurt or stricken just damages; and also shall pay such fine, as on consideration of the party smiting, or being smitten, and with what instrument, danger more or less, time, place, and provocation, shall be judged just and reasonable, according to the merit of the offence, as the justice or justices shall determine.

And if such offence be aggravated by some notorious and high-handed violences, the offender or offenders shall be bound over to the next county court, to answer for such offence.

Be it further enacted, by the authority aforesaid, that the surety of the peace, or good behaviour, as the merit of the case shall require, may and shall be granted, by any assistant or justice of the peace in this state, against all and every person or persons, who by threatening words, turbulent behaviour, or actual violence, or by any other unlawful action shall terrify or disquiet any of the inhabitants of this state; and if such offender or offenders shall neglect or refuse to find such sureties, he or they shall be committed to the common gaol of the county where the offence is committed, there to remain until he or they shall find such sureties, or be there delivered by due course of law.

Be it further enacted by the authority aforesaid, that if any person shall abuse any magistrate, or justice of the peace; or resist, or abuse any sheriff, constable, or other officer, in the execution of his office; such person or persons shall find sureties for the peace and good behaviour, until the next county court in that county; or on refusal, may be committed to the common gaol, there to remain until the next county court: which court shall take cognizance of the wrongs and abuses done to such officer or officers, by such offender or offenders and lay such penalty upon him or them (he or they being thereof legally convicted) as the merit of the offence shall deserve, appearing by the circumstances of the same, not exceeding sixty pounds.

And whereas some persons do secretly attempt mischief and hurt to others, and do commit great outrages upon them, in such manner that proof cannot easily be had.

For the detecting and punishing of which,

Be it further enacted by the authority aforesaid, that if any person shall break the peace, by secretly assaulting, beating, maiming, wounding, or hurting another; the person so assaulted and injured, making application and complaint to the next assistant, or justice of the peace, shewing him what hurt or wound he has received thereby, such assistant or justice shall forthwith grant out a writ, directed to the sheriff of the county, his deputy, or constable of the town where such assault shall be made, commanding them, or either of them, to arrest and bring before him such person so assaulting, to answer such complaint; who, upon oath being made against him of such assault, and of the wounds or bruises thereby received, by the person assaulted and beaten, shall be bound in a sufficient bond, with sureties, for his appearance at the next county court in that county, to answer to the complaint, as aforesaid: and in case of refusal to become bound, as aforesaid, such person complained of shall be committed to the common gaol of the county, there to remain till the next sessions of said county court.

And if the person so bound, or committed, shall not, on trial of the case, satisfy the court that he was at some other place, at the time the said assault was made, and was not the person who gave the assault, he shall be judged guilty, and shall be sentenced to pay the person assaulted and injured all such damages as he shall have sustained by such assault and beating; or in case such damages can not then be computed, the offender shall give bond, with sufficient surety or sureties, to pay all such damages as shall afterwards be awarded by said court at some other sessions, to which the case shall be continued, together with cost of prosecution; and also pay to the treasurer of the county such fine as the said court shall order, not exceeding the sum of thirty pounds, and stand committed till sentence is performed.

AN ACT FOR THE PUNISHMENT OF PERJURY

15 FEB 1779

Be it enacted, and it is hereby enacted, by the representatives of the freemen of the state of Vermont, in general assembly met, and by the authority of the same, that if any person or persons, either by the subordination, unlawful procurement, reward, sinister persuasion, or means of any other, or by their own act, consent, or agreement, shall wilfully and corruptly commit any manner of wilful perjury, by his or their deposition in any court of record, upon examination; that then every person or persons, so offending, and being thereof duly convicted, or attainted by law, shall, for his or their offence, forfeit the sum of fifty pounds; the one moiety thereof to the public treasury of this state, and the other moiety to such person or persons as shall be grieved, hindered or molested, by reason of any such offence, that shall sue for the same, by action of debt, bill, plaint, information, or otherwise, in any court of record in this state.

And also be imprisoned by the space of six months, without bail or mainprize.

And the oath of such person or persons so offending, shall not be received in any court whatsoever in this state, until such time as the judgment given against the said person or persons shall be reversed, by attaint, or otherwise.

And upon every such reversal, the party aggrieved to recover his or their damages, against all and every such person or persons as did procure the said judgment, so reversed, to be given against them, or any of them, by action or actions upon his or their case or cases, according to the course of common law.

And if it shall so happen that the said offender or offenders, so offending, have not goods and chattels to the value of fifty pounds, that then he or they shall be set in the pillory by the space of two hours, in some county town where the offence was committed, or next adjoining to the place where the offence was committed; and to have both his ears nailed and cut off; and from thenceforth be discredited, and disabled forever to be sworn in any court whatsoever, until such time as the judgment shall be reversed.

And all and every person or persons, who shall unlawfully and corruptly procure any witness or witnesses, by letters, rewards, promises, or by any other sinister and unlawful labor or means whatsoever, to commit any wilful or corrupt perjury, in any matter or cause whatsoever, depending, or that shall be depending, in suit and variance, by any writ, action, bill, complaint, or information, in any court, or before any committee; every such offender, being thereof duly convicted, or attainted by law, shall, for his or their offence, be proceeded against, and suffer the like pains, penalties, forfeitures, and disabilities, in all respects, as above mentioned.

AN ACT FOR ORDERING AND REGULATING PLEAS AND PLEADINGS

15 FEB 1779

For preventing unnecessary charge and delays in the several courts of common pleas in this state; and for the more regular proceeding in trials thereon,

Be it enacted, and it is hereby enacted by the representatives of the freemen of the state of Vermont, in general assembly met, and by the authority of the same, that all pleas made in abatement of writs or processes, in any of the county courts in this state, shall be made, heard, and determined, and the issue in every case joined, and an entry thereof made, before the jury is impanelled.

And in case any defendant will not make his plea, or join issue, judgment shall be given against him upon a nihil dicit.

That the general issue of not guilty, nil debet, no wrong, or diseisin, or any other general plea proper to the action, whereby the whole declaration is put upon proof, according to the nature of the case, may be made by the defendant; under which general plea, the defendant shall have liberty, upon trial of the case on such general issue, to give his title in evidence, or any other matter in his defence or justification, as the nature of the action may be; excepting only a discharge from the plaintiff, or his accord, or some other special matter, whereby the defendant, by the act of the plaintiff, is saved, or acquitted from the plaintiff's demand in the declaration.

And whensoever any party shall suppose he has missed his plea, whether the general issue, or special plea, which would have saved him in his just cause, he shall have liberty to alter his plea; and the opposite party shall have a reasonable time assigned him, for making answer thereto; and if the new plea be found insufficient for the justifying him that made it, reasonable satisfaction shall be awarded by the court before which the trial is, to the other party, for the greater delay which is made thereby, according to the interest or money, rent of land, or improvement of any other thing recovered by the suit.

Provided nevertheless, that no defendant shall, in the trial of any cause, be admitted to demur to the declaration, after he has pleaded to issue, and a judgment thereon hath been given by any court, anything to the contrary before in this act notwithstanding.

AN ACT FOR MAINTAINING AND SUPPORTING THE POOR

15 FEB 1779

Be it enacted, and it is hereby enacted, by the representatives of the freemen of the state of Vermont, in general assembly met, and by the authority of the same, that each town in this state shall take care of, support, and maintain their own poor.

And the selectmen for the time being, or overseers of the poor (where any such are chosen), shall have full power to expend or disburse, out of the town stock, or treasury, what they shall judge necessary from time to time, for the relief and support of any of the poor belonging to their towns, so far as to the amount of ten pounds; and if more be needful, the said selectmen, or overseers, or the major part of them, shall, with the advice of the authority of that town (if any there be), expend and disburse what shall be by them judged needful for the relief of the poor, as aforesaid.

And in case there be no justice of the peace in any town, the selectmen, or overseers aforesaid, of such town, may act as fully as if they had such advice in the case aforesaid, for the relief of their poor, and for the supplying them, or any of them, with victuals, clothing, firewood, or any other thing necessary for their support or subsistence.

And if any selectmen, or overseers of the poor, do neglect or refuse to give a just account, upon oath, of what he has expended as aforesaid, and of what of the town stock or money is in his custody, upon ten days warning, before an assistant or justice of the peace, when called to it by the town, and to return what is not expended to and for the use aforesaid, to the town; he or they shall be committed, by an assistant or justice of the peace, to the common goal, there to remain, at his or their own cost and charge, until he or they shall give such account, and make such return as aforesaid.

That if any poor person or persons, who have had, or shall have relief or supplies from any town, shall suffer their children to live idly, or misspend their time in loitering, and neglect to bring them up or employ them in some honest calling, which may be profitable to themselves and the public; or if there shall be at any time any family that cannot or do not provide competently for their children, whereby they are exposed to want, or extremity; or if there be any poor children in any town, belonging to such town, that live idly, or are exposed to want and distress, and there are none to take care of them, it shall and may be lawful for the selectmen, or overseers of the poor, in each town, and they are hereby impowered and directed, with the assent of the next assistant or justice of the peace, to bind out any and every such poor child or children, belonging to such town, to be apprentices, or servants, where they shall see convenient, a male child, till he comes to twenty-one years of age, and a female, till she comes to the age of eighteen years: which binding shall be as effectual, to all intents and purposes, as if any child were of full age, and by indenture of covenant had bound him or herself.

And that if any person or persons shall come to live in any town in this state, and be there received and entertained, by the space of twelve months; and if by sickness, lameness, or the like, he or they come to want relief, every such person or persons shall be provided for by that town wherein he or they were so long entertained, at said town's own proper cost and charge, unless such person or persons by law are to be provided for by some particular person or persons; or unless such person or persons, wanting relief, have, within the said twelve months, been warned as the law directs, to depart and leave the place; and if such warning be given, and the same be certified to the next superior court to be held in the same county, the said court shall and may otherwise order the defraying the charge arising about such indigent person or persons.

AN ACT FOR PROVIDING AND MAINTAINING POUNDS; AND FOR REGULATING THE IMPOUNDING CREATURES; AND FOR PREVENTING RESCUES AND POUND BREACH

15 FEB 1779

Be it enacted, and it is hereby enacted, by the representatives of the freemen of the state of Vermont, in general assembly met, and by the authority of the same, that there shall be made, and from time to time kept and maintained in every town in this state, at the charge of such town, a sufficient pound or pounds for the impounding and restraining therein all such horses, cattle, swine, and other creatures, as shall be found damage feasant, or shall be by law liable to be impounded.

And the selectmen in each town shall from time to time, as need shall require, erect and maintain a sufficient pound or pounds, as the towns have agreed, or shall agree, at the proper cost and charge of said town.

And that if any town be at any time hereafter without a sufficient pound for the purpose aforesaid, the selectmen of such town shall forfeit the sum of twenty shillings per month, for every month such town is unprovided with a sufficient pound or pounds, so agreed upon by such town or towns; one half to the county treasury, and the other half to him that shall prosecute the same to effect: any one assistant or justice of the peace, to hear and determine the same.

Provided nevertheless, that if any town have granted, or shall grant to any particular parish, vicinity, or part of any town, liberty, at their own cost and charge, to erect a pound or pounds for their conveniency (which grant such towns are hereby impowered to make) the said pound or pounds shall be maintained by the said parish, vicinity, or party of a town; and the selectmen shall not suffer, or be punishable for any defect therein.

Be it enacted by the authority aforesaid, that every person impounding any horses, cattle, swine, or other creatures, shall give notice thereof to the owners of such creatures, as soon as may be, if the owner be known, on pain or forfeiting the same penalties as are hereafter in this act expressed for such persons as having notice of their creatures being impounded, shall neglect to redeem them out of pound.

That if any horses, cattle, swine, or other creatures, shall be taken damage feasant, and impounded, and the owner thereof is not known, the impounder shall forthwith inform one of the constables of the town thereof, who shall cry such creatures, with their natural and artificial marks, by posting up the same in the town where they are impounded, and in the two next neighbouring towns from whence it may be most likely such creatures came.

And if no owner doth appear in twenty days after such creatures are cried and posted as aforesaid, then so many of the said creatures shall, by the said constable, be sold at an outcry, as may be sufficient to satisfy the damages and pounding, and meat and water, with the charges arising for crying and selling the same.

And the marks, natural and artificial, of the creatures so sold, shall be entered in the town clerk's office; together with an account of the charges arisen, and the price of the creatures, and the sum of the overplus remaining (if any be), after the town clerk is satisfied for entry; and such overplus shall be delivered to the town treasurer, to be kept for the owner: but if no owner appear within one year, said overplus shall belong to the said town's treasury.

Provided nevertheless, that all horses and cattle, that shall be impounded out of any particular inclosure, and the owner of such horses and cattle is not known, the impounder shall inform one of the constables of the town, who shall cry the same, as aforesaid.

And all horses, so impounded, shall be also cried in the town where the brand belongs that is upon such horse or horses, provided the brand belongs to any town in this state; and if no owner appear within twenty days after setting up such cries, and the fence about the inclosure out of which such creatures were impounded, do pass the view according to law, and is found sufficient by two sworn fence viewers; then such horse, horses, or cattle, may, by the constable, be sold at an outcry; and after poundage, damage, charge of viewing the fence, and all other cost arising as aforesaid, is satisfied, the overplus (if any be), to be returned to the town treasurer, to be kept for the owner: but if no owner appear within one year, the same shall belong to the town treasurer, as aforesaid.

Always provided, that if the owner or owners of such horses or cattle appear and come within said twenty days, he or they shall receive such horse kind, or cattle, paying for viewing said fence, and other damages and costs, which by this act shall be due as aforesaid.

Be it further enacted by the authority aforesaid, that if any person or persons whose creature or creatures shall be impounded, and he or they notified thereof, as aforesaid, shall not, within twenty-four hours after such notice to him or them given, either replevy or redeem his or their creature or creatures out of the pound, every such person or persons shall forfeit three shillings per head for every beast so by him or them suffered to continue in pound, and the same sum a day for every day after the first day that he or they shall suffer said creatures to continue in pound, besides all necessary charges the pound keeper shall be at, in providing and giving meat and water to such creatures so continued in pound.

All of which forfeitures as shall become due for breach of this order, shall belong one half to the pound keeper, and the other half to the town treasury (just damages and poundage being first paid); any one assistant, or justice of the peace, to hear and determine the same; and on conviction of the offender, to grant a warrant for levying the same, with cost, out of the estates of the persons convicted as aforesaid.

Be it enacted by the authority aforesaid, that all horse kind, which being suffered to go at large on the commons, that do break into any common field, or particular inclosure, and are there found damage feasant, and from thence impounded; the owner thereof (if known) shall pay for the poundage six pence per head, and damages, notwithstanding the insufficiency of the fence: and in case the owner of such horse or horse kind can not be known within the space of twenty-four hours after the impounding the same, they shall be accounted strays, and be liable to be proceeded with as such.

That upon the replevin of any such horse or horse kind, or other dispute in the law arising on any such matter, when the impounder has under oath declared the place from whence he took said horse or horse kind, that unless the owner of such horse can shew to the satisfaction of the court or justice before whom the trial is, that the said horse or horse kind were not suffered to go at large on the common and did enter into said field or inclosure through the insufficiency of some other part of the fence not adjoining to the common, judgment shall be rendered against the owners of such horse or horse kind, to pay just damages, together with cost.

Be it further enacted, that the fee to be paid by the owner or owners of all such horses, cattle, sheep, and swine, as shall be taken damage feasant and impounded (whereof three quarters shall be to the driver or impounder, and one quarter to the keeper of the key), shall be as follows, viz.—for all horse kind, and neat cattle, one shilling per head: for all sheep, two pence per head: for all swine, nine pence per head —except where the law provides otherwise.

And that if any creatures, lawfully impounded, shall escape, and get out of the pound, the owner thereof being known, shall pay all just damages and poundage, notwithstanding: which shall be as recoverable by action of debt, as any other action whatsoever.

Provided, the person or persons impounding such creatures shall give oath, that he or they took such creatures damage feasant.

And be it further enacted by the authority aforesaid, that if any person or persons shall rescue any horses, cattle, sheep, swine, or other creatures taken up as aforesaid, out of the hand or custody of any person or persons going to pound with them; or shall resist them therein; or shall by any means convey such creatures out of the pound, or custody of the law, whereby the party wronged may be liable to loose his poundage and damages, and the law be eluded, the party so offending shall, for such rescues, forfeit and pay the sum of forty shillings; and for such pound-breach, the sum of four pounds: three quarters of which shall be for the use of the town treasury of that town wherein the offence shall be committed, and one quarter thereof to him who shall prosecute the same to effect; and also shall pay all damages to the party wronged by such rescues or pound breach.

And if either of said offences be done by any person or persons not of ability to answer and pay the damages and forfeiture aforesaid, such person or persons, being convicted as aforesaid, shall, by warrant from the authority before whom the conviction is had, be whipped, not exceeding twenty stripes, for mere rescue, or pound breach, and shall be assigned in service to the wronged party, to make satisfaction for the damages he shall have sustained.

And if it appear that there were any procurement of the owner or owners of the creatures; or that they were abettors; or if it be done by their servants or children, the said owner or owners shall pay all damages and forfeitures, as if he or they had personally done the same.

Always provided, that all complaints for breach of this act, shall be prosecuted within six months after the offence is committed, and not after.

AN ACT FOR PREVENTING STALLIONS, OR STONE-HORSES, RUNNING AT LARGE IN THIS STATE

15 FEB 1779

Whereas it has been found by experience to be dangerous for stallions to run at large, and a ready way of spoiling a good breed of horses.

Which evils to prevent,

Be it enacted, and it is hereby enacted, by the representatives of the freemen of the state of Vermont, in general assembly met, and by the authority of the same, that if any person or persons shall suffer any of his, her, or their stallions (of one year old and upward) to run at large, on any of the commons or highways in this state (whether fettered, hobbled, or not), it shall and may be lawful for any person or persons, to take up, castrate, and impound every such horse, horses, colt, or colts; which castration shall be at the risque and charge of the owner or owners.

And if the owner or owners are known, the impounder shall forthwith inform him or them thereof; and the owner or owners being so informed, and shall neglect or refuse to redeem such horse, horses, colt, or colts (within twenty-four hours after such notice given), by paying all cost and charge that hath arisen by reason of said stallion or stallions being taken up, castrated, impounded, and trouble of giving information, it shall and may be lawful for the constable of the town where such horse, horses, colt, or colts, are impounded, to sell said horse, horses, colt, or colts, at an outcry, after posting them ten days before such sale; and the monies that shall be collected by such sale, after paying all necessary charges, costs, and damages (if any there be), shall be paid to the owner or owners of such horse, horses, colt, or colts.

And if the owner is not known, the constable of such town shall cry such stallions in the next three adjoining towns, by posting their natural and artificial marks; and likewise in the town or towns where such horse or horses were branded (provided the brand belongs to any town in this state), twenty days; and if no owner or owners appear within twenty days, to dispose of such horse, horses, colt, or colts, as directed in cases where the owner or owners were known, and neglected or refused to redeem them; and the monies arising from such sale or sales (if any be), over and above all cost, charges, and damages, shall be put into the treasury of such town where such horse or horses were impounded, there to be kept for the owner; and if the owner of such stallions doth not appear within one year after such impounding, the money shall belong, and be appropriated to the use of the town where such stallions were impounded.

AN ACT TO PREVENT THE SELLING OR TRANSPORTING RAW OR UNTANNED HIDES OR SKINS OUT OF THIS STATE

15 FEB 1779

Be it enacted, and it is hereby enacted, by the representatives of the freemen of the state of Vermont, in general assembly met, and by the authority of the same, that no person or persons shall directly or indirectly, sell or transport, or send away out of this state (except it to be exchange for leather), any raw or untanned hides, or skins of any neat cattle (continental property excepted), upon pain or forfeiting the sum of thirty shillings lawful money, for every such hide or skin so sold, transported or sent away; one half thereof to the complainer who shall prosecute the same to effect, and the other half to the treasury of the county where the offence is committed.

AN ACT RELATING TO WITNESSES, AND TAKING AFFIDAVITS OUT OF COURT

15 FEB 1779

Forasmuch as it is often necessary that witnesses in civil causes be sworn out of court, when by reason of living more than twenty miles distant from the place where the cause is to be tried, age, sickness, or other bodily infirmity, they are rendered incapable of travel, and of appearing at court.

To the intent therefore, that all witnesses may indifferently testify their certain knowledge, and the whole truth in the cause they are to testify unto,

Be it enacted, and it is hereby enacted, by the representatives of the freemen of the state of Vermont, in general assembly met, and by

the authority of the same, that for either of the reasons before mentioned, every assistant, or justice of the peace, may take affidavits out of court, so as a notification, with reasonable time, be first made out, and delivered to the adverse party (if within twenty miles of the place), or left at the place of his dwelling, or usual abode, to be present at the time of taking such affidavit, if he think fit.

And every such witness shall be carefully examined, and cautioned to testify the whole truth; and being sworn, the assistant or justice shall attest the same, with the day, month, and year, of the taking thereof, and that the adverse party was present (if so), or that a notification was sent him; and shall seal up the testimony, and deliver it to the party (if desired) at whose request it was taken.

And no person interested shall write or draw up the testimony of any witness in such case, nor any attorney in his client's cause: and if it manifestly appear any testimony to be written or drawn up by any interested, or the attorney in the cause; or be returned from any assistant or justice of the peace, by other hand than his own, into the court where the same is to be used, unsealed, or the seal having been broken up; all such testimonies shall be rejected by the court, and be utterly void, and of none effect in law.

That every assistant or justice of the peace, shall be, and are hereby impowered, upon request to him made, to grant summons for the appearance of any witness before him, in any civil or criminal cause, where the witness is travelling out of the state before the time of trial, and to take his deposition in such case, the adverse party being present, or notification sent him, as aforesaid.

Provided nevertheless, that witnesses to bonds, specialties, letters of attorney, and other instruments in writing under the hand of the party executing the same; or to accounts, or testimonies relating to persons out of this state, may be sworn without such notification as aforesaid.

That if any person or persons, upon whom any lawful process shall be served, to testify or give evidence concerning any cause or matter depending in any court in this state, and having tendered unto him, her, or them, such reasonable sum or sums of money for his, her, or their costs and charges, as, having regard to the distance of the place, is necessary to be allowed, as the law requires in that behalf, do not appear according to the tenor of the process or summons, having no lawful or reasonable let or impediment to the contrary, that then the party so making default, shall, for every such offence, lose and forfeit the sum of three pounds, and shall yield such further recompense to the party damaged according to the loss and hindrance that he shall sustain, by reason of the non-appearance of the said witness or witnesses; the said several sums to be recovered by the party so grieved, against the offender or offenders, by action of debt, bill, plaint, or information, in any court of record.

Be it enacted by the authority aforesaid, that no person shall be put to death for any crime committed, but by the testimony of two or three witnesses, or that which is equivalent.

And that all witnesses upon criminal cases, shall have their expenses borne and paid out of the county treasury, where the case is tried in the county courts.

And such witnesses that attend the superior courts, in criminal and capital cases, shall have their necessary expences borne and paid out of the state treasury.

And be it further enacted by the authority aforesaid, that all executors of wills, within this state, shall have liberty to have the witnesses to such wills examined and sworn in the usual form, before the next assistant or justice of the peace; which assistant or justice shall enter the oath of the witnesses on the backside of the will, and attest the same; and the oaths of the witnesses so taken, shall be accepted by the court of probate, as if they had been taken before the said court.

AN ACT CONCERNING STRAYS, AND LOST GOODS

15 FEB 1779

Be it enacted, and it is hereby enacted, by the representatives of the state of Vermont, in general assembly met, and by the authority of the same, that whosoever shall take up any stray beast, or find any lost goods, being worth five shillings, whereof the owner is not known, he shall carry a true description of such stray beast, or lost goods, with the natural and artificial marks thereof, to the register of the town where such goods or beast were found, within twelve days after the finding such goods or beast, who shall register the same, with the name of the person in whose keeping such goods or beast shall be, to the end the owners thereof, by applying to the register, may have notice thereof; upon penalty that the person so finding or keeping such goods or beast, and failing of his duty therein, shall, for such default, forfeit the value of such lost goods, or stray beast; one half to the complainer, and the other half to the town treasury.

And if the owner shall appear within six months after the registering such lost goods, or stray beast, and make good his title, he shall have restitution of the same, he paying all necessary charges for the pains and care taken about such goods or beast, as the next assistant or justice of the peace shall adjudge.

And if no owner shall appear within the said six months, the register shall appoint three freeholders, who shall, under oath, appraise said goods or beast, according to the true and just value thereof in money.

And if the owner shall appear within six months next after such appraisement, and make good his claim as aforesaid, and pay all necessary charges for the pains and care taken about such goods or beast, to that time (to be adjudged of as aforesaid), he shall have restitution of the same, or the value thereof, at the election of the finder, according to the appraisement aforesaid.

And if no owner shall appear within twelve months and a day, after the registering of such lost goods, or stray beast, the value thereof, according to the appraisement aforesaid, shall (after all just dues to the finder, keeper, and register, are defrayed) be to the use of the treasury of the town where such goods or stray beast were found.

And the selectmen of such town, are hereby fully impowered to recover and receive the same, for the use of said town.

Always provided, that the keeper of such lost goods, or stray beast, being faithful in his taking care of them, such goods or beast shall be at the risque of the owner thereof.

And that no beast shall be taken up as a stray, except it be found in a suffering condition, or manifestly straying from his owner.

AN ACT FOR THE PUNISHMENT OF DEFAMATION

15 FEB 1779

Whereas defamation and slander is a growing evil, and tends much to the disturbance of the peace:

Be it enacted, and it is hereby enacted, by the representatives of the freemen of the state of Vermont, in general assembly met, and by the authority of the same, that whosoever shall defame or slander any person or persons whatsoever, and be thereof legally convicted before any court in this state, shall pay a fine, not exceeding thirty pounds, to the public treasury of the county in which such offence is committed;

and the person or persons slandered, shall have such costs and damages as the court and jury that have cognizance of the said case, shall judge to be reasonable and just.

And whereas defaming the civil authority of the state, greatly tends to bring the same into contempt, and thereby to weaken the hands of those by whom justice is to be administered.

Which great evil to prevent,

Be it enacted by the authority aforesaid, that whosoever shall defame any court of justice, or the sentence or proceedings of the same; or any of the magistrates, judges, or justices of any such court, in respect of any act or sentence therein passed, and be thereof legally convicted before any of the general courts, or superior courts in this state, shall be punished for the same by fine, imprisonment, disfranchisement, or banishment, as the quality and measure of the offence, in the opinion of the court before whom the trial is had, shall deserve.

AN ACT FOR THE DIRECTING AND REGULATING OF CIVIL ACTIONS

FEB 1779

Be it enacted, and it is hereby enacted, by the representatives of the freemen of the state of Vermont, in general assembly met, and by the authority of the same, that the ordinary process in civil actions in this state, shall be a summons, or attachment, fairly written, signed by a magistrate, justice of the peace, or clerk of the court, mentioning the court, the time and place of appearance; therein also containing a declaration of the substance of the action: which attachments may be granted against the goods or chattels of the defendant; and for want of them, the lands or person of the defendant may be attached—provided the plaintiff, when he prays out an attachment, satisfies the said authority, by oath, or sufficient evidence, that he is in danger of losing his just dues, unless attachment is granted; and also give sufficient security to prosecute his action to effect, and answer all damages in case he make not his plea good.

And all writs and processes shall be directed to the sheriff, his deputy, or some constable, if such officer can be had without great charge or inconvenience; and in every case wherein the authority signing a writ shall find it necessary to direct the same to an indifferent person, such authority shall insert the name of the indifferent person in the direction of the writ, and the reason of such direction; and if any writ be otherwise directed, it shall abate.

Provided nevertheless, that nothing herein shall extend to affect summonses for witnesses, warrants to collectors of rates, or warrants granted by military officers.

And that no person shall be required to make answer, in any civil action, real, personal, or mixt, except the process, if returnable to the superior or county court, hath been served upon the defendant at least twelve days inclusive, before the day of the court's sitting; or if returnable to an assistant or justice of the peace, that the same hath been served six days inclusive, as aforesaid: which service shall be, if a summons, by reading the same in the hearing of the defendant or defendants, or leaving an attested copy thereof at the place or places of his or their usual abode; but if an attachment, the service shall be the attaching of the defendant's estate or person, and giving him notice by reading the writ to him, or in his hearing; or by leaving an attested copy thereof at the place of his usual abode, if that be within this state: and that all such writs as are made returnable to the county courts, shall be returned to the clerks of said courts, on the day before the sitting of such county courts, and not afterwards.

That in case any process be duly served on any defendant or defendants, and return thereof made to the court to which the same is made returnable; then, if such defendant or defendants do not appear, his or their default shall be recorded, and judgment entered up against him thereupon;—unless, before the jury be dismissed, he or they shall come into court and move for a trial; in which case he or they shall be admitted thereto, upon paying down to the adverse party, the costs to that time; and the plaintiff shall pay for entering the action anew.

But when it shall so happen that the party against whom suit is brought, is not an inhabitant, or sojourner in this state; or is absent out of the same, at the time of commencing such suit, and doth not return before the time for trial; the judges of the court before whom such suit is brought, shall continue the action to the next court; and if the defendant do not then appear (by himself or attorney) and be so remote that the notice of such suit depending could not probably be conveyed to him during the vacancy; the judges at such next court may further continue the action to the court thence next following, and no longer; but may enter up judgment of default, after such continuance or continuances: and in such cases where judgment shall be entered up by default, after such continuance as aforesaid, execution shall be stayed, and not issue forth thereon, until the plaintiff shall have given, or lodged with the clerk of said court, a bond, with one or more sufficient sureties to the adverse party, in double the value of the estate or sum recovered by such judgment, to make restitution, and to refund and pay back such sum as shall be given in debt or damage, or so much as shall be recovered upon a suit therefor, to be brought within twelve months next after the entering up of the first judgment, if upon such suit the judgment shall be reversed, annulled or altered; the security to be no further answerable than for the recovery that shall be made upon such suit to be had within twelve months, as aforesaid.

Provided also, that no real estate, taken in execution granted upon such first judgment, shall be alienated or passed away, until after the expiration of the said twelve months, or after a new trial had on a suit brought within the space of twelve months, for the obtaining restitution as aforesaid.

Be it further enacted by the authority aforesaid, that if any person who hath entered an action to be tried in any court, being called three times (after twelve of the clock on the first day of the court's sitting) shall not appear, either by himself or his attorney, to prosecute his action, he shall be non-suited, and pay all cost and charges to the defendant, and for the entry of the action, as if the same had been prosecuted in such court. And that the plaintiff, in all actions brought to any court, shall have liberty to withdraw his action, or to non suit himself, before the jury have given in their verdict; in which case he shall pay full costs to the defendant; and may afterwards renew his suit at another court, the former withdraw or non suit being first recorded.

Be it further enacted by the authority aforesaid, that there shall be free liberty of process, and the same is hereby granted in all civil actions, according to law, at any adjourned county court, as well as at the stated county courts.

And be it further enacted by the authority aforesaid, that all suits brought for the trial of the title of lands, or wherein the title of lands is concerned, shall be tried in the same county where the land lies, or facts are done concerning which the title of land may be in question. And that all other actions that may be brought before the county courts, shall be brought and tried in the county where the plaintiff or defendant dwells, if they or either of them are inhabitants within this state. And that all suits and prosecutions cognizable before an assistant or justice of the peace, shall be made and prosecuted before such authority in those towns only where the plaintiff or defendant dwells; unless there be no authority which may lawfully try the cause in either of the said towns; in which case the plaintiff may bring his suit before an assistant or justice of the peace in one of the next adjoining towns to the place of his abode.

And be it further enacted by the authority aforesaid, that all causes wherein the title of land is not concerned, and wherein the debt, trespass, damage, or other matter in demand, doth not exceed ten pounds, shall and may be heard, tried, and determined by any one assistant or justice of the peace; who are hereby impowered to hear and determine the same by jury or otherwise, according to law, and award execution on their judgment given in such cases; and that either plaintiff or defendant shall have a right to demand a jury of six men to try such causes.

Be it further enacted by the authority aforesaid, that the judges of the superior or inferior courts, assistants, and justices of the peace, shall determine matters of law, stated and referred to them by the jury in their special verdicts; which verdicts the jury in all cases wherein matters of law are to them so obscure, that they can not clearly and safely give a positive verdict, shall have liberty to give a special verdict therein, finding and presenting the facts, and thereon stating and putting the question in law, viz.: if the law be so, then we find for the plaintiff; but if the law be otherwise, then we find for the defendant.

Be it further enacted by the authority aforesaid, that the judges of the court, assistants, and justices of the peace, shall have liberty, if they judge that the jury that attend their respective courts have not attended to the evidence given in, and the true issue of the case, in their verdicts, to cause them to return to a second consideration of the case; and shall, for the like reason, have power to return them to a third consideration, and no more. And when the court have committed any case to the consideration of the jury, the jury shall be confined under the custody of an officer appointed by said court, until they are agreed on a verdict; and the court may set a suitable fine, not exceeding forty shillings, upon such officer or juryman as shall be disorderly, or neglect or refuse a due attendance of their duties respectively, during their attending the court.

And that when the parties have made their pleas in any court, and given their evidence, and the case be committed to the jury, there shall be no after plea, arguments, evidences, or testimonies, heard or received in such case.

And be it further enacted by the authority aforesaid, that if any person shall be aggrieved with the sentence or determination of any assistant or justice of the peace, he may remove his case, by appeal, to the next county court in that county where the case was first tried; the person appealing giving bond, as is hereafter provided. And if any person or persons shall be aggrieved with the sentence or determination of any county court, the party aggrieved may appeal therefrom to the next superior court to be held in the same county; or by a new process, once, and no more, may review his cause in the next session of the same county court where it was before tried; and if either party be aggrieved with the judgment or determination of the county court, upon trial of the cause by review, he may appeal to the next superior court in the same county. And if either party be aggrieved with the issue and determination of the superior court, upon the first trial of the cause, then he may, by a new process, once, and no more, review his case in the next session of the same court, there to be tried to a final issue, provided the case be brought directly to the superior court, by appeal from the first judgment of the county court: but if the case be brought to the superior court, by appeal from the judgment of the county court given on a review, it shall have a final issue by the judgment and determination of the superior court, upon the first trial there.

Always provided, that all appeals and reviews shall be entered during the time of the sitting of the court from whose judgment such appeals and reviews shall be made, and within twenty-four hours after judgment be given: and sufficient bond, with sureties, shall be given in to the said court, by the person appealing or reviewing, to prosecute his appeal or review to effect, and answer all damages in case he made not his plea good; in all which cases, execution shall be stayed until there shall be an issue of the case; and the party who shall recover his action, shall have all his just damages and cost allowed him.

Provided nevertheless, that from a judgment given by an assistant, or justice of the peace, in a case wherein the debt, damage, or other matter in demand, doth not exceed the sum of six pounds; or if the debt be due by bond, bill, or note for the payment of money or grain, avouched by one or two witnesses, and doth not exceed the sum of ten pounds, no appeal shall be allowed.

Also, that when judgment shall be given in the county court in any case brought there by an appeal, wherein the title of land is not concerned, no appeal or review to be allowed.

And that upon a judgment or determination of the county court, in suits brought directly there, upon bonds, bills or notes for the payment of money or grain, avouched by one or two witnesses, no review nor appeal shall be allowed.

And also, when either plaintiff or defendant shall in any action recover judgment upon the first and second trial, by the court and jury, the judgment on such second trial shall be a final issue, and no appeal or review shall be allowed from the same; anything in this act before to the contrary in any wise notwithstanding.

And be it further enacted by the authority aforesaid, that all appeals to any of the superior or county courts in this state, shall be entered in such courts respectively, before the second opening of such court, and not after; unless the appellant shall pay to the appellee all his cost in such case arisen to that time, to be taxed by the court; which being done, the action may be entered by the appellant, before the jury attending such court are dismissed, and not after:—which costs, so taxed and paid, shall not be considered nor allowed in making up the bill of cost in the final determination of the case.

And be it further enacted by the authority aforesaid, that any one assistant or justice of the peace, shall have full power, and they are hereby authorized and impowered to take and accept a confession and acknowledgment of any debt from a debtor to his creditor, either upon or without an antecedent process, as the parties shall agree; which confession shall be made only by the person of the debtor himself; and on such confession so made, the assistant or justice shall make a record thereof, and thereon grant out execution in due form of law. And if it so happen that such execution shall be levied on the lands of any such person confessing as aforesaid, according to the laws directing the levying executions on lands, shall be returned to, and recorded in the office of the clerk of the county court in the same county where such land lieth, provided such land lieth in a town where there is no town clerk qualified by law to record deeds; but if such land lieth in any town where there is a town clerk, qualified as aforesaid, in such case, every such execution shall be returned to, and recorded in the town clerk's office where such lands lie; and being so done and recorded, shall be good evidence of a title to such creditor for whom it shall be taken as aforesaid, their heirs and assigns,—provided no confession shall be made or taken in the manner aforesaid, for more than the value of two hundred pounds debt, together with cost. And if any debtor shall tender such confession to a creditor, and the creditor shall refuse it, he shall lose any cost that he shall, after such tender, be at in procuring judgment for his debt afterwards, unless it appear that such tender was not for the whole sum due.

AN ACT REGULATING TRIALS AND APPEALS

24 FEB 1779

Whereas no county courts have been established in this state, which makes it necessary that all such causes, or actions, as would otherwise be heard before such county courts, should now be heard and determined in the superior court.

Be it enacted, and it is hereby enacted by the representatives of the freemen of the state of Vermont, in general assembly met, and by the authority of the same, that all actions or suits that are by law directed to be heard and determined by way of appeals or otherwise, in the county courts in this state, shall be heard and determined in the same manner in the superior court in each county in this state, as they are by law directed to be heard and determined in the county courts. And the superior court shall have all the powers and jurisdictions that are by law vested in the county courts, until county courts are regularly established in each county in this state.

Be it further enacted by the authority aforesaid, that all actions that shall by virtue of this act be brought to the superior court, that otherwise would have been brought to the county court, and might by law have been appealed to the superior court; if either party be aggrieved with the judgment rendered in such case, they may have a second trial in the superior court, by way of review.

AN ACT MAKING THE LAWS OF THIS STATE TEMPORARY

23 FEB 1779

Be it enacted, and it is hereby enacted, by the representatives of the freemen of the state of Vermont, in general assembly met, and by the authority of the same, that each and every act of this state that have been passed into laws by the general assembly of this state, at their sessions holden at Bennington February 1779, be hereby declared to be temporary acts or laws, and to remain in full force until the rising of the general assembly in October next.

And be it further enacted by the authority aforesaid, that no court, or justice, shall take cognizance of any matter or thing in which the title of land is concerned, or in any action of contract where the parties appear to have made a bargain, or contract, by note, bond, debt, or agreement in writing, or otherwise, any act or law to the contrary notwithstanding.

LAWS OF VERMONT
PASSED DURING THE SESSION OF THE GENERAL ASSEMBLY
JUNE 2-JUNE 4, 1779

AN ACT TO PREVENT PERSONS FROM EXERCISING AUTHORITY UNLESS LAWFULLY AUTHORIZED BY THIS STATE

3 JUNE 1779

Whereas there are divers persons within this state, who have opposed and do continue to oppose the government threof; and who do, by every way and means in their power, endeavor to obstruct the free exercise of the powers of government within the same:

Which mischief to prevent,

Be it enacted, and it is hereby enacted by the representatives of the freemen of the state of Vermont, in general assembly met, and by the authority of the same, that if any person within this state (except continental officers) shall, after the first day of September next, accept, hold, or exercise any office, either civil or military, from or under any authority, other than is or shall be derived from this state, and be thereof convicted, shall, for the first offence, pay a fine not exceeding one hundred pounds lawful money, according to the discretion of the court which may have cognizance thereof.

And for the second offence of the like kind, shall be whipped on the naked body not exceeding forty stripes, according to the discretion of the court before whom they are prosecuted.

And for the third offence, shall have their right ear nailed to a post, and cut off; and be branded in the forehead with the capital letter C, on a hot iron.

This act to continue in force until the rising of the Assembly in October 1780, and no longer.

AN ACT TO GRANT LIBERTY OF SUING IN CERTAIN CASES THEREIN NAMED

3 JUNE 1779

Whereas it is judged inconvenient (by this assembly) to put the law for collecting of debts due from one man to another, by bond, note, book, convenants, or agreements, in force for the present.

Notwithstanding which, it is found necessary, for the support of government, and to carry on the war against our British enemy, that all obligations of what kind soever, that are given in or on account of any prosecution of any action that may by law be prosecuted; as also any covenant, promise or agreement made for the same purpose, be liable to be sued and prosecuted to final judgment and execution.

Be it enacted, and it is hereby enacted by the representatives of the freemen of the state of Vermont in general assembly met, and by the authority of the same, that all obligations, of what kind soever, that have or shall be given, in or on account of carrying on any action that may by law be prosecuted, or on account of carrying said prosecution into execution; as also all covenants and agreements made for the same purpose, may be sued for, and prosecuted to final judgment and execution, any law, usage, or custom to the contrary notwithstanding.

This act to continue in force until the rising of the assembly in October next, and no longer.

AN ACT FOR RAISING THE FEES AND FINES HERETOFORE STATED BY THE LAWS OF THIS STATE

3 JUNE 1779

Be it enacted, and it is hereby enacted by the representatives of the freemen of the state of Vermont, in general assembly met, and by the authority of the same, that all fees and fines shall be double to what they stand in the laws, the judges of the superior court only excepted; who are each to have twelve dollars per day, with the mileage the assembly-men have.

This act to remain in force until the rising of the assembly in October next, and no longer.

AN ACT IMPOWERING TWO OR THREE JUSTICES TO TRY A CAUSE OF ONE HUNDRED POUNDS; AND FORBIDDING APPEALS TO DELINQUENTS FOR NEGLECT OF MILITARY DUTY

3 JUNE 1779 (REPEALED PAGE 221)

Be it enacted, and it is hereby enacted by the representatives of the freemen of the state of Vermont, in general assembly met, and by the authority of the same, that two or three justices shall have power to try such actions as they have heretofore been impowered to try, to the amount of one hundred pounds: and that there shall be no appeal for a delinquent for neglect of military duty.

This act to remain in force until the rising of the assembly in October next, and no longer.

LAWS OF VERMONT

PASSED DURING THE SESSION OF THE GENERAL ASSEMBLY

OCTOBER 14-OCTOBER 27, 1779

AN ACT DIRECTING AND REGULATING THE CHOICE OF JUDGES OF THE SUPERIOR COURT

20 OCT 1779

Whereas no particular directions are given in the constitution for regulating the choice of judges of the superior court; in consequence of which it is necessary that some proper mode be provided by the general assembly. Therefore,

Be it enacted, and it is hereby enacted by the representatives of the freemen of the state of Vermont in general assembly met, and by the authority of the same, that in future the judges of the superior court shall be chosen in October annually, by the governor, council, and house of representatives by their joint ballot.

AN ACT IN ADDITION TO AN ACT ENTITLED AN ACT FOR THE ASCERTAINING TOWN BRANDS, AND PROVIDING AND REGULATING BRANDING AND BRANDERS OF HORSES

22 OCT 1779

Be it enacted, and it is hereby enacted by the representatives of the freemen of the state of Vermont in General Assembly met, and by the authority of the same, that the several towns hereto annexed, shall have a town brand for horses, which shall be the letters or figures following, viz.

For Tinmouth, T
For Reading, R
For Putney, P

AN ACT APPOINTING COMMISSIONERS FOR THE BETTER REGULATING TITLES OF LAND WITHIN THIS STATE, AND DECLARING THEIR POWER

22 OCT 1779

Whereas, there are many tenements, farms and tracts of land, situate within this state, claimed by sundry persons, under divers titles, occasioned partly from the unsettled situation the people of this state have heretofore been in, and partly by the avaricious views of those governors, who under the King of Great Britain, feared not to give patents directly interfering with each other, and many settlers have moved on to said lands under those different titles, and undergone innumerable hardships in settling farms, and now to dispossess them, would be cruel and unjust; while others have been intruders and trespassers from the beginning; and to establish them, in seclusion of the lawful freeholders, would be equally iniquitous and unjust.

And whereas many inconveniences must attend trials at law, in strict legal adjudications of such a multiplicity of disputes, as well to individuals as the public; such as delays of justice in many instances, increasing of broils and contentions; which great evils to prevent,

Be it enacted, and it is hereby enacted by the representatives of the freemen of the state of Vermont, in general assembly met, and by the authority of the same, that Joseph Bowker, Esq., Joseph Tyler, Esq., John Strong, Esq., Edward Harris, Esq., and Capt. Edmund Hodges, be appointed and commissionated by his excellency the governor of this state, and sworn in the form of the oath hereafter prescribed, to be commissioners for the purposes aforesaid; and that the said commissioners, or any three of them, be, and they are hereby, authorized and impowered, to do and perform the several acts, matters and things hereafter named; to wit: that the said commissioners, or any three of them, shall have power to take into consideration, and fully examine, all the evidence relating to, or respecting, the titles of controverted lands in this state: for that end, they shall have power, to send for persons, to administer oaths, to call upon the parties for charters, patents, deeds of conveyances, and all other writings respecting their title to said lands: as also to examine the parties upon oath; and shall make report to this assembly, at their next session, or at the session of general assembly in October next, which of those various claimants to the same land ought, in justice and equity, to possess and forever hold the fee of said land, with the remittances said freeholders shall make to the other claimants; together with the evidence and reasons upon which said report shall be grounded.

And be it further enacted by the authority aforesaid, that upon application made by any person, claiming lands in the actual possession of another, whereon improvements have been made, to [*Blank*] or, in his absence, to [*Blank*] they, or either of them, are hereby impowered to summon any two or more of the commissioners aforesaid, to convene in that particular town, wherein the disputed land lieth; notifying therein the time and place of convening; and also to grant a citation to the person making application, to summon the person in actual possession, to answer him in his claim, before said commissioners, at the time and place of their convening as aforesaid: which citation shall be served on the adverse party, at least twenty days before said commissioners convene: and said commissioners, after making out their reports, shall lodge a true and attested copy of each report, fourteen days before the sitting of the general assembly, at their next session, or at the session in October next, in that particular town clerk's office, in which the land lieth, that each and every party may have the perusal thereof. And said commissioners shall, on or before the opening of the general assemblies aforesaid, deliver to the clerk of said assembly, the various reports they shall have made; which reports shall be read, with the evidence and reason of each report, on the first day of the assembly's meeting, and shall then be laid on the table for each member's perusal, at least four days before they shall pass the house: after which the reports, shall be taken up the second time, and read; when all persons remonstrating against any of said reports, shall be heard; and each report that shall be approved and adjudged to be established by said assembly, and ordered to be carried into execution, a copy of the resolve of said assembly shall be sent to the town clerk's office where the land lieth; and the clerk of said town is hereby required, on the receipt of said copy from the general assembly, to record the report and resolution of the assembly, in the register book of said town; which shall be forever after deemed and considered an indisputable title to said lands, and the appurtenances thereof, in seclusion of all claims and demands whatsoever, of the party or parties in the trials aforesaid.

And be it further enacted by the authority aforesaid, that no cause for action shall be commenced or prosecuted, in which the title of land is any way concerned: and all actions now depending before any court, assistant, or justice of the peace, wherein the title of land is concerned, shall be removed from said court, assistant, or justice of the peace, in the same manner in which they now stand, to said commissioners, who are also hereby impowered to take notice of the cost that hath hitherto arisen: and all persons now in actual possession of land, shall be and remain in quiet and peaceable possession, until the general assembly shall determine the same.

And be it further enacted by the authority aforesaid, that each and every of the said commissioners, before they shall take upon them the exercise of said office, do, before an assistant, or justice of the peace, take the following oath, viz:

You, _____, being appointed one of the commissioners, according to the form and effect of an act, entitled "An act appointing commissioners for the better regulating titles of land within this state and declaring their power," do most solemnly promise and swear, by the ever living God, that you will, to the best of your knowledge and ability, without favour or affection, faithfully execute and perform, as well to justice between parties as for the benefit and advantage of the inhabitants of the state of Vermont, all and singular the power and authorities, by force and virtue of said act unto you given. So help you God.

And be it further enacted by the authority aforesaid, that the person or persons making application to the commissioners aforesaid, shall be holden to pay the same fees to said commissioners, as is allowed to the judges of the superior court: and they are hereby impowered to grant executions accordingly.

AN ACT CONSTITUTING THE SUPERIOR COURT A COURT OF EQUITY, AND DECLARING THEIR POWER

22 OCT 1779

Whereas, from the universality of the law, many cases will arise, wherein it is necessary that some further provision be made for relief in equity, than can be obtained by the rules of common law. To the intent therefore that justice and equity may be jointly administered;

Be it enacted, and it is hereby enacted, by the representatives of the freemen of the state of Vermont, in general assembly met, and by the authority of the same, that the superior court shall be, and it is hereby, constituted a court of equity, and impowered to hear and determine all cases in equity that shall be brought properly before said court, wherein the demands, dues, matter or cause in dispute, is above twenty pounds, and doth not exceed the sum of four thousand pounds, lawful money: and on consideration of the several pleas and allegations made by either party, may moderate the rigor of the law, decree and enter up judgment therein agreeable to equity and good conscience, and to award execution accordingly.

And be it further enacted by the authority aforesaid, that all cases in equity, wherein the demands, dues, matter or cause in dispute, shall exceed the sum of four thousand pounds, shall be heard and determined by the governor and council and house of representatives.

And be it further enacted by the authority aforesaid, that the form of the process in equity shall be, that the party aggrieved or oppressed, by the forfeiture or penalty annexed unto any articles of agreement, covenant, contract, bond, or other specialties, or forfeiture of estate on condition executed by deed of mortgage, or any other cause proper for a court of equity, may bring his suit for remedy and relief therein, by filing a bill, in form of a petition, in that particular court that hath cognizance of the same, therein setting forth at large the cause for relief: and shall cause the adverse party to be served with a copy of said petition, and a citation to be signed by the clerk of said court, or by an assistant, or justice of the peace, twelve days before the day of the sitting of the same.

Provided always, that the party aggrieved at any judgment to be given as aforesaid, wherein title of land is concerned, shall have liberty of review, as in other cases is provided at the common law, and shall also have the liberty of appeal from the superior court to the governor and council and general assembly.

And be it further enacted, that all causes in equity, now depending before the general assembly, wherein the demand does not exceed the sum of four thousand pounds, shall be referred to the superior court, in the same manner in which they now stand.

AN ACT APPOINTING SURVEYORS IN THE SEVERAL COUNTIES IN THIS STATE

22 OCT 1779

Be it enacted, and it is hereby enacted by the representatives of the freemen of the state of Vermont, in general assembly met, and by the authority of the same, that Abraham Ives of Wallingford, and Nathaniel Smith of Poultney, be and they are hereby appointed county surveyors for the county of Bennington; and that Timothy Bartholomew of Thetford, Joel Mathews of Woodstock, and Hazael Shepard of Halifax, be, and they are, hereby appointed county surveyors for the county of Cumberland.

AN ACT APPOINTING THE TIME AND PLACE OF HOLDING THE SUPERIOR COURT

22 OCT 1779

Be it enacted, and it is hereby enacted by the representatives of the freemen of the state of Vermont, in general assembly met, and by the authority of the same, that the time and place for holding the superior court for the year ensuing within this state shall be as follows, viz.

At Bennington, in the county of Bennington, on the third Tuesday of November.

At Westminster, in the county of Cumberland, on the third Tuesday of March.

At Tinmouth, in the county of Bennington, on the second Tuesday of June.

At Thetford, in the county of Cumberland, on the second Tuesday of September.

AN ACT DIVIDING THE SECOND AND FIFTH REGIMENTS OF MILITIA AND FORMING AND ESTABLISHING A SIXTH REGIMENT

23 OCT 1779

Whereas it has been found inconvenient for the inhabitants included within the limits circumscribing the bounds of the second and fifth regiments to continue in two entire regiments, and that it would be more convenient to form a sixth regiment within the limits of the same. Therefore,

Be it enacted, and it is hereby enacted by the representatives of the freemen of the state of Vermont, in general assembly met, and by the authority of the same, that all the military companies in the several towns and gores included in the limits hereafter described, viz. beginning at the north west corner of the township of Shaftsbury, then east on the north lines of Shaftsbury and Glastenbury, to the county line; then north in the county line to the north east corner of Harwich; then west on the north lines of Harwich, Danby and Pawlet, to the north west corner of said Pawlet; then southerly in the west lines of Pawlet, Rupert, Sandgate and Arlington, to the bounds begun at, be, and are hereby made and declared to be one entire and distinct regiment; and shall be distinguished and called by the name of the sixth regiment.

AN ACT EMPOWERING THE SEVERAL TOWNS THAT HAVE NO JUSTICES OF THE PEACE, TO CHOOSE THE SAME

27 OCT 1779

Whereas there are sundry towns in this state that are destitute of a justice or justices of the peace, and thereby deprived of the privilege of acknowledging deeds &c. in their respective towns.

Be it enacted, and it is hereby enacted by the representatives of the freemen of the state of Vermont, in general assembly met, and by the authority of the same, that each and every town within this state, that has not any justice of the peace in their respective towns; that the freemen of said towns are hereby authorized to meet, as the law directs, on or before the first Monday of December next, and make choice of a justice of the peace, and that he be commissioned by the governor, for the time being, or until others be chosen as the law directs.

AN ACT REGULATING THE CHOICE OF FIELD OFFICERS

27 OCT 1779 (REPEALED PAGE 194)

Be it enacted, and it is hereby enacted by the representatives of the freemen of the state of Vermont in general assembly met, and by the authority of the same, that whenever any regiment shall be destitute of a field officer or officers, the captain general, or in his absence, the brigadier general, shall issue his orders to the first officer in command in said regiment, to order the respective companies in the said regiment, to meet at the places where such companies usually meet in their respective towns, and give in their votes for such field officer or officers as they may be directed to as aforesaid; which votes shall be carried by the commanding officer of each company, or some person by him substituted, to a place appointed by the captain general or brigadier general, and there sorted and counted by a committee appointed by the persons who shall carry the votes.

And the chairman of said committee shall make declaration of the person or persons that shall be found to have a majority of the votes for any of said offices, and shall make return to his excellency the governor in order to their being commissioned. And in case there should be no choice for any officer or officers that shall be voted for as aforesaid, he shall make return thereof to the captain general or brigadier general, so that orders may be issued for another choice as aforesaid.

AN ACT IN ADDITION TO AN ACT, ENTITLED, AN ACT FOR THE REGULATING AND STATING FEES

27 OCT 1779 (REPEALED PAGE 221)

Be it enacted, and it is hereby enacted by the representatives of the freemen of the state of Vermont, in general assembly met, and by the authority of the same, that each juryman attending at the superior or county court, shall have one pound ten shillings for trying each cause; and each juryman for attending a justices court, one pound for trying each case. Attorneys' fees for each case in the superior or county court, six pounds. County surveyors' fees per day, six pounds ten shillings.

And be it further enacted by the authority aforesaid, that all fees and fines shall be three-folded as they stand in the laws passed before this session—except jurymen's fees, which is hereby repealed.

AN ACT TO REVIVE THE LAWS PASSED BY THE LEGISLATURE
OF THIS STATE

27 OCT 1779

Be it enacted, and it is hereby enacted by the representatives of the freemen of the state of Vermont, in general assembly met, and by the authority of the same, that each and every act and law of this state, be, and remain in full force and virtue until the rising of the assembly in March next.

LAWS OF 1780

LAWS OF VERMONT
ACTS AND LAWS PASSED AT WESTMINSTER
MARCH 1780

AN ACT FOR THE PURPOSE OF IMPOWERING THE INHABITANTS OF THE
RESPECTIVE TOWNS IN THIS STATE TO TAX THEMSELVES
ON CERTAIN OCCASIONS

14TH MARCH 1780

Whereas it is found necessary for towns, as such, to raise sums of money for the carrying on the War, to purchase Ammunition, for town stock, to support the Poor, and many other purposes which they may find necessary, not inconsistent with the Constitution of this State:

Be it therefore enacted, and it is hereby enacted, by the Representative of the freemen of the State of Vermont in General Assembly met, and by the authority of the same, that the Inhabitants of the respective towns in this State be, and they are hereby authorized to vote a tax for the purpose of carrying on the War, for procuring a town Stock of Ammunition, for the Support of the Poor of such towns, or any other Purposes which they may find necessary, not inconsistent with the Constitution of this State, at their annual town Meeting, or at any other meeting warned for that purpose: Which meeting shall be warned at least ten Days before the holding such meeting, by the Selectmen. And the respective Collector of town rates are hereby authorized to collect such taxes when directed thereto by warrant from an Assistant or Justice of the Peace; and the Collectors of such rates shall lodge the Money so collected in the Town Treasury, to be drawn out and disposed of by the Selectmen for the Purpose or Purposes for which it was raised.

(Provided always that no person be compelled by the major Vote of said Town to build or repair a Meeting House, or support a Worship, or Minister of the Gospel, contrary to the Dictates of his Conscience, Provided said Person or persons shall support some sort of religious Worship, as to them may seem most agreeable to the word of God, anything in this Act to the contrary notwithstanding.) This Proviso is not in the original but is recorded from a printed copy.

AN ACT TO PREVENT UNLAWFUL SETTLEMENT ON UNAPPROPRIATED LANDS

16TH MARCH 1780

Be it enacted, and it is hereby enacted by the Representatives of the freemen of the State of Vermont in General Assembly met, and by the Authority of the same, that if any Person or Persons shall, after the passing of this Act, presume to make Settlement, or improve any unappropriated Lands within this State, without first obtaining a legal Title to the same, shall forfeit all such Settlement, Labour and improvement to this State, and shall be obliged to give up Possession, and pay all Cost and Damage that shall accrue. Provided always that nothing in this Act be construed to debar any Person or Persons from recovering Pay for Settlement Labour &c. where it can be made to appear that such Settlement was made through mistake, or on a supposed legal Title.—And to prevent fraud in sales of Land by Persons, who pretend to a Title by virtue of their names being annexed to any Petition or Petitions on file, and lodged in the Secretary's Office for granting; all persons are hereby cautioned against such Purchases, as they are unjust in their nature, and will not be considered as legal.

AN ACT REGULATING THE TRYAL OF PERSONS WHO ON BEING ARRAIGNED FOR TREASON, FELONY, AND CRIMES AGAINST THE STATE, STAND MUTE, OR REFUSE TO PLEAD

16TH MARCH 1780

Whereas the Judgments directed by the Common Law, so far as they respect the manner of putting the Offender to Death, are marked by Circumstances manifestly repugnant to that spirit of Humanity, which should ever distinguish a free, a civilized and Christian People—For remedy whereof

Be it enacted, and it is hereby enacted, by the Representatives of the freemen of the State of Vermont, in General Assembly met, and by the Authority of the same, that in all cases of Treason, Felony, or Crimes against the State, where the party indicted, or complained of, shall, on being arraigned, obstinately stand mute, or refuse to plead, and be tried in due course of Law, such obstinately standing mute, or refusal to plead and be tried as aforesaid, shall be adjudged to amount to, and be a proper Traverse or denial of the facts, charged in the Indictment or Complaint; and the Trial shall thereupon proceed in like manner, and the same Judgment shall be given, against the said Party, if found guilty, as if he, she, or they had on being arraigned duly plead, and in proper form respectively put themselves on their Tryal.

AN ACT REPEALING A CERTAIN PARAGRAPH OF AN ACT ENTITLED "AN ACT MAKING THE LAWS OF THIS STATE TEMPORARY"

16TH MARCH 1780

Whereas, there is a certain Paragraph in said Act enacted, "that no Court, or Justice, shall take Cognizance of any matter or thing, in which the Title of Land is concerned, or in any Action of Contract, where the Parties appear to have made a bargain or Contract, by Note, Bond, Debt, or Agreement in writing, or otherwise; any Act or Law to the contrary notwithstanding."

Be it enacted, and it is hereby enacted, by the Representatives of the freemen of the State of Vermont, in General Assembly met, and by the Authority of the same, that the above recited Paragraph be and remain in full force till the first day of June next, and no longer.

AN ACT TO PREVENT THE TRANSPORTING PROVISIONS OUT OF THIS STATE

16TH MARCH 1780

Whereas large quantities of Provisions are continually exported out of this State, which, if not immediately prevented, will render it impracticable to furnish the Troops raised for the Defence of the northern frontiers.

Therefore Be it enacted, and it is hereby enacted, by the Representatives of the freemen of the State of Vermont, in General Assembly met, and by the Authority of the same, that any and all further Exportation of Wheat, Rye, indian Corn, Flour, or meal, of any kind; as also Beef, Pork, or any other Provisions whatever, that may be useful for supplying the Troops raised by this State, be and is hereby strictly prohibited and forbid to be exported out of this State (except for the use of the Continent, or that the same be permitted by the Governor with the Advice of three or more of his Council.—And all sheriffs Constables Grand Jurors, and Selectmen, in the respective Towns, and all Persons whatever within this State, are hereby authorized and required to seize any, and every, of the above mentioned Articles, which they have reason to suspect any person or Persons may be carrying out, or purchased to be carried out, of this State, contrary to the true intent of this Act; And if need be to command assistance, and make return to the next assistance or Justice of the Peace, in writing, of said Seizure: and unless said Person or persons shall satisfy the Court, before whom the Examination be had, that he or they were not conveying any of the above mentioned Articles out of this State, said Articles shall be forfeit, or such person or persons fined, not exceeding forty Pounds, at the Discretion of the Court before whom the Tryal shall be had; the one half of the forfeiture, or fine, to be to the use of this State, and the other half to the person who shall prosecute to effect.

And be it further enacted by the Authority aforesaid, that if any person or persons, shall export any of the above prohibited Articles out of this State, and be thereof convicted before any Court proper to try the same, he or they shall forfeit and pay to the Treasurer of this State, the value of said Articles so exported; to be recovered by Bill Plaint or Information: this Act to continue in force until the fifteenth Day of August next, and no longer.

AN ACT TO REVIVE THE LAWS PASSED BY THE LEGISLATURE OF THIS STATE

16TH MARCH 1780

Be it enacted, and it is hereby enacted, by the Representatives of the freemen of the State of Vermont, in General Assembly met, and by the Authority of the same, that each and every Act and Law of this State, (except those repealed by special Act of Assembly) be and remain in full force and virtue, until the rising of the Assembly in October next.

AN ACT AUTHORIZING AND DIRECTING THE SURVEYOR GENERAL TO MAKE A PLAN OF THIS STATE

16TH MARCH 1780

(This act is omitted from the original volume)

AN ACT FOR THE HEARING OF LIEUT. COLONEL JAMES CLAGHORN, AND IMPOWERING A COMMITTEE FOR THAT PURPOSE

16TH MARCH 1780

Whereas Lieut. Colonel James Claghorn of the fifth Regiment of the Militia of the State of Vermont, has remonstrated to the Assembly, that in consequence of Col⁰. Gideon Warren's Complaint to the Captain General, and Commander in chief, of the Militia of the State, purporting that said Lieut. Col⁰. Claghorn had been guilty of Misconduct in an Expedition against the Enemy on the 23ᵈ. and 24ᵗʰ of November last past, the Captain General had pleased to arrest, and suspend him from Command, until Inquiry could be made respecting the Premises.

And Whereas said Colonel Claghorn has petitioned this Assembly for a free and impartial Inquiry respecting the Premises.

To the Intent therefore that the same may be,

Be it enacted, and it is hereby enacted by the Representatives of the freemen of the State of Vermont, in General Assembly met, and by the Authority of the same, that Colonel Samuel Safford, Colonel Ebenezer Walbridge, and Captain Samuel Robinson be constituted a Committee of Inquiry; and they are hereby authorized and impowered to repair; as soon as may be, to the Town of Rutland, having first notified all parties concerned ten days before the time of the said Committee's convening; and when convened shall allow a full and impartial hearing, examine Evidences under Oath, and take all possible means to acquire Knowledge; and make report in the Premises, to this Assembly, at their next Session, with the reason and Evidence upon which they ground their Report.

AN ACT, IN ADDITION TO AN ACT ENTITLED "AN ACT FOR FORMING AND REGULATING THE MILITIA, AND FOR ENCOURAGEMENT OF MILITARY SKILL, FOR THE BETTER DEFENCE OF THIS STATE"

MARCH 1780

Whereas no Penalty is annexed, in the above Act, on the non-commissioned Officers of the several Companies of Militia, in case they, or any of them, should refuse, or neglect, to warn any such military Company to attend on muster, or other military purposes, when directed by his or their superior officer.—And whereas no Penalty has been affixed on any such non commissioned Officer, for neglecting or refusing to attend such Muster, or meeting for such other military purpose or Purposes, when duly warned therefor, by the Direction or Directions of such superior officer or officers.—Therefore,

Be it enacted, and it is hereby enacted, by the Representatives of the freemen of the State of Vermont, in General Assembly met, and by the Authority of the same, that whenever any non commissioned officer of any military Company within this State, shall refuse or neglect to warn any part of such Military Company, to attend any muster, or other meeting of such Company for military Purposes, when thereto required by Warrant, or otherwise, from his Superior Officer of such Company, and shall be thereof duly convicted, shall for neglecting to warn each such person, required to warn as aforesaid, forfeit and pay the Sum of six Pounds.—And in case any such non commissioned Officer, shall neglect or refuse to attend any such muster, or other meeting of such Company, for other military purpose or purposes, having been duly notified thereof, by the direction of his superior Officer, shall forfeit and pay for each such neglect, the Sum of six Pounds:—Which fines are to be recovered by Warrant from the Commanding Officer of each Company, and to be appropriated for the Use of such Company.— Provided always, that if any such non-commissioned officer so neglecting, shall satisfy such commanding officer, that such neglect was unavoidable, that in such case, such fines shall be relinquished.

AN ACT REPEALING AN ACT ENTITLED "AN ACT REGULATING THE CHOICE OF FIELD OFFICERS." PASSED AT MANCHESTER, OCTOBER 1779

MARCH 1780

Whereas the method provided in the above recited Act for choosing Field Officers proves very disadvantageous to the Community at large:

Therefore Be it enacted, and it is hereby enacted by the Representatives of the freemen of the State of Vermont, in General Assembly met, and by the Authority of the same, that the said Act entitled "An Act regulating the Choice of Field Officers" be and is hereby repealed.

AN ACT REGULATING THE CHOICE OF FIELD AND STAFF OFFICERS

MARCH 1780

Be it enacted, and it is hereby enacted, by the Representatives of the freemen of the State of Vermont, in General Assembly met, and by the Authority of the same, that whenever by Death, Resignation, Disqualification, or otherwise, any Regiment or Regiments shall be destitute of any Field or Staff Officer, or Officers, that it shall be the Duty of the Captain General, or in his absence of the Major General, or in their Absence of the Brigadier General, to issue his orders to the several

Captains, or officers commanding the several Companies, of such Regiment, to meet at such time and Place as the Captain General, or in his Absence the Major General, or in their Absence the Brigadier General as aforesaid, shall in such Orders direct; and that the several Companies of any such Regiment being convened, according to the Directions aforesaid, shall proceed by vote to the Choice of some suitable person or persons to supply such vacancy or vacancies; which being done, the Commanding Officer of such Regiment shall return the Name or names of such person or persons to the Governor, in order to his or their being commissioned.

LAWS OF VERMONT

ACTS PASSED AT BENNINGTON IN
OCTOBER AND NOVEMBER 1780

AN ACT FOR THE PURPOSE OF REMOVING
DISAFFECTED PERSONS FROM THE FRONTIERS OF THIS STATE

13TH OCTOBER 1780

Whereas it is found that sundry persons living in the frontier Towns of this State, who do not feel themselves in any danger from the common Enemy, and refuse their personal Assistance in the Defence of such frontier Settlement; and we have reason to fear, hold a secret and traiterous Correspondence with, and, as occassion offers, do harbour and conceal the Enemies of this and the United States—Which Embarrassment to prevent;

Be it enacted, and it is hereby enacted, by the Representatives of the freemen of the State of Vermont, in General Assembly met, and by the Authority of the same, that it shall be the Duty of the Select-men of any such frontier Towns, if they have good grounds of suspicion that any person or persons, living in such town, do secretly correspond with the Enemy; or any person or persons who do not feel themselves in danger from the Common Enemy, and refuse their personal assistance to defend said Frontier, or have for a long time neglected their Duty therein, to warn a Meeting of the Inhabitants of such Town, reciting in such Warning the names of the person or persons so suspected, and that the Design of such Meeting is to take into Consideration, whether they judge such person or persons to be dangerous to the Safety of the frontiers. And whatsoever person or persons shall be by such meeting (so warned) judged and voted to be necessary to be removed, either on Account of their Unfriendliness to the Cause of America, or their Unwillingness to support said Cause, shall be, by warrant from an Assistant, or Justice of the Peace, directed to the Sheriff of the County, his Deputy, or either of the Constables of such town, removed, with his Family and Effects, after twenty days, and within thirty days, at their own proper Cost and Charge, to the interior part of this State; Which Warrant such Magistrate is hereby directed to issue, on Application of the Select-men of such town.

Provided always, that any person voted by any town to be necessary to be removed, shall have a right of Appeal to the Governor, who, with the Advice of four of his Council (if they find that the said vote was had through mistake, or without just Grounds, against such persons, or for any other Cause than Toryism) shall have a right to order a Suspension of such removal, for such time as they shall judge convenient; Which order shall be given to the Officer who is directed to remove such Person, and shall be to him a sufficient Warrant for such Suspension, for the time specified by such Order, and no longer.

Provided also, that the Person to be removed procure such Order within twenty days from the time of such vote's being passed, and not after. And all such persons so removed, when in the interior part of the State, shall not be subject to be warned out of town, except such as have not heretofore gained a Residence in any town in this State; but shall be considered to belong to the town where he belonged before such removal; and if not of sufficient Ability to maintain themselves, and have not Relations who are by Law obliged to maintain them, they shall be supported at the Cost and Charge of the town from where they were removed. And it shall be the Duty of the Select-men of the Town where they shall reside, to see that such persons are kept to a suitable employ, in order to support themselves.—And

Be it further enacted by the Authority aforesaid, that all towns in which there are any Inhabitants, and no Selectmen, shall be under the Jurisdiction of the Select-men of the next adjoining town, or of the nearest town where there are Select-men, as far as relates to this Act.

And be it further enacted by the Authority aforesaid, that the Towns hereafter mentioned in this Act, shall be considered as Frontiers, vizt. Arlington, Sandgate, Ruport, Pollett, Wells, Poultney, Castleton, Rutland, Pittsford, Clarendon, Tinmouth, Wallingford, Danby, Shrewsbury, New-Fane, Townshend, Londonderry, Brumley, Andover, Cavendish, Pomfret, Woodstock, Bernard, Royalton, Bethel, Newbury, Barnet, Rygate, Maidstone, Guildhall, Lunenburgh, Strafford, Manchester, Reading, Weathersfield, Athens and Hartford.

AN ACT IN ADDITION TO AN ACT
17TH OCTOBER 1780

(This Act is missing in the original volume)

AN ACT DIRECTING WHAT FENCE SHALL BE DEEMED LAWFUL
19TH OCTOBER 1780

Be it enacted, and it is hereby enacted, by the Representatives of the freemen of the State of Vermont, in General Assembly met, and by

the Authority of the same, that no Fence or Fences within this State shall be deemed lawful unless they are four feet and an half high, well built with Logs, rails, stone, or Boards, or other fence equivalent.

AN ACT TO DIRECT PERSONS WITH RESPECT TO DIVISION FENCES

19TH OCTOBER 1780

Whereas many Difficulties have arisen by means of partition-fences not being properly regulated: Therefore,

Be it enacted and it is hereby enacted, by the Representatives of the freemen of the State of Vermont, in General Assembly met, and by the Authority of the same, that whenever any person or persons, having Improvements adjoining each other, the Expence of making and maintaining a lawful Fence, shall be equally divided between them. And if they can not agree to divide the same, it shall be divided by the Selectmen, or three indifferent Freeholders of such town, where such Land lyeth, each paying for their own part.—And where it shall so happen that any person or persons shall make fence against another Person's Land, that when that other person shall improve against said Fence, they shall pay the Person that built said Fence for the one half of said Fence, to be appraised by the Select-men, or three indifferent Freeholders of the town where such land lieth:—And if either of the Parties, or persons whose Improvements so adjoin each other, should refuse or neglect, to make or maintain, his, her or their proper part of said Fence, having three months notice, then the aggrieved party may enter Complaint thereof, to an Assistant, or Justice of the Peace, who is hereby directed to summon such delinquent or delinquents, to answer for his her or their neglect; and being found delinquent, shall grant Execution thereon, for Cost and Damages.

AN ACT FOR THE REVIVING AND CONTINUING IN FORCE A CERTAIN ACT OF THIS STATE PASSED AT WESTMINSTER MARCH 1780, ENTITLED "AN ACT TO PREVENT TRANSPORTING PROVISIONS OUT OF THIS STATE"

20TH OCTOBER 1780

Whereas the public necessities require the preventing Provision being transported out of this State; Therefore,

Be it enacted, and it is hereby enacted, by the Representatives of

the freemen of the State of Vermont, in General Assembly met, and by the Authority of the same, that the said Act be, and is hereby revived all and every part and paragraph thereof, except the clause prefixing the time when the Act should expire; and that the said Act shall continue in force until the rising of the next Session of this Assembly, and no longer: Provided that it also be in the power of the Governor, or Lieutenant-Governor, and two Councillors, or three Councillors, to give Permits. Provided also that it shall be in the Power of the Governor and Council to take off said Embargo, if they find sufficient Stores are procured for the Troops of this State, before the next Session as aforesaid.

AN ACT TO PREVENT TRANSPORTING PROVISIONS OUT OF THIS STATE

OCTOBER 1780

Whereas large quantities of Provisions are continually exported out of this State, which, if not immediately prevented, will render it impracticable to furnish the Troops raised for the Defence of the northern Frontiers:—Therefore

Be it enacted, and it is hereby enacted, by the Representatives of the freemen of the State of Vermont, in General Assembly met, and by the Authority of the same, that any, and all further transportation of Wheat, Rye, Indian Corn, Flour, or Meal, of any kind: as also Pork, Beef or any other Provisions whatever, that may be useful for supplying the Troops raised by this State, be, and is hereby strictly prohibited and forbid to be transported out of this State, except for the Use of the Continent, or that the same be permitted by the Governor or Lieutenant Governor, and two Counsellors, or by three Counsellors, exclusive of the Governor and Lieutenant Governor.—And all Sheriffs, Grand-Jurors, and Select-men in their respective Towns, and all persons whatever within this State, are hereby authorized and required to seize any and every of the above mentioned Articles, which they have reason to suspect any person or persons may be carrying out, or purchased to be carried out, of this State, contrary to the true Intent and Meaning of this Act: and, if need be command Assistance and make Return in writing of said Seizure to the next Assistant, or Justice of the Peace: And unless said Person or persons shall satisfy the Court, before whom the Examination shall be had, that he or they were not conveying any of the aforementioned Articles out of this State, said Articles shall be forfeit, or such person or persons fined, not exceeding forty Pounds, at the Direction of the Court before whom the Trial shall be had—the one half of the forfeiture or Fine to the Use of this State, the other half to the person prosecuting to effect.—And Be it further enacted by the Authority aforesaid, that if any person or persons shall transport any of the above prohibited Articles out of this State, and be thereof convicted before any Court proper to try the same; he or they shall forfeit and pay unto the Treasurer of this State, the value of said Articles so transported;—to be recovered by Bill, Plaint, or Information.—This Act to continue in force until the rising of the next Session of this Assembly.

Provided always, that it shall be in the Power of the Governor and Council to take off said Embargo, if they find that sufficient Stores are procured for the Troops of this State, before the next Session, as aforesaid.

AN ACT DIVIDING THE FOURTH REGIMENT OF MILITIA, AND FORMING AND ESTABLISHING A SEVENTH REGIMENT

24TH OCTOBER 1780

Whereas it has been found inconvenient, for the Inhabitants, included within the Limits circumscribing the Bounds of the fourth Regiment, to continue in one Regiment; and that it would be more convenient to form one other Regiment within the Limits of the same: Therefore.

Be it enacted, and it is hereby enacted, by the Representatives of the freemen of the State of Vermont, in General Assembly met, and by the Authority of the same, that all the military Companies in the several Towns and Gores, included in the Limits hereafter described, vizt. Beginning at the South-East Corner of Newbury, thence running on the Southerly Line of Newbury, and continuing the same Course until it strikes the County Line: Thence Southerly on the County Line so far South, that running the same Course of the Southerly Line of Norwich, will strike the South East Corner of said Norwich; Thence running said Course to said Corner; Thence running on the Bank of Connecticut River to the said South East Corner of Newbury, be, and are hereby made and declared to be, one entire and distinct Regiment; and are invested with all the Powers other Regiments in this State enjoy: and shall be distinguished and known by the name of the seventh Regiment.

AN ACT IN ADDITION TO AN ACT, ENTITLED,
"AN ACT FOR MAKING AND REPAIRING PUBLIC HIGHWAYS"

OCTOBER 30TH 1780

Whereas Team work is often times much needed in making and repairing public Highways; and as there has been no Provision made in the Law heretofore for providing Teams to work on Highways:

Therefore Be it enacted, and it is hereby enacted by the Representatives of the freemen of the State of Vermont, in General Assembly met, and by the Authority of the same, that any Surveyor of Highways, in any town within this State, shall have power, and is hereby impowered, to warn any Inhabitant to work with, or send his or her Team, Cart, or Plough, or any other Utensil, to make or repair any Highways, as the case may require, by the Direction of said Surveyor; the Owner of any such team to be allowed for a Yoke of Oxen and Cart or Plough, the same per day as is allowed for a Man.—And any person warned, and neglecting or refusing to send his or her Team as aforesaid, shall for every such neglect or refusal, pay a fine for each Day, for one Yoke of Oxen and Plough or Cart, the same as is by Law established as a fine for a man's neglect . . . . . . per Day.

AN ACT EMPOWERING ASSISTANTS AND JUSTICES OF THE PEACE, TO WARN TOWN MEETINGS, IN CERTAIN CASES THEREIN NAMED

OCTOBER 30TH 1780

Whereas it has been represented, that there are several towns within this State, that have no Select-men in the same, to warn annual Town Meetings, as the Law directs.—Therefore,

Be it enacted, and it is hereby enacted, by the Representatives of the freemen of the State of Vermont, in General Assembly met, and by the Authority of the same, that in such cases, upon the Application of four of the Freeholders of any such town, to an Assistant, or Justice of the Peace, in the County where such town lieth, requesting them to warn such meeting; any Assistant, or Justice of the Peace, upon Application as aforesaid, is hereby directed and impowered to warn such meeting in the same manner as the law directs the Select-men.

And Whereas it has been enacted that each town provide their quota of Provisions to supply the Troops of this State the Year ensuing, according to their several Lists returned:

Be it enacted by the Authority aforesaid, that such towns, not having Select-men are hereby required to hold Meetings, as soon as may be, and choose town officers, such as the law directs, to be sworn to serve until others are chosen and sworn in their room.

And that the Inhabitants of such towns give in their Lists to the Listers, within five days after being warned by the Lister: and that such Lister or Listers deliver the Lists to the Select-men within twenty days after such town meeting; who are directed to assess the Inhabitants their Quota of Provisions as aforesaid.—And that the several towns who have not sent in their Lists, are hereby directed to send their several Sums total of such List, to the next Session of this Assembly.

AN ACT FOR THE FORMING A SECOND BRIGADE

OCTOBER 1780

Whereas it is found inconvenient for the Militia of this State to be included in one Brigade:—Therefore,

Be it enacted and it is hereby enacted by the Representatives of the freemen of the State of Vermont, in General Assembly met, and by the Authority of the same, that the Militia of the State of Vermont be divided into two Brigades, in manner following (vizt.) Beginning at the South West Corner of Cumberland County; thence Easterly on the Massachusetts Bay North Line, to Connecticut River; thence northerly on Connecticut River, to Canada South Line; thence on the South Line of Canada, to the East Line of Bennington County, as it formerly stood; thence on said Bennington County East Line, to the place of Beginning, to be established one entire Brigade, to be known and distinguished by the second Brigade.

AN ACT DIRECTING WHAT MONEY AND BILLS OF CREDIT SHALL BE LEGAL CURRENCY IN THIS STATE

NOVEMBER IST 1780

Whereas no particular Money, or Bills of Credit, as yet have, by any Law of this State, been made legal Currency therein.—And Whereas not only for determining what money, and public Bills of Credit, shall be legal Currency; but also to decide, as near as may be, at what rate they severally shall pass:—Therefore

Be it enacted, and it is hereby enacted, by the Representatives of

the freemen of the State of Vermont, in General Assembly met, and by the Authority of the same, that all genuine coined Gold, Silver and Copper, shall be legal Money in this State, vizt. Gold, at the rate of five Pounds per Ounce, Silver, at Six Shillings and eight pence per Ounce, and coined Coppers, at two pence per Ounce.—And that the Bills of Credit emitted by the United States of America, before the eighteenth day of March last, be a legal tender, as Money, according to their current Value: having regard, as well to their current value at the time of making all Contracts, as at the time of rendering Judgment: To which all Courts in this State in their respective Jurisdictions are to conform themselves.

Provided no regard be had to the value of said Bills at the time of making any Contract, which was or shall be, for Gold, Silver, or money equal thereto; or for money to be made good as before the War, or for Money to be paid in any particular thing or things, at a certain Price: Any thing in this Act to the contrary notwithstanding.

AN ACT IN ADDITION TO AN ACT, ENTITLED "AN ACT DIRECTING AND REGULATING THE SERVING AND LEVYING EXECUTIONS"*

IST NOVEMBER 1780

Whereas, the Paper Currency has, for many years past, been in a fluctuating Situation, and still remains so unsettled, that it is difficult for the Legislature to fine the same on a pure Basis.—And Whereas the Gold and Silver currency is so scarce that it may render it very difficult for the People to discharge their Debts, without disposing of the necessaries of Life, and thereby disable them from doing their proportion in the present War:—therefore

Be it enacted, and it is hereby enacted, by the Representatives of the freemen of the State of Vermont, in General Assembly met, and by the Authority of the same, that, in future, the Person of any Debtor, or his personal Estate, shall not be subject to be taken, or holden, by Execution, to satisfy any Debt; Provided the Debtor tender to the Officer Lands sufficient to answer the Debt, which shall be appraised as the Law in that case directs.

Provided always, that no Creditor shall be obliged to take Lands to satisfy such Execution, unless such Debt shall amount to more than five Pounds.

---

* Repealed, April 7, 1781.

AN ACT FOR ASCERTAINING THE TITLE OF LANDS
IN CASES THEREIN NAMED

NOVEMBER 1ST 1780

Whereas divers persons late Inhabitants of this State, and others, who hold Lands by Deed or Deeds of Conveyance, within the same, have gone over to, and joined the Enemies of this and the United States of America; by which means many such Conveyances are likewise carried with such person, or otherwise by them secreted, which has put it out of the Power of the State, or Individuals, in such cases to produce such Evidence to the Title of such Lands, as the Law, in common cases, required.—Therefore

I

Be it enacted, and it is hereby enacted, by the Representatives of the freemen of the State of Vermont, in General Assembly met, and by the Authority of the same, that whenever any Action shall be brought before any Court proper to try the same, for the Surrendry of any Lands, or Tenements that were in the possession of, or occupied at, or near, the time of any such person or persons leaving this or the United States, and there going over to the Enemy; that if on such Trial the Defendant shall make it appear, by Evidence, to the Satisfaction of the Court or Jury, that the Person or Persons who have gone to the Enemy as aforesaid, was at the time of his leaving this or any of the United States, the just and rightful Owner of any such Lands and Tenements, and produce a Deed of Conveyance from under the hand and Seal of any person duly impowered by the Authority of this State to convey the same; that in every such case, Judgment shall be rendered for the Defendant: and a Copy of such Judgment, together with such deed, recorded in the Town Clerk's Office where such Land lieth, shall be deemed good and sufficient Evidence to the Title of any such Land or Tenements.

II

And be it further enacted by the Authority aforesaid, that if any Person or Persons that have been heretofore, or that may in future, be appointed to sell any such Lands; or any person claiming Land by Deed from any such Person, shall bring his Action for the Recovery of any such Lands as may be in the Possession of any other person or persons, it shall be determined in the same manner.

AN ACT APPOINTING AND IMPOWERING COMMISSIONERS TO SELL AND DISPOSE OF FORFEITED ESTATES, AND THE BETTER REGULATING THE SAME

2ND NOVEMBER 1780

I

Be it enacted, and it is hereby enacted, by the Representatives of the freemen of the State of Vermont, in General Assembly met, and by the Authority of the same, that there shall be appointed twelve Persons, Commissioners in this State, to wit, in the County of Cumberland, in the half Shire of Cumberland, three; in the half Shire of Gloucester, three; in the County of Bennington, in the half Shire of Bennington, three; in the half Shire of Rutland, three; whose duty it shall be, upon the State's Attorney's certifying to them the Condemnation of any Estate by the respective County Court, to set up a public Notification in some public Place, describing the Land, and Article for Sale, at least ten Days; and shall then proceed to sell the same to the highest Purchaser, giving absolute Deeds of Warranty, in behalf of the freemen of this State.— Provided always, that not less than two of said Commissioners shall be assenting to the Bargain.

II

And be it further enacted by the Authority aforesaid, that all Commissioners heretofore appointed by the Court of Confiscation, be dismissed, and the Contracts which they have made, and not executed, shall be referred by them, as soon as may be, to the Commissioners abovesaid, who are hereby authorized to fully execute the same.

AN ACT TO MAKE THE TRUSTEES OF CLIO-HALL A BODY POLITIC AND CORPORATE IN LAW

3RD NOVEMBER 1780

Whereas a number of Persons, for the laudable Purpose of promoting Literature, have entered into a voluntary Association and Subscription for erecting an Academy, or Seminary of Learning in this State, to be kept, for the time being, at Bennington, but afterwards at such place as the Legislature shall direct: to be called and known by the name of Clio-Hall, and have appointed a Board of Trust for the well managing its Police and Government.

And whereas said Board of Trust have petitioned this Assembly, that they, and their successors in office, may hereafter be known and acknowledged in Law, to all Intents and purposes, as a Body politic and corporate, by the Name of the Trustees of Clio-Hall.

Therefore Be it enacted, and it is hereby enacted, by the Representatives of the freemen of the State of Vermont, in General Assembly met, and by the Authority of the same, that Thomas Chittenden Esqr. Governor, Timothy Dwight M. A., the reverend David Avery, Isaac Tichenor Esqr. the honorable Moses Robinson Esqr. the honorable Jonas Fay Esqr. Ezra Myles Junr. Esqr. Stephen Ron Bradley Esqr. the revr. Mr. Daniel Collins, Colo. Benjamin Simonds, Bela Turner Esqr., and Thomas Porter Esqr.—constituted a Board of Trust for Clio-Hall be, and they hereby are, for themselves and Successors in office, created a Body politic and corporate, to be known and acknowledged in Law, to all intents and purposes, and called the trustees of Clio-Hall.

AN ACT DIRECTING IN WHAT MONEY JUDGMENTS OF COURT SHALL BE GIVEN IN THIS STATE

3RD NOVEMBER 1780

Whereas it is highly necessary and convenient, that all Judgments for Money should be in that Currency which is most permanent, and least subject to change.—Therefore,

Be it enacted, and it is hereby enacted, by the Representatives of the freemen of the State of Vermont, in General Assembly met, and by the Authority of the same, that all Judgments given by any Court, or Justice of the Peace, in this State, for any sum of Money, on any Account whatsoever, shall be for Gold and Silver; and at the same time the said Court, or Justice, shall make a Rule at what rate the Bills of Credit, made a tender in this State, shall be received in satisfaction thereof, having special regard to the Act which makes said Bills a lawful tender; and all Execution to issue accordingly including therein the said Rule.

Provided nevertheless, the said Court or Justice, when the said Judgment remains unsatisfied, till the said Bills materially alter in value, may, on proper Application, alter said Rule, as Justice shall require.

AN ACT FOR REGULATING FEES

NOVr. 3RD 1780

Whereas the Fees heretofore granted to Officers of Government, and others, have been stated in Continental Currency, which is so far depreciated, that it does not answer the purpose intended: And it is also found that the fees, in some instances, as formerly stated, were not adequate to the Service:—Therefore,

Be it enacted, and it is hereby enacted, by the Representatives of the freemen of the State of Vermont, in General Assembly met, and by the Authority of the same, that the Establishment of the Fees belonging to the several officers of this State, be as follows vizt.

Assistants Fees

	£	S	D
For attending the General Assembly and Council, when convened, per Day	0	7	0
Travel, per Mile out	0	0	4

Representatives Fees

	£	S	D
For attending the General Assembly, per Day	0	6	0
Travel, per Mile out	0	0	4

Superior Court's Fees

	£	S	D
Chief Judge while sitting, per Day	0	18	0
Assistant Judge while sitting, per Day	0	15	0
Travel, per mile out	0	0	4
To the Jury, for each Action tried	1	4	0
And there shall be paid into the Clerk of the Superior Court's Hands, for the Benefit of the Treasury of this State, for each Action tried in the Superior Court	0	18	0
For each Default or Confession	0	10	0

Clerk of Superior Court's Fees

	£	S	D
Entering each Action and Judgment	0	2	6
Filing each Testimony	0	0	2
Each Execution	0	1	3
Entering Judgment acknowledged	0	0	9
Copy of each Testimony	0	0	4

County Court Fees

	£	S	D
Chief Judge while sitting, per Day	0	10	0
Justice of the Quorum, per Day	0	7	0

	£	S	D
Travel, per Mile out	0	0	4
To the Jury, for each Action	0	18	0
And there shall be paid into the Clerk of the County Court's hands, for the benefit of the Treasury of the County, for each Action tried in County Court	0	10	0
For each Default or Confession	0	4	0
For Licence to each Tavern-keeper (whereof to the Clerk)	0	4	0

Clerk of County Court's Fees

	£	S	D
Entering each Action	0	0	3
Entering each Judgment	0	1	0
For Attachments, Summons, and Execution, and other things proper to him, as in the Assistant's and Justice's Fees.			

Assistants and Justices Fees

	£	S	D
Attachments or Summons for Action	0	1	0
When Bond is given	0	1	3
Summons for Witnesses	0	0	6
Entry and Tryal of each Action	0	3	0
If by a Jury	0	6	0
Every Execution	0	1	3
Every Warrant for Criminals	0	1	3
Bond for Appeal	0	0	6
Copy of Evidence	0	0	6
Copy of Judgment	0	0	8
Every Recognizance	0	0	9
Judgment on Confession or Default	0	1	0
Affidavits taken out of Court	0	0	9
Taking the Acknowledgment of a Deed, Mortgage &c.	0	0	7
Each complaint	0	0	9

Court of Probate's Fees

	£	S	D
For granting Administration, to the Judge	0	1	6
For receiving and Probate of every Will and Inventory or fifty Pounds, or under	0	2	0
To the Clerk	0	0	9

	£	S	D
Receiving, and Probate of every Will and Inventory, above fifty Pounds	o	3	o
To the Clerk	o	1	o
Each Quietus, or Acquittance	o	1	o
To the Clerk	o	o	6
Recording every Will and Inventory, of fifty Pounds, or under	o	2	6
Also three pence per hundred for every hundred Pounds after the said fifty Pounds; and half so much for Copy of the same			
Each Bond for Administration	o	1	o
Each Letter of Administration	o	1	o
Each Citation	o	o	6
For making out a Commission, receiving and examining the Claims of Creditors to insolvent Estates, and registering the same	o	1	3
Registering the Commissioners Report, for each page of twenty eight Lines, and ten Words to each Line	o	o	8
For entering an Order upon the Administrator, to pay out the Estate in Proportion unto the several Creditors, returned by the Commissioners	o	o	8
Allowing of Accounts, settling and dividing of intestate Estates	o	2	o
Appointing Guardians, and taking Bond	o	1	3

Secretary's Fees

	£	S	D
For recording Laws and Orders of Public Concernment, in the State Records, each	o	1	o
Affixing the State Seal, each time	o	1	o
For each Military Commission	o	1	o
Each Commission for the Justices of each County	o	3	o
Commission for Judges of the Superior Court	o	2	o
For each Commission for Judges of County and Probate Courts	o	1	o
Each Petition or Memorial to the General Assembly	o	o	6

Fees to the General Assembly

	£	S	D
For each Petition or Memorial, between Party and Party	1	o	o

Town Clerk's Fees

	£	S	D
For recording a Deed	o	1	o
For the Copy of a Deed	o	1	o
For a Survey-Bill	o	o	6
For recording a Marriage, Birth or Death	o	o	3
For recording each Mark	o	o	6

Attorney's fees

	£	S	D
In taxing Bills of Cost, the Parties that recover, for Attorney's fees, at County Court	o	4	o
In the Superior Court	o	6	o

Post Wages

	£	S	D
For Man, Horse, and Expence, each Mile out	o	o	4

Sheriff's and Constable's fees

	£	S	D
Serving every Summons	o	o	4
If by Copy	o	o	6
Serving every Attachment	o	o	6
Bail Bond	o	1	o
For levying each Execution, to be one Shilling for one pound or under, and three Pence on the Pound for every pound above			
For attending at a Justice's Court, when, obliged to attend, for each Action tried	o	1	3
Each mile Travel out, to be computed from the Court	o	o	4
Sheriff's attending the General Assembly, Superior or County Court, per day	o	6	o
Constable for like Service, per day	o	4	6
Fees for Plaintiff or Defendant: attending any Court, per day	o	2	o
Witnesses, for attending any Court, per Day	o	3	o
Travel for Plaintiff, Defendant, or Evidence in any Court, per mile	o	o	3
Fees for a Jury employed in laying out Highways shall be for every Juror, per day	o	3	o
The Sheriff attending on said Jury, per day	o	4	o
Jury for a Justice's Court, for each Action tried	o	9	o

Brander and Recorder of Horses fees

	£	S	D
For branding and recording every Horse-kind	o	o	6
For each Copy of Record	o	o	6

Goaler's Fees

For Commitment of a Prisoner	o	1	o
For discharge of a Prisoner	o	1	o
For dieting of a Prisoner, per week	o	5	o

County Surveyor's Fees

For himself and Horse, per Day, besides Expences	o	6	o

Sheriff's and Constable's Assistant's Fees

For each man that attends the Sheriff or Constable, per Day	o	4	o

AN ACT AGAINST INIMICAL CONDUCT

3RD NOVEMBER 1780

Whereas it has been represented, that many persons who are Enemies of the Liberties of this, and the United States of America, are continually using their utmost Exertions to discourage and dishearten the good friends to the Liberties aforesaid, by making and spreading false News, and speaking diminutively of the Proceedings of the Friends aforesaid.—Therefore

Be it enacted, and it is hereby enacted, by the Representatives of the freemen of the State of Vermont, in General Assembly met, and by the Authority of the same, that if any person shall speak any Word, do any Act or thing, with design, against this Country, that shall have a direct or indirect tendency, to discourage the good People of this State from nervously exerting themselves in the cause of this Country; or shall speak words disrespectful of said Cause, or the measures taken to support it; or shall by any Words or Actions, with design as aforesaid, encourage or shew themselves disposed to encourage the disaffected persons in this State; or shall spread, or endeavour to spread, false news with regard to the Strength or Success of the Enemy, or with regard to any disadvantage they would insinuate the Army or Armies of this; or the United States to be under; and be thereof convicted before one or more Assistant, or Justice of the Peace, (who are hereby impowered to try the same) he or they shall be punished by Fine, not exceeding ten Pounds, Whipping not exceeding ten Stripes, or imprisonment not exceeding twelve Months; or either, or all of them, according to the nature of the offence, at the Discretion of the Court, before whom the Trial may be had.

AN ACT FOR THE PURPOSE OF PROCURING PROVISION FOR THE TROOPS, TO BE EMPLOYED IN THE SERVICE OF THIS STATE FOR THE YEAR ENSUING

3RD NOVEMBER 1780

Whereas, the state of the present Currency, or Medium of trade, is such that it is difficult to procure necessaries to supply the Army, without calling on each town for a Quota of such Supplies, Therefore,

I

Be it enacted, and it is hereby enacted, by the Representatives of the freemen of the State of Vermont, in General Assembly met, and by the Authority of the same, that there be seventy two thousand, seven hundred and eighty one Pounds of good Beef, thirty six thousand, three hundred and eighty nine pounds of good salted Pork, without Bone, except Back bone and Ribs, two hundred and eighteen thousand, three hundred and nine Pounds of good merchantable Wheat Flour, three thousand and sixty eight Bushels of Rye, six thousand, one hundred and twenty five Bushels of Indian Corn, collected at the Cost and Charge of the respective towns in this State, and at the rates or quotas hereafter affixed to such towns:

And that there be a Commissary General appointed, who shall take the charge of the same.—And it shall be the Duty of the Select-men of each respective town, to procure such quota by the time or times hereafter directed by this Act: Which Select-men are hereby impowered to levy a tax on their respective towns, for the procuring such Quota; and also such quantity of Salt, and number of Barrels, as shall be found necessary for that purpose, and all the attending Charges, either in the Articles before described, on in Silver or Paper Currency.

II

Be it further enacted by the Authority aforesaid, that if the Select-men of any town neglect their Duty herein, it shall be in the Power of the Governor and Council, to issue their Warrant to the Sheriff of the County, or his Deputy, commanding him to levy of the Goods or Chattels of such Select-men, and dispose thereof according to Law, a sufficiency to procure such Quota; except it does appear to them that the People of the Town, or one third part thereof, were opposed to the Select-men in procuring such Provision:—in which case it shall be in the power of the Captain General to issue his Warrant to the said Commissary General, by himself, or his Deputy, to repair to such town, and there seize, transport, and dispose of, a quantity of any of the necessary Articles, to the amount of such quota, belonging to such Persons as have opposed the said Select-men.

Provided always, that the said Select-men shall be accountable to the Commissary-General, for the part of those who have not opposed such Select-men.

And Whereas, there are several towns in this State, the Inhabitants of which have not chosen, or do not choose, Select-men according to Law, and which towns the Commissary General may have no person to call on:—Which difficulty to remove,

III

Be it enacted by the Authority aforesaid, that it shall be in the Power of the Governor and Council, from time to time, to nominate and appoint a person or persons, in every such town, who shall have it in their power to transact the Business in this Act prescribed for Select-men: and whose duty it shall be, to notify and acquaint the Inhabitants of such town or towns, of the tenor of such Act.

Provided, that such persons be not liable to be levied on as the Selectmen. But it shall be in the Power of the Captain General, in case of such towns failing to furnish their Quota as aforesaid, to issue his Warrant to the said Commissary General, directing him to repair to such town, by himself or his Deputy, and there seize, transport, or dispose of, a quantity of any of the necessary Articles, to the Amount of such quota, belonging to any person, Inhabitants of such town.—And it shall be the duty of such Commissary General, to see that such Provisions be forwarded in such quantity, and at such time or times, as it shall be wanted for the Use of the Troops. And if it be found that there be a Surplusage of Provision for the Army in Service, it shall be in his power, with the Advice of the Board of War, to barter or exchange such part of such Provision as will appear necessary, for Rum, Salt, Powder, Lead, or other necessaries for the Army.

IV

And be it further enacted by the Authority aforesaid, that whatever Select-men, or other person appointed by the Governor and Council, shall embezzle, or be concerned in embezzling, or misapplying any Provision, collected for such quota, he shall forfeit and pay, treble the value thereof, one moiety to the public, for the purpose of procuring Provision as aforesaid, the other to the person who shall prosecute to effect: and shall suffer Disfranchisement.

That if any Select-men, or other person appointed by the Governor and Council, shall collect, store up, or deliver to the Commissary General, or his Order, any Provision, except such as is of a good quality, and well packed and saved; or of any other than the quality required in this Act, and be thereof convicted, he shall pay treble the value of the Article he should have procured, to be disposed of as aforesaid; unless it appears that it was not through his neglect, or for want of properly attending to his Duty.

Provided always, it shall be the Duty of the Select-men to warn a town meeting, and consult the Inhabitants on the method of procuring such Provision.

That the time for the Flour, Pork, Rye and Indian Corn, to be provided and stored in each town, be the first day of January next: That the time for the Beef to be provided and delivered, be, for the towns of Manchester, Sandgate, and to the Northward in the County of Bennington, the eighteenth day of December: That the time for the Beef to be provided and delivered for the towns of Arlington, Sunderland, and all the towns to the Southward thereof in said County, be, on or before the fifteenth day of January next;—that the time for the Beef to be provided and delivered for the County of Cumberland, be, on or before the fifteenth day of January next.—And that all such Beef be delivered on the Foot, except such towns shall otherwise agree with the Commissary.

Provided always, that the Constables of the respective towns shall be obliged to attend to the Orders of the Select-men, with regard to collecting such Provision.—And in towns where there are no Constables appointed, it shall be in the power of said Select-men, or such other person or persons as shall be appointed by the Governor and Council, to appoint a Constable in every such town, who shall have equal Powers in collecting said Articles, with other Constables chosen in the usual manner.

V

And be it further enacted by the Authority aforesaid, that if the Commissary or his Deputy, be impeded or resisted in collecting the Articles aforesaid, he shall call to his assistance such part of the Militia as he shall judge necessary, at the Cost of the person or persons so impeding.—And it shall be the duty of the said Commissary, or his Deputy, to seize so much of the Delinquent's Property, as will pay said Cost, and rate, being sold at Vendue.

VI

And be it further enacted by the Authority aforesaid, that to the end it may be known which town is guilty of embezzling, or misapplying, or being any ways concerned in collecting, storing up, or delivering to the Commissary, any Provision, except such as of a good quality, and well packed as aforesaid; each town shall mark their Barrels of Provision, to be delivered as aforesaid, with the same Mark as is established by Law to brand their Horses.

VII

And be it further enacted by the Authority aforesaid, that this Act be forthwith printed, and Copies thereof sent to the respective towns in this State.

And Whereas the Sum total of the Lists of several towns, have not been brought in according to Law; for which reason they have been assessed at the Discretion, and according to the best Judgment of this Assembly; by which means some of such towns may be aggrieved.

VIII

Therefore, Be it further enacted by the Authority aforesaid, that on the Application of any such town to the General Assembly, at their session in October 1781, shewing that such town was assessed higher than of right it ought to be, it shall be the duty of such future Assembly to make proper Allowance to such town, of Account of their next rate or tax. And if it be found that any town is not rated high enough, that matter shall be also rectified by a future Assembly.

That the Quotas for each town be as follows:

Towns	Pounds W^t of Flour.	Pounds of Beef.	Pounds of Salted Pork.	Bushels of Indian Corn.	Bushels of Rye.
Pownal	10,543½	3,514	1,757	294	147
Bennington	16,025	5,341½	2,670¼	413	206½
Stamford	750	250	125	24	12
Shaftsbury	12,559	4,186½	2,093¼	354	177
Arlington	5,356	1,785	892½	150	75
Sandgate	514	180	90	18	9
Sunderland	2,707½	902½	451¼	78	39
Manchester	6,867	2,289	1,144½	188	94
Ruport	3,256	1,089	544½	90	45
Dorset	3,000	1,000	500	84	42
Pawlet	3,220½	1,073	536½	90	45
Danby	4,284	1,428	714	123	61½
Harwich	75	25	12½	6	3
Wells	1,800	600	300	54	27
Poultney	2,795	932	466	78	39
Castleton	2,031	677	338	57	28½
Tinmouth	4,272	1,424	712	120	60
Clarendon	5,119	1,706½	853½	144	72
Rutland	5,818	1,939½	969	162	81
Shrewsbury	300	100	50	9	4½
Wallingford	1,672	557	278½	48	24
Pittsford	900	300	150	24	12
District of Ira	1,500	500	250	42	21
Hinsdale	3,000	1,000	500	84	42
Guilford	7,500	2,500	1,250	210	105
Halifax	4,500	1,500	750	126	63
Whitingham	1,500	500	250	42	21
Brattleborough	6,750	2,250	1,125	186	93
Marlborough	2,100	700	350	60	30
Dummerston	5,250	1,750	876	147	73½
New Fane	3,000	1,000	500	84	42
Townshend	3,750	1,250	625	105	52½
Putney	6,000	2,000	1,000	168	84
Westminster	6,750	2,250	1,125	186	98
Athens	900	300	150	28	15
Rockingham	6,150	2,050	1,025	174	87
Thomlinson	300	100	50	12	6
Chester	3,000	1,000	500	84	42
Londonderry	1,500	500	250	42	21
Springfield	3,000	1,000	500	84	42
Andover	300	100	50	12	6
Cavendish	600	200	100	18	9
Weathersfield	1,611	537	268	48	24
Wilmington	2,338	779½	389	66	33
Windsor	11,813	3,937½	1,969	324	162
Reading	351	117	58½	12	6
Hertford	3,198	1,066	533	90	45
Woodstock	3,543	1,181	590½	99	49½

Hartford	3,750	1,250	625	105	52½
Pomfret	2,400	800	400	66	33
Bernard	1,200	400	200	33	16½
Norwich	6,000	2,000	1,000	168	84
Sharon	1,200	400	200	33	16½
Royalton	1,392	262	232	39	19½
Bethel	600	200	100	18	9
Thetford	3,000	1,000	500	84	42
Strafford	2,200	800	400	66	33
Fairlee	900	300	150	33	16½
Moretown	1,500	500	250	42	21
Newbury	5,700	1,900	950	162	81
Corinth	900	300	150	33	16½
Ryegate	1,800	600	300	54	27
Barnet	750	250	125	24	12
Peacham	750	250	125	24	12

AN ACT FOR THE BETTER REGULATING PROCESSES IN ACTIONS OF TROVER AND CONVERSION

3RD NOVr 1780

Whereas many times it so happens, in Case of Trover and Conversion, that the Property is transferred through a number of persons hands, before the other Claimant makes Suit in Law after it. And Whereas the Claimant generally takes the Person who has the Property in Possession.—And Whereas there has not yet been made any Law for the Defendant to cite the first supposed Trespasser to answer the Suit, which makes him obliged to sue his Voucher, and so to the first Trespasser by which means great loss is needlessly made.—Which to prevent in future.

Be it enacted, and it is hereby enacted, by the Representatives of the freemen of the State of Vermont, in General Assembly met, and by the Authority of the same, that when any person or persons shall be prosecuted in any Action of Trover, the Defendant shall cite the person who first purchased the Property in Dispute, if he may be found in this State, by a Notification from an Assistant, or Justice of the Peace; and such Citation or Notification being served by a proper Officer, and returned to the Court, such person cited as above, shall be holden to Trial, as though he had been first summoned to appear at said Court, and answer to such Action: any Law, Custom, or Charge, to the contrary notwithstanding.

AN ACT TO ENABLE ASSIGNEES OR INDORSEES OF NEGOTIABLE NOTES,
TO MAINTAIN ACTION THEREON, AS ON INLAND BILLS OF EXCHANGE;
OR AS THOUGH SUCH NOTE WERE TAKEN IN HIS, HER, OR THEIR OWN
NAME

4TH NOVʳ 1780

Whereas not only for the Benefit of Trade, Paper Credit, and the Ease and Conveniency of Process on negotiable Notes, but also for continuing the former Custom concerning such Notes;

Be it enacted, and it is hereby enacted, by the Representatives of the freemen of the State of Vermont, in General Assembly met, and by the Authority of the same, that all promissory Notes, payable to Order or Bearer, may be assigned or indorsed, and action maintained thereon, as on inland Bills of Exchange:—and that Action may, in the same manner, be maintained on all such Notes as have already been assigned or indorsed as aforesaid.

AN ACT TO LIBEL CONFISCATED ESTATES

4TH NOVEMBER 1780

Whereas, many persons, heretofore possessed of real and personal Property in this State, have joined the open Enemies of this and the United States, and, by their treasonable Conduct, have justly forfeited their Estates to the good People of this State.—To the Intent, therefore, that the same may be legally condemned, and appropriated to the use of the People of this State, to enable them vigorously to prosecute the War against Great Britain, in Conjunction with the United States:

I

Be it enacted, and it is hereby enacted by the Representatives of the freemen of the State of Vermont, in General Assembly met, and by the Authority of the same, that the County Courts, within their respective Counties, be, and they are hereby constituted Courts to judge and determine of all forfeiture, that have or may accrue to this State, by reason of any Treason, or misprison of Treason, against the same. And that in all cases wherein persons have gone, or shall hereafter voluntarily go, from this, or any of the United States, and join the open Enemy, or commit any overt Act of Treason against this, or the United States, and shall flee and escape from Justice, so that they can not be proceeded against in due form of Law; that then, and in every such case, it shall be the

Duty of the Sheriffs, Selectmen, Grand-Jurors, and all informing officers, to make due Presentment of all real and personal Estate of, or belonging to, any person or persons as aforesaid, to the Clerk of said Court, in the respective County where the Estate may be found; which said Clerk, by order of the Judge of said Court, shall libel each and every Article of said Estate, in Westminster Gazette, at least twenty four days before the day of the Court's sitting; notifying the time and place of the Court's sitting, and requiring all who have any Claim or title to said Estate, real or personal to bring in and defend the same against the State.—And all Tryals of Forfeiture shall be by Jury; any Law, Usage, or Custom to the contrary notwithstanding.—Provided nevertheless that nothing herein before contained shall be construed to extend to any Goods or Estate heretofore condemned, and appropriated to the Benefit of this State by the Court of Confiscation.

II

And be it enacted, by the Authority aforesaid, that it shall be the duty of the State's Attorney, in the respective Counties, to prosecute all Trials for Forfeiture to final Judgment; and certify all such Estates, real or personal, against which Judgment shall be rendered to Commissioners appointed by the General Assembly to sell the same.

III

And be it enacted, by the Authority aforesaid, that the Court shall have Power to appoint Auditors, to hear and examine the Claims of the Debtors and Creditors to or from such Estate, as have been, or shall be, adjudged forfeited to the use of this State as aforesaid; and certify the Balance due from such Estates to any person or persons, to the Court appointing said Auditors; and shall certify all Debts due to said Estates, to the State's Attorney, (taking his Receipt for the same) who is hereby authorized to sue for the same.

AN ACT IN ADDITION TO, AND EXPLANATION OF, THE LAST PARAGRAPH OF AN ACT, ENTITLED "AN ACT AGAINST HIGH TREASON"

6TH NOVEMʳ 1780

I

Be it enacted, and it is hereby enacted, by the Representatives of the freemen of the State of Vermont, in General Assembly met, and by

the Authority of the same, that if any person or persons shall know of any of the Enemies of this or the United States, to be any way lurking about in this State, either in the Woods, or in the House or Houses of any of the disaffected people, or any other place; or shall harbour any of the aforesaid Enemies, and conceal the same, or neglect immediately to acquaint the Authority, and be thereof convicted before the County or Superior Court, shall be punished by fine, according to the nature of the Offence; and shall be imprisoned, at the Judgment of said Court, in any of the Goals in this State, not exceeding ten Years.—And

II

Be it further enacted by the Authority aforesaid, that on the Complaint of any County, or town informing Offices, made to an Assistant, or Justice of the Peace, that any person or persons have for more than one year last past, appeared by their conduct to be inimical persons, and likely to do Mischief, if they are suffered to go at large; he shall issue his Warrant, and call such person or persons before him, to answer such Complaint; and also call to his Assistance one or more assistants or Justices of the Peace: And if on Examination, it be judged by the said Court, or a Jury of six Men, that the said person or persons are dangerous persons to go at large, they shall pay Cost of Prosecution, and be committed to any of the Goals within this State, during the Pleasure of the Court, at their own Expence.

Provided always, that such person or persons shall have liberty to apply to the Superior Court for Relief, who shall grant such Relief as they judge best.

AN ACT TO PREVENT THE TRIAL OF THE TITLES OF LANDS

8TH NOVr. 1780

Whereas there is such a variety of interfering Claims or Titles to Land within this State, it is judged necessary to prevent Trials of the Titles of Lands for the present.—Therefore,

Be it enacted, and it is hereby enacted, by the Representatives of the freemen of the State of Vermont, in General Assembly met, and by the Authority of the same, that no Court or Justice shall take Cognizance of any matter in which the Title of Land is concerned.—Provided, that the foregoing Paragraph shall not be construed to exclude a Trial concerning Wilmington and Draper.

AN ACT TO REPEAL CERTAIN ACTS HEREIN AFTER DESCRIBED

8TH NOVEMr 1780

Be it enacted, and it is hereby enacted, by the Representatives of the freemen of the State of Vermont, in General Assembly met, and by the Authority of the same, that the following Acts, vizt., An Act entitled "An Act for the regulating and stating Fees", an Act entitled "An Act to prevent the return to this State of certain persons therein named, and others who have left this State, or either of the United States, and joined the Enemies thereof"; an Act entitled "An Act impowering two or three Justices to try a cause of one hundred Pounds, and forbidding Appeals to Delinquents for neglect of military Duty"; and An Act entitled "An Act in Addition to an Act, entitled, an Act for the regulating and stating Fees", be and they hereby are, repealed.

AN ACT TO REVIVE THE LAWS PASSED BY THE LEGISLATURE OF THIS STATE

8TH NOVEMBER 1780

Be it enacted, and it is hereby enacted, by the Representatives of the freemen of the State of Vermont, in General Assembly met, and by the Authority of the same, that each and every Act and Law of this State (except those repealed by special Act of Assembly) be and remain in full force and virtue, until the rising of the Assembly in October next.

ARTICLES, RULES, AND REGULATIONS, FOR PRESERVING ORDER, GOOD GOVERNMENT, AND DISCIPLINE AMONG THE MILITIA, AND OTHER FORCES OF THIS STATE; WHEN CALLED TO ACTUAL SERVICE, FOR THE DEFENCE AND SECURITY OF THE SAME, AND WHEN CALLED UPON WITH RESPECT TO GOING INTO SERVICE &C.

NOVEMr. 8TH 1780

Be it enacted, and it is hereby enacted, by the Representatives of the freemen of the State of Vermont, in General Assembly met, and by the Authority of the same, that the following Articles shall be observed for the purpose aforesaid.

SECTION I

Art. I. All Officers, non-commissioned Officers, and Soldiers, when the Safety, the good of the Service, and Conveniency permits, shall, with Decency and Reverence, attend divine Service, at the place appointed for that purpose, on penalty of being, by the Judgment of a Court martial, mulct of the whole of his or their Wages for one day, respectively.

Art. II. Any Officer, non commissioned Officer, or Soldier, who shall use any unlawful Oath or Execration, shall incur the penalty expressed in the first Article.

Art. III. Any Officer, non commissioned Officer, or Soldier, who shall behave himself with Contempt or Disrespect towards the General or Generals, or Commander in chief, or shall speak words tending to his or their Dishonour, or shall begin, excite, cause or join in any Mutiny or Sedition in the Regiment, Troop, Company, Garrison, Party, Post, Detachment or Guard to which he belongs, or in any other Corps or Party of the Militia, or forces of this State, or the United States, or shall not use his utmost Endeavours to suppress any Mutiny or Sedition when he is present; or knowing of any Mutiny or intended Mutiny, shall delay to give Information to the Commanding Officer; such Officer, non-commissioner Officer, or Soldier shall suffer such Punishment as shall be inflicted, according to the nature of the Offence, by the Sentence of a Court martial.

Art. IV. Any Officer or Soldier, who shall strike his Superior Officer, or shall draw, or offer to draw, or lift up any Weapon, or offer any Violence against him, being in the Execution of his Office, or shall disobey his lawful Command, shall suffer such Punishment as shall be inflicted, according to the nature of the Offence, by the Sentence of a Court-martial.

Art. V. Any non-commissioned officer or Soldier, who shall desert, or without leave of his Commanding Officer, absent himself from the Troop, Company, or Party, to which he belongs, shall be liable to pay all reasonable Cost, arising for the Recovery of any such Soldier so deserting, as well as such reasonable sum as may be offered by his Commanding officer, as a Reward or Encouragement for apprehending and returning any such Deserter; which cost shall be deducted out of such Deserter's pay, if a Sufficiency be due for his Services; otherwise to be recovered by Bill, Plaint or Information, before any Court proper to try the same; and shall suffer such other Punishment as shall be inflicted by the sentence of a Court-Martial.

Art. VI. Any Officer or Soldier, being convicted of advising or encouraging any other Officer or Soldier to desert, shall suffer such Punishment as shall be ordered by the Sentence of a Court-martial.

Art. VII. All Officers shall have right to quell Quarrels, Frays and Disorders, though in any other Corps, and to order in Arrest or Confinement the Persons concerned; and whosoever shall offer any Violence to such Officer, (though of an inferior Rank) shall be punished at the discretion of a Court-martial.

Art. VIII. Whatsoever Officer, either in actual Service of the State, or of the Militia at home, who shall be guilty of Disobedience of Orders, and be thereof convicted before a General Court-martial, shall be cashiered; and if not in actual Service, to pay Cost of Prosecution.

Art. IX. All Challengers, duellers, and Seconds, and all who shall aid or abet therein, shall be dealt with according to the nature of his offence, Agreeable to the Laws of War, by the Judgment of a Court-martial.

Art. X. Any Officer or Soldier, who shall use any reproachful or provoking Speeches or Gestures to another, or shall behave disorderly, or use any menacing Words or contemptuous Carriage, in the presence of a Court-Martial, shall be punished according to the nature of his offence.

Art. XI. Any non-commissioned Officer or Soldier, who shall in Camp Garrison, Quarters, or on a march, offer any violence to any Inhabitant, or commit any Outrage on him or his Goods; or shall plunder any house, or other building, or any Field, Garden, or Lot, of any Effects; or shall kill, wound, or destroy, any Cattle, Sheep, Hogs, Fowls, or any other creature, belonging to any of the good People of this State; or shall, by threatening, or otherwise, force or compel any of the Inhabitants to loan, give, or sell any Horse, Carriage, Victuals, Liquor, Entertainment, or any other thing, shall be punished, according to the nature of his offence, by the Judgment of a Court-martial; and Reparation shall be made by the Offender to the party injured, by paying him the Wages due to the Offender, or by delivering him over to the civil Authority, to be dealt with according to the Law of the Land, as the case may require: And any officer who shall command on a March, or in Camp, Garrison, or Quarters, who shall neglect to see Justice done herein, shall on Proof thereof before a General Court-Martial, be cashiered, and otherwise suffer such Penalties as such offenders ought to have done.

Art. XII. No non-commissioned Officer or Soldier, shall be found one Mile from the Camp without leave in writing from his Superior

Officer. No Officer or Soldier shall lie out of his Camp or Quarters, without leave from his commanding Officer. All non-commissioned Officers and Soldiers shall, at Retreat-beating, retire to their Quarters. All Officers, non-commissioned Officers, and Soldiers shall, at the time prefixed by the Commanding Officer, immediately repair to the Parade, Alarm-Post, or other Place of Rendezvous, and there shall remain until duly dismissed or relieved: Any who shall offend herein, shall be punished according to the nature of his Offence, by the Judgment of a Court martial.

Art. XIII. If any Officer or Soldier shall think himself wronged by his Superior Officer, and shall, upon due Application made by him, be refused Redress, he may complain to the General, or Commander of the Camp, Post, or Garrison, who is hereby required to examine into the matter, and see that Justice be done.

Art. XIV. Any Commissioned Officer found drunk on Guard, or other Duty under Arms, shall be cashiered. Any non-commissioned Officer or Soldier, so offending, shall suffer such Punishment as shall be inflicted by the Sentence of a Court-martial.

Art. XV. Any Centinel found sleeping on his Post, or who shall leave his Post before relieved, shall suffer such Punishment as a Court-martial shall order.

Art. XVI. Any person who shall designedly make a false Alarm, or any officer or Soldier who shall, without urgent necessity, leave his Platoon or Division, shall be punished, according to the nature of his offence, by the Judgment of a Court-martial.

Art. XVII. Any Officer, non commissioned Officer, or Soldier, who shall leave his Post in time of an Engagement, to go in Search of Plunder, shall suffer such Punishment as a Court-martial shall see cause to inflict.

Art. XVIII. Any Officer or Soldier, who shall, by his Influence, cause or excite the officers or Soldiers of any Post, to compel the Commanding Officer of any Post, or Garrison, to give it up to the Enemy, or to abandon it, shall suffer Death, or such other Punishment as a General Court martial shall inflict.

Art. XIX. Any Officer or Soldier, who shall make known the Parole or Countersign, to any one who is not entitled to receive it; or shall give a false Parole or Watch-Word to any who are entitled to receive it, shall suffer Death, or such other Punishment as a General Court-martial shall inflict.

Art. XX. Whatsoever Officer or Soldier, when in Service, shall relieve the Enemy with Money, Victuals, Arms, or Ammunition; or shall knowingly harbour or protect the Enemy, or shall hold a Correspondence, or give Intelligence to the Enemy, either directly or indirectly, shall suffer Death, or such other Punishment as a General Court-martial shall inflict.

Art. XXI. Whatever Officer or Soldier, in time of an Engagement, shall traiterously and evidently, be aiming to decoy or betray any Corps, Party, or Detachment into the hands and Power of the Enemy, shall suffer Death.

Art. XXII. Whatsoever Officer or Soldier shall shamefully abandon any Post committed to his Charge, or endeavour by Words to induce others to do the like, in time of Engagement, shall suffer Death, or such other Punishment as a General Court-martial shall inflict.

Art. XXIII. No non-commissioned Officers or Soldiers shall sell, waste, destroy, or embezzle any Arms, Ammunition, or other warlike Stores, belonging to, and delivered to him for the Service of this State, on pain of being punished, according to the nature of his offence, and of paying the value of the thing so sold or wasted, to be stopped out of his Pay, by the sentence of a Court martial, or recovered by Action in civil Law.

Art. XXIV. Whatsoever Officer shall be convicted before a Court-martial of behaving in a scandalous, infamous manner, such as is unbecoming the Character of an Officer and a Gentleman, shall be discharged the Service.

Art. XXV. All Spies from the Enemy, found in any of our Camps, Garrisons, or Forts, or in the neighbourhood thereof, either lurking in Woods, or among the Inhabitants, with or without Arms, and who shall be thereof convicted by General Court-martial, shall suffer Death.

Art. XXVI. All Crimes not capital, and all Disorders and neglect, which Officers and Soldiers may be guilty of, to the Prejudice of good Order, and military Discipline, though not mentioned in these articles, are to be punished by Court martial, according to the nature and Degree of the Offence.

SECTION II,

Art. I. Whensoever a General Court-martial shall be necessary in Camps or Garrison, and there is no General Officer in Command there, such Court martial shall be called by the Captain General; or in his Absence the next Officer in Command in the State. And no Court-martial shall be held in the State, except in Camp or Garrison, without

Orders from the Captain General: And in necessary cases, court-martial may be held in any part of the State, when and where the Captain General shall direct.

Art. II. Every General Court martial shall consist of thirteen Members, the Senior in Rank to be the President, who shall not be under the rank of a Field Officer.

Art. III. All Courts martial, not general, shall be appointed, and the Members named, by the Colonel or Commanding Officer of the Regiment or Detachment, to which the Offender, who is to be tried, belongs.

Art. IV. The Sentence of any Court-martial shall not be put in Execution, until the same be approved, and the Execution ordered, by him who appointed the said Court:—and no Sentence for a capital offence, shall be put in Execution without being first laid before the Captain General for the time being, and by him approved of.

Art. V. All members of a Court martial shall behave with Decency and Calmness; and shall begin with the youngest in rank to give their Opinions.

Art. VI. All Regimental Courts-martial shall consist of five Members, unless in cases where not more than three can be had.—All shall be commissioned Officers.

Art. VII. No Field Officer shall be tried but by a General Court-martial; nor in those cases shall any member be below the Degree of a Captain.

Art. VIII. No regimental Court martial shall sentence any Prisoner to receive a greater Punishment than thirty nine stripes for one Offence.

Art. IX. All Offenders who are confined, shall have their Trial as soon as the nature of the Case, and the situation of the Service, will admit; and the Crime shall be given in writing before the relieving of the Guard.

Art. X. Every Officer commanding the Guard, when an Offender is committed, shall within twenty four Hours, report the Prisoner, and the Crime he is charged with, to the Commanding Officer of the Post, that speedy Justice may be done.

Art. XI. All Sutlers, and others, who keep with the Troops in Service, shall be subject to these rules and Regulations.

Art. XII. Any Officer who shall make a false return, for the purpose of obtaining more Pay, Provisions, or Stores, than his just due, shall, on Conviction thereof, be cashiered, and rendered incapable of holding any military Commission thereafter in this State; and shall also be holden to reimburse any Money, or other Articles drawn by virtue of such false Return.

Art. XIII. All members sitting in Courts martial, shall be sworn by the President and the President shall himself be sworn by the next officer in rank, in said Court. The Oath to be taken previous to their Proceeding to the Trial of any offender, in the form following, vizt.

You A B, swear, that you will well and truly try, and impartially determine the cause of the Prisoner now to be tried, according to the rules and regulations for the preserving Order, good Government, and Discipline, among the Militia, and other forces of this State. So help you God.

Art. XIV. All persons called to give Evidence in any case before a Court-martial, who shall refuse to give Evidence, shall be punished for such Refusal, at the Discretion of such Court-martial. The Oath to be administered in the form following, vizt.

You swear, the Evidence you shall give in the case now in hearing, shall be the Truth, the whole Truth, and nothing but the Truth. So help you God.

Art. XV. When this State's Troops and Militia are called to do Duty together, the Officers in the State's Service for any term of time, shall command the Militia Officers of equal Rank; but a Militia Officer shall take the Command of those Officers of inferior Rank.

AN ACT APPOINTING TIMES AND PLACES FOR THE SITTING OF THE SUPERIOR COURT, FOR THE YEAR ENSUING

8TH NOVEMᵣ 1780

Be it enacted and it is hereby enacted, by the Representatives of the freemen of the State of Vermont, in General Assembly met, and by the Authority of the same, that the Superior Court the Year ensuing shall sit at the times and Places following, vizt. at Bennington in the County of Bennington, on the first Tuesday of December next:—At Westminster in the County of Cumberland, on the third Tuesday of December next:—At Thetford in the County of Cumberland on the last Tuesday of December next:—And at Tinmouth in the County of Bennington on the third Tuesday of January next.

AN ACT REGULATING AND STATING THE FINES AND PREMIUMS IN THE
SEVERAL LAWS OF THIS STATE

OCTOBER SESSION 1780

Whereas the Fines and Premiums, or Rewards, in the several Laws of this State, have been formerly stated in Continental Currency, which has so far depreciated, that it does not answer the Intent of the Law.— And it is also found, that in some Instances the Fines and Rewards, as formerly stated, were not adequate to the purpose intended.—Therefore

Be it enacted, and it is hereby enacted, by the Representatives of the freemen of the State of Vermont, in General Assembly met, and by the Authority of the same, that the several Fines and Rewards in the Laws of this State, be, and they hereby are, stated as follows, vizt.

	£	S	D
In the Act regulating Marriages, Fine	20	0	0
In the Act directing Listers in their Office and Duty, Fine	10	0	0
In the Act directing Proceedings against forcible Entry and Detainer, Fine	1	0	0
In the Act for forming and regulating the Militia, Fine for the Clerk's neglect	3	0	0
Fine for a Soldier refusing to muster	6	0	0
When draughted, and refusing to march, fine	9	0	0
Non-commissioned Officer neglecting to warn such person, Fine	0	6	0
Officers disobeying Orders from the Commander in Chief, fine	50	0	0
Non-commissioned Officers neglecting to attend, Fine	0	9	0
In the Act for the due Observation and keeping the first day of the Week as the Sabbath, &c.—Penalty for working	1	0	0
Penalty for rude Behaviour	2	0	0
for travelling on said Day,	1	0	0
for walking abroad &c.	0	6	0
for keeping the outside of the Meeting-house &c.	0	6	0
for convening in Companies &c.	0	6	0
In the Act for regulating Mills and Millers, Fine for taking more toll than the Law directs	1	0	0
In the Act to encourage the destroying of Wolves and Panthers, Fine for taking out of Pit or Trap	4	0	0

	£	S	D
In the Act for the Punishment of Theft, Penalty	2	0	0
In the Act for regulating the Election of Governor, Deputy-Governor, Council, &c. Constable's Fine	4	0	0
For illegal voting, Fine	1	0	0
In the Act directing Town-Clerks in their office and Duty, Penalty for neglect	0	4	0
In the Act for laying out and altering Highways, Fine for neglect	1	0	0
In the Act for making and repairing public Highways, Fine for refusing or neglecting	0	3	6
In the Act for the Appointment and regulating Attornies, Penalty on Transgressors	5	0	0
In the Act for the Punishment of Drunkenness, Fine	0	8	0
In the Act against profane swearing and cursing—Fine	0	6	0
In the Act directing Constables in their Office and Duty, Constable's neglect, fine	0	5	0
For refusing assistance, fine	0	10	0
For contemptiously refusing, Fine	2	0	0
For Constables and other persons refusing to prosecute Hue—and Cries, fine	2	0	0
An Act for authenticating Deeds and Conveyances, Fine for town Clerk's neglect	5	0	0
An Act for the punishing Trespasses on divers cases, &c. for cutting, felling &c., Fine	0	10	0
for leaving down Bars &c. Fine	0	10	0
In the Act for the Settlement of testate and intestate Estates, for Executor's neglect, fine	3	0	0
In the Act concerning sudden and untimely Death, Juror neglecting.—Fine	0	6	0
In the Act for the Preservation of Deer, fine for transgressing	4	0	0
In the Act for preventing and punishing Riots and Rioting, Fine	10	0	0
In the Act for appointing of Sheriffs &c., Officer's refusal &c. Fine	10	0	0
Soldier's refusal,—fine	2	0	0
Wages for Captain per Day	0	6	0
for Lieutenant	0	4	6
For centinel	0	3	0

	£	S	D
For obstructing &c. fine	15	0	0
In the Act regulating Juries and Jurors, fine for default	1	10	0
In the Act regulating Proprietors meetings, fine for neglect	5	0	0
In the Act regulating Fisheries, fine	4	0	0
In the Act concerning Delinquents, fine	4	0	0
In the Act to prevent unseasonable Night-Walking, &c., fine	0	10	0
In the Act against Barratry and common Barrators, fine	20	0	0
In the Act against Gaming,—fine for Tavern-keepers	2	0	0
For persons convicted of Gaming,—fine	0	10	0
In the Act for ascertaining Town-brands &c. for branding at any other place than the Town Pound,—fine	1	10	0
For branders refusing to brand,—fine	0	6	0
For counterfeiting a Brand.—fine	5	0	0
In the Act for the marking Cattle, Swine &c.—fine	0	2	0
In the Act to prevent Encroachments on Highways &c. fine	3	0	0
In the Act concerning Grand-Jurymen, fine for refusing to serve	1	5	0
Fine for neglect	1	10	0
Fine for not presenting	0	12	0
For neglecting to choose Grand-Jurors—fine	5	0	0
In the Act for the Punishment of Lying, fine	2	0	0
In the Act for licensing and regulating houses of public Entertainment &c.—first fine	1	10	0
Fine for not getting Sureties	0	10	0
Fine for selling Liquors without License	0	10	0
In the Act against breaking the Peace, fine for abusing any Magistrate	30	0	0
For private Assault—fine	10	0	0
In the Act for the Punishment of Perjury—fine	30	0	0
In the Act for providing and maintaining Pounds &c. Fine on Select-men for neglect	0	6	0
Fine for neglect to redeem out of Pound	0	1	6
for rescuing out of Pound	1	0	0
In the Act to prevent the selling or transporting raw or untanned Hides or Skins out of this State,—Penalty	0	15	0
In the Act relating to Witnesses &c.—fine &c.	1	0	0

	£	S	D
In the Act for the Punishment of Defamation, fine	10	o	o
In the Act in Addition to the Militia Act—fine	2	o	o
In the Act to prevent persons from exercising authority, unless lawfully authorized by this State—fine—	40	o	o
In the Act to encourage the destroying of Wolves and Panthers, Bounty for each Wolf or Panther,	3	o	o
For each Whelp that sucks	1	10	o
In the Act against counterfeiting Bills of public Credit, Coins &c.—the Reward	5	o	o

INDEX OF CONSTITUTION

INDEX

VERMONT CONSTITUTION, 1777

(NOTE: Roman numerals refer to sections' numbers either in Chapter I or II according to the Arabic page numbers listed next to them. Index of the Laws is printed separately.)

INDEX OF LAWS

INDEX

LAWS OF 1778-1780

NOTE: The Index of the Constitution, 1777 is printed separately, supra page 235.

The Numbers refer only to the page which contains the *Title* of the Act in which the subject matter appears.